Romantic Globalism

Romantic Globalism

BRITISH LITERATURE AND
MODERN WORLD ORDER, 1750–1830

Evan Gottlieb

THE OHIO STATE UNIVERSITY PRESS
COLUMBUS

Copyright © 2014 by The Ohio State University.
All rights reserved.

Library of Congress Cataloging-in-Publication Data
Gottlieb, Evan, 1975– author.
Romantic globalism : British literature and modern world order, 1750–1830 / Evan Gottlieb.
pages cm
Includes bibliographical references and index.

ISBN-13: 978-0-8142-1254-7 (cloth : alk. paper) ISBN-10: 0-8142-1254-9 (cloth : alk. paper)
ISBN-13: 978-0-8142-9357-7 (cd-rom) ISBN-10: 0-8142-9357-3 (cd-rom)

1. English literature—18th century—History and criticism.
2. Globalization in literature.
3. Romanticism—Great Britain. I. Title.
PR149.G54G68 2014
820.9'006—dc23
2013037404

Cover and text design by Juliet Williams
Type set in Adobe Minion Pro

♾ The paper used in this publication meets the minimum requirements of the American National Standard for Information Sciences—Permanence of Paper for Printed Library Materials. ANSI Z39.48–1992.

9 8 7 6 5 4 3 2 1

CONTENTS

Acknowledgments   vii

INTRODUCTION   Recovering Romantic Globalism   1

CHAPTER ONE   Going Global: The Scottish Enlightenment
               Theorizes Modernity   17

CHAPTER TWO   The Global Gothic: Sympathy, Cosmopolitanism,
               and Tolerance in Radcliffe's Romances   44

CHAPTER THREE Fighting Words: British Poetry and the
               Napoleonic Wars   68

CHAPTER FOUR   The Clash of Civilizations and Its Discontents:
               Byron, Scott, and the East   95

CHAPTER FIVE   Modern Sovereignty and Global Hospitality in
               Scott's European Waverley Novels   121

CONCLUSION   Romanticism, Mediation, Globalization   147

Notes   155
Bibliography   188
Index   206

ACKNOWLEDGMENTS

At the conclusion of a long process of drafting, writing, and revising, it is a true pleasure to thank the many people who helped me along the way. At the very forefront stand Anthony Jarrells and Matthew Wickman, who not only read and critiqued draft chapters of *Romantic Globalism* but subsequently (and unbeknownst to me) generously agreed to serve as its anonymous reviewers for OSU Press. I also owe a huge debt of thanks to Samuel Baker, who twice provided invaluable advice for reframing the book's argument. Adam Beach, Yoon Sun Lee, James Mulholland, Pam Perkins, and Paul Westover each read draft chapters and gave me much-appreciated feedback. Many other colleagues provided insights and encouragement at various stages, including Liz Bohls, Miranda Burgess, Jim Carson, Alex Dick, Ian Duncan, Penny Fielding, Deidre Lynch, Ken McNeil, Robert Miles, Rob Mitchell, Steve Newman, Susan Oliver, Padma Rangarajan, and Juliet Shields. I am also grateful to the various scholarly organizations, societies, and conferences under whose collegial auspices I gave conference papers related to this project: the American Society for Eighteenth-Century Studies, the North American Society for the Study of Romanticism, the Northeast and Northwest ASECS chapters, the International Walter Scott Conference, and the 2006 Scottish Romanticism in World Literatures conference at UC Berkeley.

While the process of formulating and sharpening ideas may take place across a range of locales, real and virtual, the writing process (for me at least) is firmly rooted at home. Accordingly, I want to thank my colleagues in the School of Writing, Literature, and Film at Oregon State University, especially Richmond Barbour, Peter Betjemann, Neil Davison, Ray Malewitz, Jillian St. Jacques, and Tara Williams for their ever-available good cheer and good sense. My students, both undergraduate and graduate, provided many opportunities for me to try out parts of what follows in their courses. I have also consistently received tangible institutional support for the research and writing of *Romantic Globalism*. My sincere thanks go to department chairs and school directors both past and present (Kerry Ahearn, Tracy Daugherty, Anita Helle, and Bob Schwartz); Dave Robinson, Wendy Madar, and everyone else at the Oregon State University Center for the Humanities, where both the first and last chapters of this book were drafted; Dean Larry Rogers and the College of Liberal Arts for a Faculty Research Grant; and the OSU Valley Library for additional travel funds. I also want to acknowledge the many office staff and specialists at Oregon State University who have helped me repeatedly with arrangements for course schedules, leave time, travel reimbursement, and many other small but vital tasks: Jenny Bunch, Shelley Fell, Ann Leen, Felicia Phillips, Alison Ruch, and Aurora Terhune.

Special thanks are due to everyone at The Ohio State University Press who helped bring this project to fruition, including Rebecca Bender, Malcolm Litchfield, Eugene O'Connor, and especially Sandy Crooms. I am also grateful to Scott Smiley for preparing this book's index.

Finally, no set of acknowledgments could be complete without thanking my family for their incredible support, frequent cheerleading, consistent interest in my work, and unconditional affection. This book is dedicated to Lynette, with all my love, always.

A version of parts of Chapter Three was previously published as "Fighting Words: Representing the Napoleonic Wars in the Poetry of Hemans and Barbauld," *European Romantic Review* 20.3 (July 2009): 327–43. Reprinted by permission of the publisher (Taylor & Francis Ltd, http://www.tandf.co.uk/journals).

INTRODUCTION

Recovering Romantic Globalism

SAMUEL Taylor Coleridge's "Fears in Solitude" announces its historical context in its subtitle, "Written April 1798, During the Alarm of an Invasion." The poem's nationalistic sentiments are equally displayed on its surface. Coleridge, angry at having been under suspicion (along with his friend William Wordsworth) of spying for the French, loudly announces his patriotism: "But, O dear Britain! O my mother Isle! / Needs must thou prove a name most dear and holy / To me . . . who revere / All bonds of natural love, and find them all / Within the limits of thy rocky shores."[1] What troubles Coleridge, however, is that those apparently "natural . . . limits" of the nation-state, his beloved Britain, are in danger of being breached by outside forces. The domestic peace that Britons have come to take for granted—"[p]eace long preserv'd by fleets and perilous seas" (84)—is under threat in a manner that imperils the identities of citizen and country alike:

> My God! it is a melancholy thing
> For such a man, who would full fain preserve
> His soul in calmness . . .
> . . . that he must think
> What uproar and what strife may now be stirring
> This way or that o'er these silent hills—Invasion, and the thunder and the shout,

And all the crash of onset; fear and rage,
And undetermined conflict . . . (29–31, 34–39)

The poet's inability to determine the origins of these imagined cries and tumult indicates Coleridge's profound disorientation as he forecasts the unraveling of the social fabric that would accompany a foreign invasion. But if Britain is threatened externally, Coleridge suggests, this is the inevitable consequence of its having already compromised its internal integrity through morally dubious activities like the slave trade: "Ev'n so, my countrymen! have we gone forth / And borne to distant tribes slavery and pangs, / And, deadlier far, our vices . . . " (50–52). Having made a habit (and an industry) of breaching other nations' borders, Coleridge implies, Britain cannot expect to remain impermeable forever.

The full-scale French invasion Coleridge feared never materialized; instead, Britain emerged from the Revolutionary and Napoleonic wars as Europe's most dominant nation-state, a position it held mostly unchallenged until World War I. What "Fears in Solitude" forecasts accurately, however, is a future in which Britons no longer have the luxury of imagining they exist in splendid isolation from the rest of the world. Although Coleridge expresses a penultimate wish to be left to "my own lowly cottage, where my babe / And my babe's mother dwell in peace!" (222–23), the poem's concluding lines not only hint at the futility of that desire (since Coleridge's domestic life was in reality anything but peaceful), but also highlight the artificiality of the speaker's prophesied withdrawal into the purely local and immediate. For no sooner does he shut the door to his cottage, than Coleridge opens his heart and mind "to indulge Love, / and the thoughts that yearn for human kind" (228–29). "Fears in Solitude" may explicitly express a yearning for protective isolation, but implicitly it speaks to the inevitability of human contact, over distances and at speeds and intensities hitherto unknown. It speaks, that is, to the experience of globalization.

Neither Coleridge nor any Romantic-era author would have used "globalization" to describe the cluster of hopes and anxieties expressed by "Fears in Solitude," since the term was not coined until well into the twentieth century.[2] Nevertheless, the fundamental argument of this book is that many British writers of the long Romantic era were aware of the global processes and dynamics that were increasingly reshaping their lives, their nation, and their world. I argue that a number of the most influential and popular authors of this period—including David Hume, Adam Smith, Ann Radcliffe, Felicia Hemans, Anna Laetitia Barbauld, Lord Byron, and especially Walter Scott—wrote texts that not only encouraged readers to think globally, but also strove (albeit in different ways, and with differing degrees of ambivalence) to explore the ethical imperatives of such thinking. This emergent global imaginary is what I call "Romantic globalism."[3]

GLOBALIZATION: THE LONG VIEW

Later in this introduction, I discuss some of the unique developmental characteristics of Romantic globalism. First, I want to specify what is meant by "globalization," since this term has become so ubiquitous in both popular and scholarly discourse. Generally speaking, globalization refers to the ways in which, primarily as a result of new technologies that reduce the time it takes for people, goods, money, and information to cross large distances, the world has effectively grown smaller and more interconnected. In Zygmunt Bauman's words, "The term 'time/space compression' encapsulates the ongoing multi-faceted transformation of the parameters of the human condition."[4] Regarding the specific qualities of this transformation, Manfred Steger elaborates: "Globalization refers to a multidimensional set of social processes that create, multiply, stretch, and intensify worldwide social interdependencies and exchanges while at the same time fostering in people a growing awareness of deepening connections between the local and the distant."[5] Steger's stress on the social and perceptual changes wrought by globalization is particularly useful for thinking about how literary and cultural texts both reflect and influence these processes; at the same time, it arguably underplays the economic and political dynamics of globalization. Steger's definition should be supplemented by Bill Ashcroft's more pointed assertion that globalization "has most often been invoked to demonstrate the processes of supranational movements of capital, transnational corporate power and the diffusion of the global economy."[6]

Ashcroft's linking of globalization to transnational corporations is typical of those theorists—including Arjun Appadurai, Carlo Galli, Michael Hardt, Fredric Jameson, and Antonio Negri—who closely associate the global with the (post)modern.[7] Although they do not speak with one voice regarding the specific causes of what they see as contemporary globalization's decisive rupture with the past, such critics generally support Appadurai's assertion that "the modern world . . . is now an interactive system in a sense that is strikingly new."[8] Throughout *Romantic Globalism*, I borrow critical insights from many of these theorists of contemporary globalization. My interest in exploring the history of global thinking, however, has led me to be more influenced by those who view globalization as a long-durational phenomenon. Defined broadly enough, of course, globalization is a process that has been going on since the first humans began migrating across the planet.[9] For the sake of critical specificity, however, I think it's more useful to treat globalization in its more recent manifestation, as a set of interlinked processes that grows out of—and, as we will see, alongside—the era of modern nation-state consolidation. There is debate about precisely when to locate this moment, or whether it is even productive to talk about a single "age of nationalism."[10] Nevertheless, the mid-eighteenth century is a logical moment to locate the origins of the industrialization that historians of nationalism like Benedict Anderson and Ernest Gellner identify as an important catalyst—along with rising literacy rates, effective print technologies, and the relative decline in authority of traditional social elites and religious institutions—for modern Western nation-building.[11]

Moreover, 1750 is a productive starting place for a study of Romantic globalism because it also corresponds to the start of what Roland Robertson identifies as the second, "incipient" phase of long-durational globalization.[12] One need not accept every detail of Robertson's timeline to agree that recognizably modern globalizing processes, notwithstanding their unprecedented acceleration and convergence since the 1970s, have been taking place for at least several centuries. In this context, one of the best-known frameworks for describing and analyzing long-durational globalization is the "world-systems analysis" methodology developed by Immanuel Wallerstein. Although sometimes criticized for relying too heavily on a Marxian base-superstructure model,[13] world-systems analysis is undeniably effective at tracking the ways in which global processes, especially those that contribute to making the world feel smaller and more interconnected, are intimately tied to the global spread of capital. Although Wallerstein locates the origins of our modern world system in the sixteenth-century Mediterranean trading world—a milieu well beyond the scope of this study—I follow his basic insight that global processes and perspectives are immanent to the workings of capital. (This is an insight, as we will see in Chapter One, which Enlightenment thinkers like Hume and Smith developed early.[14])

Taking a long view of globalization allows other historical continuities to emerge as well. Our contemporary geo-political era is frequently characterized as being marked by the decline of the autonomous nation-state; in one of the strongest versions of this thesis, Hardt and Negri claim that "we are witnessing today [a transition] from traditional international law . . . [to] a new sovereign, supranational world power," which they term "Empire."[15] Viewing globalization as a set of interlinked economic, political, technological, and socio-cultural transformations that has been developing for several centuries, however, makes visible the extent to which it has long been altering or weakening some elements of nation-state sovereignty, while in fact strengthening or facilitating the creation of others. This is yet another insight that, I will argue, was first developed by the Scottish Enlighteners; its present form is well articulated by Saskia Sassen, who observes that "[g]lobal processes are often strategically located/constituted in national spaces.... The material and legal infrastructure that makes possible the global circulation of financial capital, for example, is often produced as 'national' infrastructure—even though increasingly shaped by global agendas."[16] Recognizing the long-durational, deep-seated imbrications of national and global frameworks helps connect our contemporary experiences of globalization with those of earlier eras—connections we especially need to make if we wish to leverage the weight of historical experience in order to intervene critically in our own moment.

In recent years, critics and scholars of contemporary literature and culture have begun to apply the analytic insights of globalization studies.[17] This book is indebted to such studies, which provide diverse models of how to think the literary and the global together. Yet it differs fundamentally by declining to treat globalization as a primarily contemporary phenomenon. In this sense, *Romantic Globalism* has at least as much in common, methodologically speaking, with several recent historical studies. C. A. Bayly's *The Birth of the Modern World, 1780–1914*, for example, builds a strong case for recognizing that "the networks of what I am calling here 'archaic [i.e. pre-eighteenth century] globalization' and 'early modern' [i.e. 1760–1830] globalization persisted under the umbrella of the nineteenth-century international system."[18] For reasons of clarity, I do not adopt Bayly's nomenclature. Nevertheless, I share his conviction that the decades on either side of 1800, which witnessed a succession of world-changing technological and political revolutions (agricultural, industrial, American, French, and Haitian, to name only the most important for the West), constitute a crucial era for what Bayly calls "the forces promoting global interconnections."[19]

Recognizing the historicity of these forces has, in turn, prompted historians to rethink the traditional narrative of the rise of European imperialism. James Belich argues that eighteenth- and nineteenth-century Euro-British expansionism mobilized three overlapping but theoretically distinctive forms: "*networks*, the establishment of ongoing systems of long-range interaction, usually for trade; *empire*, the control of other peoples, usually through conquest; and *settlement*, the reproduction of one's own society through long-range migration."[20] Because Victorian imperialism not only depended on previously established trade routes (global networks), but also held sway in most parts of the world for a relatively brief period of time, Belich argues that it was the last of these forms—"the settler revolution . . . the creation of new societies, not the control of old ones"—that made the deepest and longest-lasting impact on our contemporary world order.[21] Combined with his identification of an under-regarded "demographic revolution" that saw Britain's population triple between 1750 and 1850 (despite several waves of emigration), Belich's account challenges us to revise our conventional understanding of both the historical consistency and the long-durational effects of European expansionism in this period.[22]

Bayly and Belich are not the only historians to suggest that most iterations of modern European imperialism were far less unified or hegemonic in practice than they may have appeared, even to their participants. The conventional story of the rise of the second (i.e. post-1776) British Empire is familiar: following the abandonment of its North American ambitions after the humiliation of the American Revolution, Britain emerged triumphantly from the Revolutionary and Napoleonic wars to find itself, by the early 1830s, in a position of worldwide dominance unparalleled since ancient Rome. John Darwin, however, has recently argued that Britain's imperial ambitions and rhetoric should not be taken at face value. This does not mean reviving the old chestnut that the British Empire was acquired in a fit of absent-mindedness; rather, it means recognizing that "the Empire" as we know it was never fully "acquired" at all. As Darwin states, "British imperialism was a global phenomenon . . . its fortunes were governed by global conditions; and . . . its power in the world derived rather less from the assertion of imperial authority than from the fusing together of several disparate elements."[23] Imperialism, in other words, was not only always already global, but was consistently disrupted, diluted, and even derailed by developing globalization. Furthermore, Bernard Porter contends that for many Britons (especially from the working classes), the Empire never loomed particularly large in their daily consciousness; Britain may have been—or may have aspired to be—a world-historical power by the mid-nineteenth century, but an awareness of its imperial ambitions seems never to have thoroughly pervaded the majority of its citizens' lives.[24] As a result, imperial historians have begun to conclude that "empire was something of a perpetual chimera for the British."[25]

The time is thus right to review with fresh eyes some of the past decades' most important analyses of "the macropolitics of Romanticism."[26] Most such studies owe a collective debt to *Orientalism*, Edward Said's groundbreaking 1978 history of the West's aggressive "othering" of the East as a means of simultaneously establishing and justifying its own superiority.[27] Drawing especially on Michel Foucault's theorization of the knowledge-power dyad, and rerouting these insights through the terrain of colonial relations previously mapped by Frantz Fanon, *Orientalism*—alongside subsequent studies by Gayatri Chakravorty Spivak, Homi Bhabha, Ania Loomba, Robert Young, and others—made postcolonial discourse studies an essential critical methodology for literary historians of the 1980s and 1990s. *Culture and Imperialism*, Said's follow-up to *Orientalism*, even takes a Romantic-era text as one of its central examples: analyzing Jane Austen's supposed *sangfroid* in *Mansfield Park* (1814) regarding the Bertrams' financial reliance on their slave-operated Antiguan plantations, Said finds further evidence of early nineteenth-century Britons' assumption of "the avowedly complete subordination of colony to metropolis."[28]

Postcolonial theory has come a long way since Said's originary works; some of its recent iterations, in the works of critics like Spivak and Vivek Chibber, so challenge and complicate Said's initial dualisms (colonizer/colonized, metropole/colony) as to render them nearly unrecognizable.[29] Nevertheless, the postcolonial influence on the study of Romanticism has been profound. Probably the strongest version of this perspective is articulated in Saree Makdisi's *Romantic Imperialism: Universal Empire and the Culture of Modernity*. Although Makdisi acknowledges that "the great European empires" of "the end of the nineteenth century" were "in the romantic period . . . just beginning their worldwide expansion," he nevertheless reads most of the canonical male Romantic poets (and a lone novelist, Walter Scott; women hardly enter the picture at all) as engaged in negotiating their relations to a globe-spanning Britain that is imagined as fully imperial in intent if not also in practice. For Makdisi, even the "spots of time" that a poet like William Wordsworth creates to shelter himself textually from the onslaught of modernity ultimately confirm empire's inevitability.[30] In this reading of Romanticism's relationship to globalization, the latter is almost entirely conflated with imperialism, becoming a malevolent, unstoppable force that can only be cravenly justified or vainly resisted.

Makdisi has subsequently nuanced some of his positions, clarifying that there was a range of Romantic attitudes toward imperialism.[31] This agrees with the general direction taken by other long-eighteenth-century and Romantic scholars since the 1990s. Often drawing on postcolonial (and post-*Orientalism*) theories of hybridity and performativity, scholars have paid increasing attention to British anxieties in the face of contact with other nations and peoples. In lieu of an exhaustive literature review, a mostly chronological glance at a few key monographs must suffice to sketch the contours of these developments. In *Bardic Nationalism: The Romantic Novel and the British Empire*, Katie Trumpener offers a portrait of British national identity that coalesces by co-opting, rather than excluding, the identities and literary genres of the so-called "Celtic Fringe"; in *British Romantic Writers and the East: Anxieties of Empire* and *Curiosity and the Aesthetics of Travel Writing, 1770–1840,* Nigel Leask examines a variety of more-or-less unstable cultural and discursive strategies through which British writers negotiated their positions vis à vis the rest of the world; in *Romanticism and Colonial Disease,* Alan Bewell delineates the impact of colonial exchange on Western ideas and anxieties regarding global epidemiology; and in *Fair Exotics: Xenophobic Subjects in English Literature, 1720–1850; Imperial Characters: Home and Periphery in Eighteenth-Century Literature; Britain's Chinese Eye: Literature, Empire, and Aesthetics in Nineteenth-Century Britain;* and *Freedom's Empire: Race and the Rise of the Novel in Atlantic Modernity, 1640–1940,* Rajani Sudan, Tara Ghoshal Wallace, Elizabeth Chang, and Laura Doyle (respectively) explore the destabilizing effects on British identity of foreign contact and conflict, especially in relation to India, China, and the Atlantic world.[32]

These studies have been joined by others that, while not forgetting the lessons and insights of postcolonial theory, foreground the growing globality of Britain's mid-eighteenth-century situation. Ian Baucom's *Specters of the Atlantic: Finance Capital, Slavery, the Philosophy of History* is a watershed critical exploration of Romanticism's relation to the "triangle trade" of money, goods, and slaves between Britain, Africa, and the Caribbean that greatly facilitated Britain's rise to global hegemony despite the British slave trade's official abolition in 1807. Although Baucom's primary critique is of finance capital and its "culture of speculation"—the logic, he argues, behind "that procedure by which value detaches itself from the life of things"[33]—his book also models how to consider the literary, political, and ethical implications of Britain's increasing imbrications in the Romantic era's world order, without presuming that the British Empire was entirely stable or unified at the time. Similar in scope, if not in aim or tone, is Samuel Baker's recent *Written on the Water: British Romanticism and the Maritime Empire of Culture.* Focusing largely on the Lake Poets, through careful contextualization and interpretation Baker conclusively demonstrates that, despite their reputation for insularity, the works of Wordsworth, Coleridge, and their peers are thoroughly saturated by the interests and anxieties aroused by the increasing extension of Britain's global (and specifically oceanic) interests.[34] An analogous interplay of local and global dynamics is also described and interrogated in Mary Favret's *War at a Distance: Romanticism and the Making of Modern Wartime,* in which British Romantic texts and visual art produced in the context of the Revolutionary and Napoleonic wars are read in relation to "the ways distant war invades and becomes implicated in the most familiar forms of the everyday."[35] Favret's method, in turn, resonates with Kevis Goodman's in *Georgic Modernity and British Romanticism: Poetry and the Mediation of History*, particularly her reading of William Cowper's *The Task* (1785), which reveals the reclusive poet busily engaged in selectively transforming the "noise" of world events into his famously conversational verse.[36]

Although they do not employ precisely the same critical terms, these recent studies (as well as others by scholars like Penny Fielding, Richard Maxwell, Michael Wiley, and Esther Wohlgemut) share an interest in exploring how Romantic-era literature was deeply invested in negotiating global issues—without assuming that such negotiations were always already entirely framed or contained by the overlapping ideologies and practices of colonialism and imperialism.[37] This critical balancing act accords with what Paul Jay has recently deemed the necessity of "questioning the whole idea of a historical break separating postcolonialism from globalization," a questioning that can begin only once "the histories of colonization, decolonization, and postcolonialism are [understood as] part of the long history of globalization."[38] Endorsing this position does not mean denying or marginalizing the exploitation of overseas territories, peoples, resources, and trade routes that was being actively pursued, sometimes by official policy and sometimes via mere opportunism, by certain British elements during the long Romantic era. Rather, it is to begin to recognize that such activities took place as part of a much larger historical transformation—globalization—that has become visible only retroactively. As Jürgen Osterhammel and Niels P. Petersson observe, "[t]he history of imperialism and colonialism is a particularly important cornerstone for the history of globalization."[39]

Likewise, I make no claim that Romantic-era Britons invented or were the first to experience globalization; on the contrary, there is already a significant body of scholarship demonstrating that Britain's history of negotiating its position with regard to the rest of the world goes back at least to the sixteenth century.[40] I am also well aware that this study neither moves beyond the more-or-less established canon of British Romantics, nor into the ambit of English-language texts published outside Britain in the period.[41] Instead, by focusing on the global dynamics represented and negotiated, first by some of the Scottish Enlighteners and later by a number of popular Romantic-era authors, *Romantic Globalism* seeks to contribute to the change of intellectual emphasis whereby, as Kapil Raj indicates, "recent historiographical developments and understandings" make it possible "to re-examine the nature of . . . knowledge making in the globalized space of early modernity in the context of European expansion."[42]

RECOVERING ROMANTIC GLOBALISM

Deploying the long-durational understanding of globalization outlined above, the following chapters explore how a number of influential British writers of the long Romantic era encouraged readers to adopt a recognizably modern global mindset, and learn to think of themselves as members of a nation-state whose economic, political, and socio-cultural development is inextricably intertwined with that of the rest of the planet. I do not posit a single set of attributes that determines whether a Romantic-era text is sufficiently global in orientation; such a checklist might have heuristic advantages, but would be reductive as well as overly formulaic. Instead, what the texts and authors I focus on share—besides an interest in navigating and representing ideas, themes, characters, and plots that frequently exceed national bounds or borders—is a commitment, implicit or explicit, to teach readers to think globally in ways that emphasize the horizontality, transversality, or mutually constitutive nature of the relations between peoples and nations.

This broad criterion opens a second, related argument of this book: that in the century before the Victorian zenith of the British Empire, global thinking frequently took shape as an alternative to, rather than merely an elaboration or anticipation of, imperialism.[43] I coin the phrase "Romantic globalism," rather than simply adopt a more neutral pre-existing term like "global imaginary," to underscore that the authors on whom I focus not only were aware of the global processes transforming their world, but also were frequently interested in promoting markedly progressive, egalitarian ways of conceptualizing and influencing them. I am interested, in other words, in connecting Romantic globalism to the perspective of theorists like Jacques Derrida and Jean-Luc Nancy when they assert their preference for the French term "mondialisation" over the English "globalization." As Derrida explains, he prefers the former because it "gestures toward a history, it has a memory that distinguishes it from that of the globe . . . a certain oriented history of human brotherhood," whose sympathetic features Derrida would retain as a bulwark against the largely inhuman "techno-science" that, he fears, appears increasingly to determine the course of contemporary globalization.[44] Nancy concurs, emphasizing that "*mondialisation* would rather evoke an expanding *process* throughout the expanse of the *world* of human beings, culture, and nations."[45] Although the Romantic globalism I articulate in this book does not look the same in every case—in particular, I claim that it undergoes a significant transformation around the years of the Napoleonic Wars—it is unified to the extent that all of its authors share the ethical impulse that animates Derrida's and Nancy's inclinations to support "mondialisation" over "globalization." To some, this may appear overly optimistic, utopian, or even naïve. Nevertheless, I follow Robert Mitchell's view that recovering Romantic-era perspectives on globalization can help reassert into public consciousness "the question of the kind of life we want to live on the one earth that we currently occupy."[46] Especially given its frequent engagements with the aesthetic and ethical dimensions of globalization—dimensions that are too often lost when we allow entirely economic definitions of globalization to dominate public discourse—there is much to gain by recognizing both the world-shaping stakes, and the ethical imperative, of Romantic globalism.

My first chapter lays the groundwork for these contentions by demonstrating that some of the most important cognitive features of modern globalization—in particular, a recognition of the intrinsic interdependence of nations, and a conception of different nations as existing in a homogenous temporal framework—were developed and theorized by the Scottish Enlightenment. As Bauman, Jameson, and others assert, globalization both creates and requires alterations in the way people conceive of their relations to each other, spatially as well as temporally. Significantly, space and time also form the primary axes of the interdisciplinary investigations of the Scottish Enlighteners. Adam Smith's *The Wealth of Nations* (1776) inaugurates the modern discipline of economics by recognizing the obsolescence of older mercantilist dogma, which encouraged countries to hoard specie to achieve economic self-sufficiency. Smith's free-market theories are among the first systematic attempts to delineate the emerging world system of global capital. At the same time, Smith and his fellow Enlighteners develop ideas regarding the chronological stages through which they believe all societies progress, from the primitive (hunting and gathering) to the more advanced (agricultural and commercial). This fundamental alteration in the way history can be conceived makes it possible to think of various societies as occupying different historical stages simultaneously within a unified temporal framework. By recalibrating time and space as secular, modern, and homogenous, I argue in Chapter One, the Scottish Enlightenment creates the knowledge techniques adequate to a modern conceptualization of globalization. They also pave the way for the political ideas of Immanuel Kant, whose ideas signal a transition between earlier, Westphalian ideas of national sovereignty and the rise of more cosmopolitan models of international relations.[47]

In the years immediately following the Scottish literati's major treatises, Romantic globalism largely expressed itself as an extension of such cosmopolitanism. Some of its most influential expressions, moreover, found an unlikely vehicle in Ann Radcliffe's highly popular Gothic romances. Today, her novels are frequently understood as xenophobic confirmations of Britons' difference from and superiority to the foreign (frequently Catholic and European) characters populating their pages. By contrast, I argue in Chapter Two that Radcliffe's romances synthesize key Enlightenment insights to model a tolerant appreciation of foreign landscapes, cultures, and peoples. Although relatively little is known about Radcliffe's personal history, what we do know of her biography supports reading her novels as progressive, liberal-minded documents. Furthermore, close attention to her major novels—*The Romance of the Forest* (1791), *The Mysteries of Udolpho* (1794), and *The Italian* (1797)—reveals their increasing investment in what I call "sympathetic cosmopolitanism." This early form of Romantic globalism is predicated on a notion of tolerance whose usefulness as a discourse of global concord, I will suggest, is ultimately compromised. In the wake of the Terror and the ensuing wars with revolutionary France, moreover, both Radcliffe's tolerant ethic and her generic discretion are eclipsed by the abrasive Gothic horror of writers like Matthew Lewis.

Even as Radcliffe's sympathetic cosmopolitanism appeared increasingly outmoded and outmaneuvered, opportunities for writers to influence Britons' perceptions of their global situation continued to arise, albeit with ever-higher stakes. Government repression in the form of the suspension of *habeas corpus* (1794), the Gagging Acts (1795), and the Combination Act (1799) created an atmosphere in which questioning the motives or methods of war was increasingly dangerous. Critics have justly blamed this political environment for the poor reception given to Anna Laetitia Barbauld's *Eighteen Hundred and Eleven* (1812), a poem that prophesizes Britain's imminent collapse. In the middle of my third chapter, I analyze several elements of Barbauld's text to bring out some specific elements that might have seemed most disturbing to her contemporaries; in preceding and subsequent sections, I focus on two lesser-known poems—one written before and one after *Eighteen Hundred and Eleven*—that take up Barbauld's concerns with the national and global stakes of Britain's wartime efforts, but to very different ends. By putting Barbauld's poem back into dialogue with Felicia Hemans' *England and Spain; or, Valour and Patriotism* (1808) and Anne Grant's *Eighteen Hundred and Thirteen* (1814), I try to shed light not only on how these authors engaged in a critical public conversation regarding Britain's prospects during and after the Napoleonic Wars, but also on their differing views regarding the proper roles of both poetry and women during those turbulent times. The chapter concludes by considering the effects of Walter Scott's explicitly martial wartime poems, *The Vision of Don Roderick* (1811) and *The Field of Waterloo* (1815), which together cemented the establishment version of Britain's wartime identity.

Although the peace negotiations that were supposed to conclude the Napoleonic Wars were disrupted by the Hundred Days of Bonaparte's unexpected return, plans were already underway for the redistribution of European and worldwide territories. What was to be Britain's new geopolitical role in the post-Napoleonic era? Famously maligned by Percy Shelley and Byron, Viscount Castlereagh nevertheless successfully used the Congress of Vienna to secure conditions for Britain's global flourishing in the nineteenth century. But in the short term, Napoleon's final defeat at Waterloo in June of 1815 found Britain entering a period of renewed national anxiety. With the French threat removed, internal conflicts previously submerged or sublimated by the pressures of war rose to the surface once again. A massive influx of decommissioned soldiers, the nascent labor movement, and the general discontent among the newly industrialized working poor combined to make the fifteen or so years between Waterloo and the passing of the first Great Reform Bill in 1832 domestically tumultuous.

Faced with the prospects of increasing internal instabilities and evergreater foreign commitments, Romantic-era Britons (not unlike some of their present-day counterparts in America, Europe, and elsewhere) were frequently tempted to simplify their global perspective by adopting an "us versus them" mentality. Franco Moretti, for example, has demonstrated that the years surrounding Waterloo produced an unprecedented abundance of military novels, nautical tales, and historical and oriental romances that generally both confirmed and justified Britain's newfound ascendancy, usually at its enemies' and rivals' expense.[48] Not all such publications, however, adopted this perspective. In Chapter Four, I contend that several of Byron's so-called Orientalist productions—*Lara* (1814), *The Siege of Corinth* (1816), and *Sardanapalus* (1821)—critically respond to this "clash of civilizations"-style worldview. In these works, Byron repeatedly explores the theme of the European who has "gone native" or "turned Turk" and assumed the habits and customs of the Eastern lands where he or she has sojourned. Adapting Srinivas Aravamudan's concept of "levantinization," I argue that the main characters of these Byronic texts represent versions of the cosmopolitan, hybridized identity that Byron admired. Their inevitably tragic ends coincide with the poet's recognition that such levantinization is continuously threatened by the polarized mentality that saturated his cultural moment. Although Byron's famous irony repeatedly highlights the injustices of this situation, it proves unusable for engendering alternative imaginings. I conclude this chapter, then, by turning to Scott's *The Talisman* (1825), a savvy and self-conscious novelistic negotiation of Britain's post-Napoleonic role as a world power set in pre-modern Palestine. Here, Scott repeatedly disrupts British readers' assumptions of their ancestors' moral and theological superiority over their Muslim counterparts, thereby problematizing the dualistic mindset that threatened to render such global contact inevitably hostile.

If Scott's oeuvre repeatedly takes center stage in the second half of *Romantic Globalism*, this is warranted by the fact his poetry and prose saturated the later decades of the Romantic era to an unmatched, unprecedented degree.[49] For most of his late-twentieth-century critical revival, scholars remained focused on Scott's best-known, Scottish-themed novels. Yet as Robert Crawford observes, Scott's European novels "became part of the way Europe came to imagine its constituent parts and the relationship between them," and are thus equally deserving of consideration.[50] My final full-length chapter focuses on how two of Scott's later novels, *Quentin Durward* (1823) and its quasi-sequel *Anne of Geierstein* (1829), use historical settings that pre-date the Napoleonic Wars to identify and explore some of the most significant European developments on the path to contemporary state sovereignty and a Eurocentric global order. In *Quentin Durward*, Scott highlights both the progressive and repressive dynamics of modern nation-building; I read the novel's main plot—in which a wily Louis XI seeks to centralize the nascent French state by playing its feudal lords against one another—in light of the frame narrative's interest in the transition from pre- to post-Enlightenment modes of identity. *Anne of Geierstein* takes up similar themes, but countervails the structural violence of state sovereignty—this time embodied in the conflict between the Swiss Cantons and Charles of Burgundy—by emphasizing the importance of what I call "global hospitality": a formal acceptance of otherness that holds out the possibility of greater accord between individuals as well as nations, without eliding their differences. The promise of such hospitality points the way forward (or back, as it were) to a more ethical attitude toward globalization—a neo-Romantic globalism, the possibility of which I take up briefly in my conclusion.

My account of the development of Romantic globalism thus runs through the Scottish Enlightenment's theorizations into Radcliffe's sympathetic cosmopolitanism, pivots on Napoleonic wartime poetry, and ends in a moment of global hospitality. This is not intended to be a definitive or complete account, either of the evolution of Romantic globalism or of the variety of Romantic-era attitudes toward Britain's expanding role on the world-stage. In part because I have chosen to focus primarily on writers whose works were immediately popular—or, as in the case of Barbauld's *Eighteen Hundred and Eleven*, immediately provocative—some authors whose globalizing views are no doubt worth considering more carefully (for example, Mary Shelley and Charlotte Smith) are largely absent from my account. Some excellent macropolitical scholarship on these and other figures has already begun to appear, and *Romantic Globalism* is intended to spur more scholarship on the subject, rather than to provide a final or definitive account.[51] Furthermore, while there were doubtless some Romantics who simply paid little attention to their world's globalizing, there were certainly others, like Edmund Burke, who actively opposed most progressive or speculative movements. Again, my relative silence with regard to Burke and his anti-Enlightenment, anti-Jacobin peers (except for a glance in their direction near the end in Chapter Two) is not meant to deny their existence or influence. Their resistance to many aspects of British modernity has been well marked by others, although again I suspect that such resistance itself would benefit from more attention to its properly global context.[52]

My use of the adjective "properly" in the preceding sentence prompts one more reflection on the implicitly comparative historicizing framework on which this book rests. For reasons I hope are already becoming clear, *Romantic Globalism* throws its weight behind bringing out the connections and continuities between the global experiences and attitudes of those who lived and wrote in Britain circa 1750–1830, and our contemporary situation. Nevertheless, on several occasions I suggest ways in which our experiences of globalization necessarily differ from those of the Romantics. Although I feel strongly that globalization needs to be understood as a long-durational rather than an exclusively or even primarily contemporary phenomenon, I am fully aware that today's globalizing processes take place more quickly and are more deeply, complexly intertwined in people's daily lives than ever before. As discussed above—and as I hope is apparent in what follows—the Romantics' experiences of globalization were usually felt from within the boundaries of the nation-state; to adopt Manuel Castells' important distinction, whereas the Romantics were beginning to experience a "linked" world order, today we live in a much more fully (albeit unevenly) "networked" global society.[53] But this is not to say that our experiences of globality today are somehow unmediated; if the greatly enhanced speed of today's telecommunications frequently makes differences of time and space irrelevant, for example, then as Paul Virilio has argued, speed itself must be recognized as an ideologically charged matrix of perception.[54] Especially given the greater degrees of obvious interference attendant on global exchanges in prior eras, Romantic-era globalization was much more explicitly mediated than today's version; moreover, the forms that mediation took were much more textually driven than those of today's predominantly image-based popular culture.[55] The attention that I pay to genre in this study should be understood as one way to account for the Romantics' differently mediated experiences of globalization. As Bruno Latour has tirelessly articulated, the modes and methods of interaction between actants may change historically, but networks themselves have always been with us (which is one way of understanding why "we have never been modern").[56]

Over a decade ago, Immanuel Wallerstein coined the term "utopistics" to chart a course away from the traditional utopias of past ages—"breeders of illusions and therefore, inevitably, of disillusions"—and toward "the serious assessment of historical alternatives, the exercise of our judgment as to the substantive rationality of alternative possible historical situations."[57] If, as I contend throughout this book, Romantic-era authors experienced and critically negotiated some of the most profound aspects of early modern globalization, then we are the inheritors of their decisions and representations. Just as they faced fateful questions about how to respond to their changing global situation, the choices we confront today are equally grave—perhaps more so, given contemporary force multipliers like nuclear weaponry and climate change. Recovering the global dimensions and dynamics of British Romanticism, I suggest in my conclusion, sheds light on some of the most progressive, forward-looking aspects of its works and worldviews. It may also help illuminate the full range of our contemporary global choices, at a time when their stakes are higher than ever.

CHAPTER ONE

Going Global

THE SCOTTISH ENLIGHTENMENT THEORIZES MODERNITY

*H*ISTORIANS have long remarked on the unlikely fact that the relatively remote, politically powerless nation of Scotland became one of the world's centers of eighteenth-century learning. Even the members of what was eventually called the "Scottish Enlightenment" were aware of this improbability.[1] As Hume wrote to a friend in 1757,

> Is it not strange that, at a time when we have lost our Princes, our Parliaments, our independent Government, even the Presence of our chief Nobility, are unhappy in our Accent and Pronunciation, speak a very corrupt Dialect of the Tongue which we make use of; is it not strange, I say, that, in these Circumstances, we shou'd really be the People most distinguished for Literature in Europe?[2]

Hume's comments are perhaps as much "a wish, indeed a self-fulfilling prophecy" as a description of reality, since at mid-century the bulk of the Scottish literati's voluminous output still lay in the future.[3] Nevertheless, he was surely right to recognize that something extraordinary was taking place in Edinburgh, Glasgow, Aberdeen, and Scotland's other centers of higher education. Bereft of their Parliament since the 1707 Act of Union with England, the Scots relied on their remaining civil institutions—religious, legal, and educational— for their sense of national identity. Building on the intellectual foundations of

Scotland's seventeenth-century men of letters,[4] and following Hume's call in *A Treatise of Human Nature* (1739–40) to develop "the science of man" on the "solid foundation" of "experience and observation,"[5] the writers and thinkers of the Scottish Enlightenment—backed by relatively progressive academic and religious organizations, intrepid and entrepreneurial booksellers, and a literate middle-class reading public committed to self-improvement—produced influential works in a variety of modern humanistic and social scientific disciplines.[6]

Elsewhere, I have written about the implications for British national identity of the Scottish literati's theorizations of sympathy, and in the next chapter I argue that a version of these theories is deployed in Radcliffe's romances for specifically cosmopolitan ends.[7] In this chapter, however, I focus on the domains of Enlightened inquiry—specifically, Hume's and Adam Smith's writings on political economy, and Hume's, Smith's, Henry Home's (Lord Kames'), and John Millar's conjectural histories—that set the conceptual coordinates for Britons to apprehend the nature and scope of globalization. In doing so, I build on the generally accepted idea that Enlightened thought plays a foundational role in the cognitive edifice of Western modernity. As opposed to the condemnatory judgments of Adorno, Heidegger, and others, I follow Jürgen Habermas' more positive assessment of the Enlightenment's legacy as the unfinished "philosophical discourse of modernity."[8] Exemplary here is Jonathan Israel's recent crediting of the Enlightenment with "the emergence of an interlocking complex of abstract concepts of which individual liberty, democracy, freedom of expression, comprehensive toleration, equality racial and sexual, freedom of lifestyle . . . together with a wholly secular morality based on equity" are the most significant.[9] Where Israel claims that these progressive concepts were developed primarily in the work of Spinoza and other members of "the radical Enlightenment," however, I argue that the economic and historical theories of Hume, Smith, and their fellow literati are at least equally important to our modern worldview, especially its global modality as "the intensification of consciousness of the world as a whole."[10]

My argument also takes its cue from Fredric Jameson's classic essay "The Realist Floor-Plan," which reminds us that the Enlightenment "assume[s] the emergence of a new space and a new temporality, a whole new realm of measurability and Cartesian extension, as well as of measurable clock time, a realm of the infinite geometrical grid, of homogeneity and equivalence."[11] Because his endpoint is the nineteenth-century realistic European novel, Jameson does not elaborate here how this "new space" and "new temporality" were theorized in any specific Enlightenment texts.[12] In fact, as Matthew

Wickman shows, Scottish Enlightenment mathematicians like Colin Maclaurin played integral roles in defending and popularizing the Newtonian calculus that facilitated these cognitive advances.[13] By paying close attention to the secondary, more concrete articulations of these concepts in the economic and anthropological works of Hume, Smith, Kames, and Millar, I aim to demonstrate their engagement in mapping the conceptual coordinates of modern globalization (even as some of their compatriots were literally mapping the globe).[14] After considering the ramifications of their economic and historical inquiries, I conclude with a brief analysis of Kant's influential writings on the prospect of world society. Kant's vision, I argue, both consolidates many of the literati's insights and anticipates even more modern forms of global thinking.

HUMEAN ECONOMICS AND NASCENT GLOBAL THINKING

In his own day, Hume was best known as a historian and an essayist; his many collections of essays and multi-volume *History of Great Britain* (1754–62) initially far outsold his original *Treatise on Human Nature*. Nevertheless, to understand Hume's contribution to Romantic globalism, his *Treatise* is the place to begin. Much of it is devoted to explaining epistemological skepticism, a philosophical position with admittedly little immediate bearing on geopolitical questions. Yet even Hume's abstract philosophizing bears the clear imprint of what Uday Singh Mehta, speaking of both Hume and Smith, calls "a security that stems from the knowledge that the religious and political convulsions of the seventeenth century are behind them, along with a blissful ignorance of the industrial and French revolutions that are still just beyond the horizon."[15] The Scottish Enlighteners' historical situation—on the cusp of Western modernity, as well as the border between a Scottish past and a British present[16]—is both the limiting condition and the enabling source of their theoretical insights.

When Hume turns in Book Three of the *Treatise* to consider the origins of government, his first priority is to refute the social contract theory developed by earlier thinkers like Hobbes and Locke. Despite their differences, these men shared the belief that, in order to receive the protections to person and property afforded by government, people must voluntarily give up some of their natural liberty and effectively enter into a contract with their leaders. Hume argues that social contract theory, insofar as it considers the origins of nations to be essentially endogamous, overlooks a central element in the formation of the earliest governments: inter-national relations. In so-called primitive societies like those of Native Americans, Hume conjectures, conditions may be egalitarian enough, and people's desires humble enough, that everyone's needs more or less harmonize, and even petty disagreements "will have but small tendency to disturb society" (539).[17] Only in times of war, Hume asserts, do societies need strong, top-down leadership to organize fighting against external enemies and prevent civil strife from the stress of conflict: "And so far am I from thinking with some philosophers, that men are utterly incapable of society without government, that I assert the first rudiments of government to arise from quarrels, *not among men of the same society, but among those of different societies*" (539–40; my italics). Once such structures of authority are established, moreover, they prove difficult to dismantle:

> This authority instructs [the primitives] in the advantages of government, and teaches them to have recourse to it, when either by the pillage of war, by commerce, or by any fortuitous inventions, their riches and possessions have become so considerable as to make them forget, on every emergence, the interest they have in the preservation of peace and justice. (540)

Later, we will see how this account of the origins of what Foucault calls governmentality—the bureaucratization of modern society[18]—differs from those of Kames and Millar. More immediately, what stands out is the elementary function Hume grants to relations *between* societies in the process of their institutionalization. They do not organize themselves first and then later declare war on each other, as we might suppose; rather, inter-societal conflicts necessitate robust and ultimately durable governments. Furthermore, it is not only war that calls permanent administrative frameworks into existence: "commerce" and, more vaguely, "any fortuitous inventions" also produce the conditions in which governmentality takes root. What war and commerce similarly require is that societies and, by extension, states have close, extended contacts with one another. Hume's argument for the origin of government in the *Treatise*, in other words, is already fundamentally global in orientation insofar as it recognizes that states' political and economic institutions always develop in relation to those of others.[19]

This essential insight informs Hume's later, more popular writings on political economy.[20] His great model in essayistic endeavors, Joseph Addison, had already treated such questions for an earlier generation. In *The Spectator* #69 (1711), Addison's speaker marvels at London's growing centrality to global trade and praises the "mutual Intercourse and Traffick among Mankind."[21] Nevertheless, the former continues to think of such exchanges as transactions between individual merchants, which leave the "British Territories" themselves essentially unchanged. Hume, by contrast, encourages readers to adopt a worldview that is more dynamic as well as expansive.

In "Of Commerce," the opening essay of his *Political Discourses* (1752), Hume establishes the foundation for a recognizably modern economic state infrastructure by explaining that public and private interests, already scandalously conjoined by Bernard Mandeville's *The Fable of the Bees* (1714), may legitimately be reconciled if one adopts a sufficiently elastic view of the value of the labor force produced by a given state's commercial investments.[22] Hume then mounts a more provocative argument: as important as the development of domestic commerce is to state growth, foreign commerce is even more crucial. Much as inter-national conflict produces governmentality, Hume argues that foreign commerce effectively stimulates its domestic counterpart: "If we consult history, we shall find that, in most nations, foreign trade has preceded any refinement in home manufactures, and given birth to domestic luxury" (263). Whereas domestic commodities generally improve slowly, superior foreign products can be imported, used, and immediately enjoyed. Meanwhile, through exports of superfluous goods, large profits can be realized. As a result, says Hume, "men become acquainted with the *pleasures* of luxury and the *profits* of commerce; and their *delicacy* and *industry*, being once awakened, carry them on to father improvements, in every branch of domestic as well as foreign trade" (264). In short, the maturation of a nation-state depends, not so much on the development of a central, immutable core of identity, but rather on the continuous (and in the case of commerce, quite literal) give-and-take of goods, services, people, and ideas with other, equally permeable territorial entities.

Although Hume's view would be challenged by the "blood and soil" national discourses of the nineteenth and twentieth centuries, it clearly anticipates Saskia Sassen's contemporary definition of the global as that which "simultaneously transcends the exclusive framing of national states yet partly inhabits national territories and institutions."[23] This is not to deny that Hume's thinking is almost always marked by national commitments. Rather, I am suggesting that Hume's recognition that global forces and flows precede the consolidation of national entities and institutions looks forward to the insights (although not the skeptical attitude) of contemporary critics of globalization like Carlo Galli, who sees the "*intrinsically unstable* and *profoundly indeterminate*" nature of "modern political spatiality" as a product of contemporary economic globalism.[24]

Hume's commitment to global commercial progress develops in *Political Discourses*' subsequent essays, which Eugene F. Miller notes "generally . . . condemn domestic market restrictions" and assert the mutual advantages of free trade—that is, trade that does not discriminate between domestic and foreign goods—between nation-states.[25] Furthermore, by recognizing that "market adjustment tends to maintain a supply of money that is generally proportioned to the levels of industry among different nations,"[26] Hume demonstrates the futility of mercantilism's attempts, primarily through trade restrictions and tariffs, to control the sum total of money in a given state. Assuming a gold standard, Hume shows in "Of the Balance of Trade" that when the amount of specie in a given country goes up, prices rise as well, leading to a decrease in exports, which in turn reduces the amount of money in circulation. This theory, which economists call the "price-specie-flow mechanism," effectively overturns mercantilism's core policy of hoarding currency, and argues instead for letting the effects of free trade—the cornerstone of economic globalism—"naturally" regulate a nation's monetary supply.[27] Hume's commitment to free trade is powerfully expressed in the following passage near the conclusion to "Of the Balance of Trade":

> From these principles we may learn what judgment we ought to form of those numberless bans, obstructions, and imposts, which all nations of Europe, and none more than England, have put upon trade. . . . Could anything scatter our riches, it would be such impolitic contrivances. But this general ill effect, however, results from them, that they deprive neighbouring nations of that free communication and exchange which the Author of the world has intended, by giving them soils, climates, and geniuses, so different from each other. (324)

Needless restrictions on trade violate the natural order of things. As if to drive home this point, Hume's claim to know the intentions of the world's "Author" rhetorically conveys the intensity of his belief, not so much in God (whose existence Hume personally, infamously doubted), but in the cause of the freest possible international trade.[28]

This cause is furthered in "Of the Jealousy of Trade," placed behind "Of the Balance of Trade" in 1758, where Hume demonstrates, again *contra* mercantilism, that states need not resent or attempt to stifle others' economic successes. Domestic industry, Hume explains, cannot be injured by neighboring nations' rising prosperity: "I go farther, and observe, that where an open communication is preserved among nations, it is impossible but the domestic industry of every one must receive an encrease from the improvements of the others" (328). Having already established that foreign imports both provide desired luxuries and stimulate domestic improvements, Hume now argues it is in a given state's best interest that others be equally economically advanced, because "if our neighbours have no art or cultivation, they cannot take [our surplus commodities]; because they will have nothing to give in exchange" (329). Hume then repeats in truncated form his earlier description of the implicitly international design of the world: "Nature, by giving a diversity of geniuses, climates, and soils, to different nations, has secured their mutual intercourse and commerce, as long as they all remain industrious and civilized" (329).

Admittedly, Hume's arguments here are far from disinterested: he clearly means to encourage Britain's flourishing. Yet as John Robertson indicates, Hume's reasoning implicitly relies on the presupposition "that no one nation would acquire the political and military power forcibly to distort the pattern of trade over a long period."[29] In this light, the rise of British and other European imperialisms represents a swerve away from the most desirable course of global progress; and in a subsequent essay, "Of the Balance of Power," Hume indeed condemns "[e]normous monarchies" and other projects of national expansion as "destructive to human nature" (340–41). In a manner that can be difficult to recognize given our contemporary conflation of neoliberal economic policies and globalization, Hume's support of free trade actually makes him an enemy of incipient imperialism. For Hume, smart political economy means encouraging Britons (and Europeans in general, since his *Political Discourses* were quickly translated on the Continent) to think of their world as united by common economic interests and goals, rather than merely by unending competition. It also problematizes the too-easy assumption that globalization is at bottom little more than a pretext for yet another round of Western domination and exploitation. On the contrary, Hume's early disarticulation of imperialism and globalization—a strong version of what Karen O'Brien calls "the ambivalent, underdetermined relationship of [the Enlightenment's] global imagining[s] to incipient imperialism"—suggests that the latter is not only perfectly possible without the former, but also theoretically incompatible with it.[30] Hume's economic theories thus set important precedents for the egalitarian, even idealistic tenor of later Romantic globalism.

THE ETHICS OF SMITHIAN FREE TRADE

Like his friend Hume, Adam Smith was fortuitously positioned on what Mehta calls "the cusp that Britain was crossing."[31] The oft-omitted full title of Smith's most famous text, *An Inquiry into the Nature and Causes of the Wealth of Nations,* is revealing in several ways. Rather than announcing that he has single-handedly solved the problem of political economy, as some of his followers later claimed, Smith's title echoes the speculative, hypothetical register of many of the literati's treatises. Smith also knew he was not the first to attempt to uncover political economy's fundamental mechanisms; not only did he have Hume's example and the work of the French physiocrats before him, but he was also well aware of James Steuart's influential, mercantilist *Inquiry into the Principles of Political Economy* (1767).[32] Whereas Smith uses the definite article for his earlier major work, *The Theory of Moral Sentiments* (1756; 6th ed. 1790), he opts for an indefinite pronoun ("an") and a more tentative noun ("inquiry" rather than "theory") when naming his economic treatise. Equally striking is the plural noun at the title's conclusion, which signals—in a way that has too often been overlooked—that this is not a text about a particular nation's wealth, or about each nation considered in isolation, but about the wealth of nations considered together, as an interconnected network of relations. Smith's choice of title thus reflects not only what Donald Winch calls Smith's "broad comparative and cosmopolitan ambitions,"[33] but also his Humean awareness that, to understand how an individual nation becomes wealthy and sustainable, one must comprehend the mechanisms that determine the economic fates of *all* nations.[34]

The basic mechanisms that exist within each national economy—the division of factors of production (land, labor, capital) and their categories of return (rent, wages, profit), the distinction between "natural" and "market" price, the difference between "productive" and "unproductive" labor—as outlined in the first three books of *Wealth of Nations* have been exhaustively analyzed elsewhere.[35] More important for my purposes are Books Four and Five, in which Smith launches a series of withering attacks on the mercantilist policies of his day and intermittently analyzes Britain's economic relationship with its North American colonies, which had recently begun their historic rebellion. By further demolishing mercantilist arguments for hoarding precious metals and specie, Smith sets the course for the creation of a more fully integrated global economic system. He thus not only anticipates but also helps facilitate the conditions for Wallerstein's recognition that "[c]apitalism as a system of production for sale in a market for profit . . . has only existed in, and can be said to require, a world-system in which political units are not coextensive with the boundaries of the market economy."[36]

In a letter to a friend a few years after the initial publication of *Wealth of Nations,* Smith describes it as a "very violent attack . . . upon the whole commercial system of Great Britain."[37] He begins Book Four by pointing out that mercantilism is based on the flawed premise that wealth is equivalent to money. Instead, Smith asserts that real wealth must be understood, first and foremost, in terms of "the annual produce of [a nation's] industry,"[38] for as he points out earlier in the same chapter, trying to hoard coinage is a vain endeavor: "When the quantity of gold and silver imported into any country exceeds the effectual demand, no vigilance of government can prevent their exportation" (I.436). From passages like this, subsequent generations of economists learned to venerate Smith as the free market's great defender—although, as many have pointed out, this is a highly partisan and selective reading of Smith, who in fact calls for ample government intervention and spending in areas like public education and infrastructure.[39]

Mercantilism is not just founded on faulty principles: it simply doesn't work. In succeeding chapters, Smith demonstrates the ways in which mercantilism's imposition of restraints and high taxes on imports, combined with its obsession with encouraging excessive exports, are not only wrongheaded but also destructive of a given country's "real wealth and revenue" (I.451). Like Hume, Smith understands that trade is not a zero-sum game, since one country does not win and another lose when there is an uneven balance of trade between them. Rather, in the absence of "bounties and monopolies" (whose creation Smith always opposes), "that trade which, without force or constraint, is naturally and regularly carried on between any two places, is always advantageous . . . to both" (I.489). Hence Smith agrees with Hume that it is in all nations' best interests to see their neighbors elevated to similar states of improvement. Indeed, Smith seems to believe unfettered international commerce to be the best method of ensuring both peace and prosperity: "Commerce . . . ought naturally to be, among nations, as among individuals, a bond of union and friendship" (I.493). Such sentiments sound familiar to us, of course, because they are still consistently deployed by today's proponents of economic globalism.[40]

Given the extent to which Smith's theories and policy recommendations have come to seem inextricably linked to neoliberal economics, it is worth remembering that in his own day and immediately afterward his ideas appeared quite radical.[41] Smith's enumeration of the benefits of free trade between France and England to both countries "without either mercantile jealousy or national animosity" (I.495), for example, arrived at the end of nearly a century of war between these nations. The advent of the French Revolution only confirmed for some that Smith's ideas were subversive of authority and hierarchy; as Dugald Stewart recalled, "[t]he doctrine of a Free Trade was itself represented as of a revolutionary tendency" by those who opposed democratic reforms.[42] Smith recognized that his recommendations were not likely to be fully carried out, remarking that "[t]o expect, indeed, that the freedom of trade should ever be entirely restored in Great Britain, is as absurd as to expect that an Oceana or Utopia should be established in it" (I.471). This admission is not a retraction: Smith's use of the verb "restored" artfully suggests that total free trade would merely return Britain to a more natural state of affairs. It also insinuates that his ideas are simply ahead of their time; in Richard F. Teichgraeber's words, Smith "meant, about all else, that a policy of laissez-faire, whatever its considerable intellectual merits, ran far ahead of actual social developments in eighteenth-century Europe."[43]

Smith's belief in the many virtues of unfettered free trade led him to take other progressive political positions, most notably on Britain's relationship with its North American colonies. Indeed, as *Wealth of Nations* went to press just months before the signing of the American Declaration of Independence, it is difficult to overstate the timeliness of Smith's reflections on the future of Britain's colonial relations. In sum, while he admits that "there are no colonies of which the progress has been more rapid than that of the English in North America" (II.571), Smith believes that in the long run neither Britain nor America can realize its full economic potentials within their uneven arrangement. Although they were taxed at a lower rate than their British counterparts, the Americans were forbidden from establishing any competitive manufactures with Britain, and from using ships other than British ones for trading with the mother country.[44] Smith's recognition that these "Navigation Acts" had benefits for Britain did not prevent him from seeing that the resultant monopolization of the colonies' foreign trade was actually stunting Britain's growth in other areas (see II.596). Furthermore, he condemns the ways in which Britain has warped its own manufacturing capacities to fit the North American market:

> In her present condition, Great Britain resembles one of those unwholesome bodies in which some of the vital parts are overgrown, and which, upon that account are liable to many dangerous disorders. . . . A small stop in that great blood-vessel, which has been artificially swelled beyond its natural dimensions, and through which an unnatural proportion of the industry and commerce of the country has been forced to circulate, is very likely to bring on the most dangerous disorders upon the whole body politick. (II.604–5)

Following a long British tradition of "exploit[ing] the venerable metaphor of the body politic,"[45] Smith apotropaically wields the figure of the unbalanced, unhealthy organism against the prospect of economic collapse. Ultimately, he suggests that there is something immoral about Britain's monopolizing relationship with her colonies; how else to explain the biting tone of his

observation that "[t]o found a great enterprise for the sole purpose of raising up a people of customers, may at first sight appear a project fit only for a nation of shopkeepers. It is, however . . . extremely fit for a nation whose government is influenced by shopkeepers" (II.613)?

Between the strains on the British financial system (especially the growing national debt), the stifling of the colonies' economic potential (not to mention their political freedoms), and the escalating political tensions between them, Smith foresaw that Britain and America would have to alter their relationship, probably permanently, for the survival of both. A best-case scenario meant the creation of a true union, one that would institute a policy of free trade (II.935) as well as provide additional benefits to each side: Britain would be able to tax its former colonies in a way that would help relieve its growing national debt, while America (with fair representation in British Parliament) would find the "tranquility" it needed to prosper (II.945). Smith even imagines that were such a union to occur, "[t]he seat of the empire" might eventually move to the North America, since the (former) colonies would likely outpace Britain economically in the long run (II.625–26).

Although the loss of the North American colonies marked the end of one stage of Britain's colonial endeavors, it indirectly facilitated the eastern-oriented ventures that followed. Yet the conclusion of *Wealth of Nations* makes clear that Smith does not approve of imperial projects in any guise.[46] Recognizing that "[t]he territorial acquisitions of the East India company" might seem to offer some recompense for Britain's growing expenses, Smith nonetheless recommends that "[i]t might, perhaps, be more proper to lighten, than to aggravate, the burden of those unfortunate countries"; to this end, he warns against increasing their taxation, and instead counsels ending "the embezzlement and misapplication of the greater part of those which they already pay" (II.946). Having condemned the current state of colonial affairs and warned against increasing the exploitation of Britain's Eastern colonies, Smith then launches a final attack on colonial policy in general. Calling the colonies "a sort of splendid and showy equipage" that will never be profitable despite the fantasies of the British elite, Smith counsels that they "should awake from [this golden dream] themselves, and endeavour to awaken the people" before it is too late (II.946–47). Although it would take two twentieth-century "world wars" for his prophecy to be realized, Smith was surely correct to recognize that Britain's future lay not "with the imagination that [it] possessed a great empire," but rather with the recognition that it must "endeavour to accommodate her future views and designs to the real mediocrity of her circumstances" (II.947). Attempts at empire-building would merely delay the true integration of Britain's economy into the world-system.

I have argued that Hume's and Smith's favored visions for Britain's economic development were always broadly global rather than specifically imperial, but there were limits, of course, to their prescience. They were not to have the last words on the question of the role of free trade in global economic progress; David Ricardo's later formulation of the theory of "comparative advantage" (which states that trade between countries will always be beneficial as long as each partner focuses on those activities in which it has a relative advantage) in his *Principles of Political Economy and Taxation* (1817), for example, was highly influential and inevitably encouraged competition between nations, even if this was not Ricardo's intent. Furthermore, although Hume and Smith clearly anticipate economic globalization in the general sense, both still think within the limits of "*internationalization*"—defined by Geoffrey Ingham as "an acceleration of the flow of goods, money, and other financial assets *between* nation states"—rather than toward what Ingham calls "genuine *globalization*": "economic processes and forms of organization . . . which *transcend* the territorial limits of states."[47]

Finally, Hume and Smith arguably overlook, or at least underestimate, the destabilizing long-term effects of the global market forces they were among the first to theorize. From the left-wing perspective articulated by Slavoj Žižek, for example, it now seems clear that "[c]apitalism has no 'normal,' balanced state: its 'normal' state is the permanent production of an excess; the only way for capitalism to survive is to expand."[48] Moreover, Hume and Smith seem to have been relatively blind to the geo-political inequalities that were being exacerbated even as they wrote. As Wallerstein indicates, along with the "basic dichotomy" of "bourgeois versus proletarian"—which concerned Smith enough that he recommends government-funded universal education to keep workers from falling into mental lethargy—the other fundamental binarism produced by the capitalist world-system

> was the spatial hierarchy of economic specialization, core versus periphery, in which there was an appropriation of surplus from the producers of low-wage (but high supervision), low-profit, low-capital intensive goods by the producers of high-wage (but low supervision), high-profit, high-capital intensive, so-called "unequal exchange."[49]

This is precisely the kind of hierarchy that promoters of economic globalism, from Hume and Smith to Thomas Friedman, believe can be overcome by "flattening" the world's economic relations.[50] According to most critics of globalization, however, what unequal exchange produces in real geographical terms is the related phenomenon of "uneven development": the process, according to David Harvey, by which "'[d]ifference' and 'otherness' are *produced* in space through the simple logic of uneven capital investment, a proliferating geographical division of labor, and increasing segmentation of reproductive activities and the rise of spatially ordered (often segregated) social distinctions...."⁵¹ Especially for its skeptics, economic globalization is thus akin to the Derridean *pharmakon*: it is simultaneously the potential cure of the world's inequality and its root cause and intensifier.⁵² If such ambivalence is not frequently explicit in the politico-economic writings of Hume and Smith, their clear-sighted theories nonetheless bring into focus many of the ideas, terms, and conditions that have framed debates over globalization ever since.

FROM GLOBAL ECONOMICS TO CONJECTURAL HISTORY

So were the Scottish Enlighteners simply unaware of capitalism's destabilizing, inequitable tendencies at the international and global levels, or did they recognize them implicitly? In this section, I contend that the literati implicitly acknowledged these propensities and, moreover, attempted indirectly to explain and even justify them. They pursued these goals, and thereby further established the conceptual framework for thinking globally, through the conjoined deployment of a methodology of conjectural history and the theoretical framework of stadial history.⁵³ Granted, these two elements of Scottish "speculative history" are not usually separated out, and it was the generation after Hume and Smith that specifically denominated these concepts. But temporarily detaching conjectural history from stadial theory will help us analyze their functions separately before recombining them, allowing me to ask: what did this partnership of practice and theory allow the Scottish Enlighteners to think? My answer will be that it allowed them to think globality, *mondialisation*, "worldwideification," with an unprecedented degree of sophistication.

If political economy forms a quintessential vector of the Scottish Enlightenment, history forms an intersecting line of conceptual force. Like Foucault in the twentieth century, the literati were primarily interested in writing "histories of the present," that is to say, in exploring the development of the traditions, institutions, and ways of being that set the cognitive and affective parameters of their era.⁵⁴ This was accomplished by combining their belief in the universality of human nature—an Enlightenment shibboleth—with the recognition that such nature is nevertheless susceptible to change depending on geographical and other circumstances. As James Chandler and others have observed, the Scottish Enlighteners recognized that conceptualizing one's own historical moment or situation depends on one's ability to frame or contextualize that situation in relation to those of others, whose situations in turn demand similar treatment.[55] Beginning with the stadial historical theory of Hume and Smith, and then via more extended exercises in conjectural history by Kames and Millar, we can trace the development of an increasingly sophisticated globalism: one that accounts for uneven geographical development by positing it as an inevitable feature of humanity's incomplete march to modernity.[56]

Hume's primary argument in his 1741 essay "Of the Study of History," to quote Alexander Broadie's succinct paraphrase, is that history is "a precondition of almost all intellectual development."[57] Given the relative brevity of our individual lives, says Hume, "we would forever be children in understanding, were it not for this invention [i.e. historiography], which extends our experience to all past ages, and to the most distant nations; making them contribute as much to our improvement in wisdom, as if they had actually lain under our observation."[58] Hume deftly associates the study of history with the cognitive mastery of both time ("all past ages") and space ("the most distant nations"). But an obvious question loomed: how does one write the histories of times and places one has not personally witnessed? One answer was to use the printed record, and the Enlighteners frequently depended on older historical sources and travelers' accounts for their texts. But they also readily recognized that the historical record is necessarily incomplete, since at a certain remove from the present no accounts survive. The solution to this problem is already implied in Hume's statement that the best histories allow readers "to be transported into the remotest ages of the world, and to observe human society, in its infancy": some things simply have to be extrapolated. Years later, Dugald Stewart would summarize this insight as follows: "In this want of direct evidence, we are under a necessity of supplying the place of fact by conjecture; and when we are unable to ascertain how men have actually conducted themselves upon particular occasions, of considering in what manner they are likely to have proceeded, from the principles of their nature, and the circumstances of their external situation."[59] Given the assumed constancy of human nature, knowledge of specific circumstances could generate a reasonably accurate or at least plausible account of what transpired at a given time and place, no matter how remote.[60]

Conjectural history was a methodology, but to function effectively it needed a theory undergirding it. The basic structure of stadial theory is outlined clearly by Smith in his 1762–63 lectures at the University of Glasgow, in which he states that humankind passes through "four distinct states" or stages: "1ˢᵗ, the Age of Hunters; 2ᵈˡʸ, the Age of Shepherds; 3ᵈˡʸ, the Age of Agriculture; and 4ᵗʰˡʸ, the Age of Commerce."⁶¹ The well-known significance of Smith's sequence lies not only in its progressive scaffolding of stages of social development, but also in its predication of those developments on changes in a society's mode of subsistence. The influence of this schema on Marx's conception of historical materialism is well known. Less well known, however, is that Smith immediately follows this initial outline with a remarkable thought experiment in which he invites his audience to imagine how a dozen people stranded on a deserted island would, over time, develop increasingly sophisticated means for sustaining and organizing themselves: "[T]he first method they would fall upon for their sustenance . . . would be the chase. This is the age of hunters. In process of time, as their numbers multiplied, they would find the chase too precarious for their support. . . . Hence would arise the age of shepherds" (14–15). Smith then makes a remarkable leap from "the indefinite, isolated location of this group of castaways . . . to a generalizable model":⁶² in the middle of what is clearly a conjectural history he suddenly shifts to consider the contemporary world, stating that "[w]e find accordingly that in almost all countries the age of shepherds preceded that of agriculture. The Tartars and Arabians subsist almost entirely by their flocks and herds" (15). More details about the productive arrangements of these modern-day "primitive" nations follow—Smith notes, for example, that North American Indians do not strictly follow this framework, since they use some agriculture without keeping herds—before conjecture returns: "But when a society becomes numerous they would find a difficulty in supporting themselves by herds and flocks. Then they would naturally turn to the cultivation of land" (15).

To understand what this slippage between conjectural history and stadial theory signifies, let's recall that Smith was not the first thinker to theorize that societies move through incremental stages of development on their progress to modernity. Vico's *New Science* (1725) and Montesquieu's *Spirit of the Laws* (1748), for example, each anticipates Smith's break with the older traditions that saw human history as primarily cyclical or a narrative of decline.⁶³ But this first recorded appearance of the Scottish Enlightenment's stadial theory is multiply suggestive. Smith's seemingly unselfconscious use of a clearly conjectural, hypothetical scenario (castaways learning to survive together) as evidence for his model of historical change confirms the mutually reinforcing, essentially circular relation between conjectural history and stadial theory: each both presupposes and establishes the other's truth. It also displays one of the signature innovations of Scottish Enlightenment historiography: the ability to think of different nations or societies as inhabiting distinct stages of development simultaneously. Although stadial theory outlines a supposedly natural progression from primitivism to civilization—and for Smith and his fellow literati, the benefits of commercial progress (greater civility, peace, and prosperity) almost always outweigh its costs (loss of martial vigor and civic virtue, attenuation of the bonds of society or nation)—it does not guarantee progress as inevitable.[64] Theoretically, any people or nation could become stuck in a given developmental stage; in practice, such judgments were frequently reserved for African and Asian social orders, which from an eighteenth-century British perspective often appeared stalled in "earlier" stages.

Where the famous opening line of L. P. Hartley's novel *The Go-Between* (1953) asserts that "[t]he past is a foreign country; they do things differently there,"[65] Smith's combination of conjectural history and stadial theory anticipates this observation with a chiasmatic twist: foreign societies offer the opportunity to witness the past in the present. The synthesis of conjectural history and stadial theory thus facilitates what Chandler identifies as the most distinctive aspect of the new sense of historicism that would persist well into the Romantic era: "the quality and extent of its interest in what might be called 'comparative contemporaneities.'"[66] By teaching readers to apprehend that societies could co-exist in space yet seem to occupy different historical moments, Smith and those who took up his ideas were giving Britons the cognitive tools to grasp their world as an interconnected albeit uneven whole.[67]

RE-WRITING WORLD HISTORIES

Stamped by Smith's not-so-invisible hand, the combination of conjectural history and stadial theory became the central driver of the Scottish Enlightenment's historiographical, sociological, and anthropological innovations. As Roxann Wheeler notes, if in the 1760s and 1770s, when Smith was giving the lectures that would become the basis of *Wealth of Nations,* stadial theory "became culturally influential," then "between 1780 and 1800, it became more like an orthodoxy."[68] Two of the works that helped establish this dominance—although each complicates it as well—are Lord Kames' three-volume *Sketches of the History of Man* (1774) and John Millar's *Observations Concerning the Distinction of Ranks in Society* (1771; changed to *The Origin of the Distinction of Ranks* for the revised third edition of 1779).

One of the most prolific writers of the Scottish Enlightenment, Kames was an early supporter of Smith and corresponded with Hume, to whom he was distantly related, for nearly twenty years. Having already published influential volumes on legal, critical, philosophical, and even agricultural themes, *Sketches* was intended to be Kames' crowning achievement. Its overarching theme is humanity's progress through the stages of development introduced by Smith, and its volume titles—"Progress of Men independent of Society," "Progress of Men in Society," and "Progress of Sciences"—duly seem to promise a commitment to stadialism.[69] But even in the initial sketch (originally entitled "Diversity of Men and Languages," and later separated out as a "Preliminary Discourse concerning the Origin of Men and Languages"), Kames' commitment to stadial theory is clearly tempered by other interests and allegiances. Mark Salber Phillips notes that *Sketches* is as much a "theodicy" as an Enlightened treatise insofar as its frequently ramshackle construction "is held together by a conviction that every part of God's design manifests a necessary order."[70] Kames' desire to accommodate stadial theory to his Presbyterianism helps explain why phrases like "the finger of God," "destined by Providence," "Providence intends . . . " and "Providence extracts order out of confusion" appear with regularity (I.56, I.69, I.266, II.362). It also may explain his decision—not endorsed by most other literati—to account for humankind's racial and linguistic diversity by positing not one but multiple points of origin.

In his "Preliminary Discourse," Kames begins by setting out what he takes as proof of humanity's polygeneticism. Mocking both Linnaeus' classificatory methods and Montesquieu's climatic theories of racial difference, Kames surveys physical differences between Africans and Europeans and concludes that "beyond any rational doubt . . . there are different races or kinds of men, and . . . these races or kinds are naturally fitted for different climates" (I.47). His challenge then becomes how to square this view with the biblical account of Adam and Eve, and Kames' solution is to posit that humankind's original racial unity was fractured by God after Babel. This position was not popular—indeed, it apparently failed to convince most of his readers—but it reminds us that despite its reputation for disenchanting the world, not all Enlightenment writers were satisfied keeping theological and secular worldviews mutually exclusive.

Although Kames' polygeneticism places him outside the Enlightened mainstream, his persistently comparative approach is undeniably modern, as is his recognition that his conclusions (however misguided) could be finally validated only by "an extensive survey of the inhabited parts of our globe" (I.45). The next sketch, in which Kames considers the progress of humanity regarding "Food and Population" (I.53), further demonstrates his willingness to open stadial theory to other contributing factors. Despite his initial mockery of Montesquieu's and Buffon's climatic theories, Kames repeatedly explores how climate variations affect human development. In line with stadial theory, he first conjectures that people move from hunting to pastoralism when overconsumption leads to scarcity and "[m]en, thus pinched for food, are excited to try other means to supply their wants" (I.55). There follows a hypothetical population boom, which leads to inter-tribal conflict abated by the invention of agriculture, which in turn necessitates private property, laws, government, and eventually the stimulation of commerce (I.57). As an "honest observer,"[71] however, Kames cannot help but wonder whether this stadial schema applies equally well around the globe. Noting that most produce grows best in moderate temperatures, for example, Kames infers that these "circumstances make it highly probable, that agriculture first became an art in temperate climes" (I.57), and that stadial theory is best borne out "in all temperate climates of the Old World," where "progress . . . [has] been precisely uniform" (I.59). In colder environments where nutritious crops will not grow in abundance, by contrast, Kames thinks that social development likely stops at the pastoral stage, whereas in the tropics, he believes that neither hunting nor pasturage was generally practiced; instead, "the inhabitants, at present, subsist on vegetable food; and probably did so from the beginning" (I.61). While never abandoning stadial theory altogether, Kames' commitment to accounting for the world's geographical diversity leads to significant modifications of the standard Enlightenment progress narrative.

Kames' willingness to amend stadial theory in the light of real-world evidence is clearest in Book Two of *Sketches,* where he turns to consider "The Origin and Progress of the American Nations." Native Americans were of particular interest to Scottish Enlightenment thinkers, who saw American Indians as "living examples of an earlier stage of society" and thus often placed them at the origins of their histories.[72] But Kames is not convinced that such aboriginals fit the stadial trajectory as neatly as other writers assumed. His perception of their distinct physical characteristics—including their lack of body hair, "copper colour," and, most alarmingly, their tendency "to be born with down upon the skin, which disappears the eighth or ninth day, and never grows again" (II.556–57)—leads Kames to hypothesize that Native Americans, like Africans, form a separate race. Other phenomena prove puzzling too, including the fact that "[t]he North-American tribes are remarkable with respect to one branch of their history, that, instead of advancing, like other nations, toward the maturity of society and government, they continue to this hour in their original state of hunting and fishing" (II.561). Kames can solve this mystery only by conjecturing that, since population density is not a problem in North America, the natives never needed to develop pasturage. This hypothesis, however, only creates further problems: to explain the paucity of the American Indian population, for example, Kames is forced to fall back on Buffon's dubious theory that Native American men have weak generative powers and little interest in the opposite sex (II.562–63). Moreover, Kames is at a loss to explain how, despite lacking pasturage, many Indian tribes nevertheless developed certain varieties of agriculture, effectively skipping a historical stage: "The fact however is singular, of a people using corn before tame cattle: there must be a cause, which on better acquaintance with that people will probably be discovered" (II.566). Finally, there is the unaccountable fact that South America, despite being less temperate than North America, has witnessed much greater civilizational progress (see II.566–67). If Kames is ultimately unable to provide satisfactory answers to the puzzling questions these observations raise, he at least shows a salutary willingness to admit their existence. What Wheeler calls Kames' "intellectual meanderings and revisions"[73] might better be understood as evidence of his Enlightened willingness to let the facts (as he understood them) complicate and even contradict his theories.

In this, as in much else, Kames was an important influence on an even greater proponent of stadial theory: John Millar. Like Kames, Millar—a student of Smith's before himself becoming Regius Chair of Civil Law at Glasgow University—was a polymath. (He also lived for a time in the Kames' household as a tutor.) But it was his analysis of the nature of authority in *Origin of the Distinction of Ranks* that truly made Millar's reputation. Although the first edition was only a moderate seller, he expanded and revised the text over the next decade, and it went on to reach a wide audience in Britain, Europe, and America (where James Madison, among others, owned a copy).[74] *Distinction of Ranks* displays all the hallmarks of the global thinking that characterizes the powerful, Enlightened conjunction of conjectural history and stadial theory.

In his brief preface to the first edition, Millar immediately registers his comparativist leanings by noting "the amazing diversity in the manners of different countries, and even of the same country at different periods" (284). Nevertheless, he is certain that the careful observer will be able to account for these differences by considering a range of variables, including "how much the character of individuals is influenced by their education, their professions, and their peculiar circumstances" (284). Combined with Millar's later assertion that "general improvements ... proceed from a gradual reformation of the manners, and are accompanied with a correspondent change in the condition of society" (285), he clearly introduces a great deal of flexibility into stadial theory's account of the number and hierarchy of factors that influence social development.[75] In Millar's view, a society's subsistence mode is merely one contributing factor to its growth and progress. Accordingly, he anticipates later developments in Marxian theory inasmuch as for Millar the relation between base and superstructure is multi-directional. This theoretical flexibility is extended in the revised introduction to the third edition of *Distinction of Ranks,* where Millar further develops his catalogue of factors that contribute to social diversity[76] before concluding that "[t]he variety that frequently occurs in these, and such other particulars, must have a prodigious influence upon the great body of a people; as, by giving a peculiar direction to their inclinations and pursuits, it must be productive of correspondent habits, dispositions, and ways of thinking" (84).

Millar's expanded introduction to *Distinction of Rank*'s third edition is also notable for its truly global outlook. At its outset, and very much in a fully Enlightened spirit, he invokes his intent to "survey the present state of the globe" in order to investigate humanity's "natural progress from ignorance to knowledge" (84–85). At the same time, he declares that current peoples who are "destitute of culture" can be profitably compared with those in "the remote history of polished nations" who were also in "a state of the same rudeness and barbarism" (84). Chandler points out that Millar's sensitivity to the possibilities of both past and present "barbarism" opens up modern comparativism insofar as it attempts to take into account "the different *global circumstances* of such states of a nation. . . . "[77] In this regard, at least, it seems clear that Millar's methodology ultimately better supports the connotations of *mondialisation,* which Nancy says "keep[s] the horizon of a 'world' as a space of possible meaning for the whole of human relations," than those of the English "globalization," which according to Nancy presupposes "the idea of an integrated totality" and is thus less open to "the expanse of the *world* of human beings, cultures, and nations."[78]

A good example of such openness can be found when Millar, again in materials added to the third edition of *Distinction,* considers one of the phenomena that so interested Kames: the effects of climate.[79] Like Kames, Millar feels certain that climate must be apprehended by stadial theory: "Among the several circumstances which may affect the gradual improvement of society, the difference of climate is one of the most remarkable" (87). Millar is even more skeptical than Kames, however, of just how far such influence can be said to reach. After reviewing some of the evidence in favor of climatic theory, and weighing whether different climates have different effects on their inhabitants' constitutions, Millar can only conclude that "[h]ow far these conjectures have any real foundation . . . seems difficult to determine" (89). He then uses his comparativist approach to question climate theory's veracity, pointing out, for example, "the mildness and moderation of the Chinese, with the rough manners and intolerant principles of their neighbours in Japan" (89). However misguided these characterizations might appear to us today, Millar's commitment to comparativism—which Rey Chow calls a key ally of the "aspirations toward global peace, cosmopolitical right, and intercultural hospitality"[80]—effectively undermines climate theory by demonstrating the existence of (supposedly) substantial differences in national characters despite similar climatological environments.

The remainder of *Distinction of Ranks* focuses precisely on these differences. Of its six final chapters, all of which employ stadial theory in their examinations of social development, the longest by far is "Of the Rank and Condition of Women in Different Ages." Here, Millar reviews the evolution of women's social positions from their roles as secondary partners in the primitive marriages of hunter-gatherers, to the elevation of "those female virtues which, in a polished nation, are supposed to constitute the honour and dignity of the sex" (99). For the most part, he enthusiastically endorses the standard Scottish Enlightenment belief that the present state of British society represents the current zenith of "the gradual advancement of a people in civilized manners" (169): women gain freedom, the tyranny of patriarchs and monarchs is reduced, democracy advances, and the arts and commerce flourish. At the same time, Millar is not convinced that progress is an absolute good; late in *Distinction of Ranks,* for example, he remarks that although "the effects of opulence and refinement . . . [have] a tendency to inspire the people with notions of liberty and independence," they simultaneously "furnish the king with a standing army, the great engine of tyranny and oppression" (240). (His later *Historical View of the English Government* [1787; final edition 1803] makes many observations concerning the loss of valor and vigor among so-called polite peoples.[81]) Millar also occasionally suggests that "barbarous" nations have certain advantages over their more developed counterparts, including "greater freedom and plainness of behavior, according as they are farther removed from luxury and intemperance" (105). Significantly, Millar subsequently proposes that so-called savage nations are probably better off that way, given the environment in which they must subsist:

> When men are in danger of perishing for hunger; when they are exerting their utmost efforts to procure the bare necessities of life . . . their constitution would surely be ill-adapted to their circumstances, were they endowed with a refined taste of pleasure, and capable of feeling the delicate distresses and enjoyments, accompanied with all those elegant sentiments, which, in a civilized and enlightened age, are naturally derived from that passion. (114)

By treating "savagery" not as a moral failing, but as a stage of social development well suited to the actual material conditions in which people find themselves, Millar anticipates the ethos of modern social scientific disciplines.

Ultimately, however, it is Millar's methodological innovations, rather than his (often wayward) conclusions, that give his text its distinctly modern, global feel. I've already noted that, in Millar's opinion, progress can be taken too far; he does not hesitate, for example, to condemn the "strong disposition to pleasure" he detects in the peoples of modern-day France and Italy, which he fears will have "similar consequences to what [it] produced in ancient Rome" (155). Such juxtapositions of the ancient and the modern occur throughout *Distinction of Ranks*; on almost every page, Millar mixes examples from past and present to reinforce his arguments regarding the changing nature of social authority over time. Many sections in *Distinction of Ranks* also include comparisons between geographically disparate peoples or nations. Describing matrilineal traditions of naming among ancient Lycians, for example, Millar remarks that "[t]he same custom took place among the ancient inhabitants of Attica; as it does at present among several tribes of the natives of North America, and that of the Indians upon the coast of Malabar" (117). Here, temporal and spatial planes of comparison are granted equal importance; the following pages refer to Hottentots, the populations of the islands of Formosa and Ladrone, and North American Indians, before returning to "the ancient inhabitants of Attica" once more (118–19). Later, addressing the natural authority of fathers, Millar cites Caesar's account of the Gauls, followed by the customs of "ancient German nations," "the early laws and customs of Arabia," and "the empire of Russia" under Peter the Great, before considering evidence drawn from present-day accounts of "parts of Tartary," "the coast of Africa," and "the savages of South America" (164–66). Again, my interest is not in the legitimacy (or lack thereof) of Millar's various claims and comparisons, but rather in the habit of mind fostered by his repeated mapping of various cultural phenomena onto an implicit graph whose axes are homogeneous, linear time and contiguous, global space. This mindset both encourages and privileges the ability to grasp the "complex connectivity" which, according to Tomlinson, characterizes globalization in its most fundamental sense. *Distinction of Ranks* thus precisely substantiates Reinhart Koselleck's argument that the Enlightenment witnessed a significant shift in people's understanding of their own historicity: "With the opening up of the world, the most different but coexisting cultural levels were brought into view spatially and, by way of synchronic comparison, were diachronically classified."[82]

If they read Millar's text carefully, moreover, readers would learn both to apprehend and to accept the unequal global distribution of wealth. Indeed, by recognizing that the natives of Tartary, Africa, or South America coexist with those of Europe and Britain, while understanding that they simultaneously occupy less advanced stages of societal organization, readers would potentially accept uneven development as a natural feature of globality.[83] After all, if all nations are on the path to modernity but some of them fail to reach that zenith and plateau at a lower evolutionary level, then there is nothing to be done beyond learning to appreciate them for what they are. (The subsequent Victorian-era position that savages and heathens should be Christianized, thus justifying imperialism on moral grounds, would be extremely problematic as well.) Insofar as our current global mindset takes its cues from our Enlightened predecessors, it remains the case that the line between appreciating global diversity and naturalizing uneven development remains blurry. To the extent that globalization today continues both to create and to reinforce uneven development around the world—an argument put forward most frequently by its critics on the Left[84]—it clearly retains the ideological conservatism embedded in the worldview promulgated by literati like Millar.

Nonetheless, it is noteworthy that *Distinction of Ranks* concludes with a powerful, forward-looking condemnation of slavery. After reviewing the dismal conditions of workers in "the primitive ages of the world" (244)—which includes reflections on such modern "primitives" as "Tartars" and "the negroes upon the coast of Guinea" (247)—Millar demonstrates how, with the passage of time and concomitant steps up the stadial social ladder, laborers generally gain some measure of freedom and independence from their masters: "In this manner domestic slavery, having gradually declined for ages, has at last been exploded from the greater part of Europe" (268). Mustering his synthetic abilities, Millar subsequently brings together his economic, moral, and historical arguments to attempt to prove that "[i]n whatever light we regard the institution of slavery, it appears equally inconvenient and pernicious" (272). As far as Millar is concerned, the abolition of slavery is an inevitable feature of the gradual perfection of society "in the present age, [which] has of late contributed to the removal of many prejudices, and been productive of enlarged opinions" (279). Writing some three decades before the British slave trade would be abolished, Millar's anti-slavery sentiments, even more than Hume's and Smith's cerebral anti-imperialisms, stand as one of the most positive legacies of the Scottish literati's commitment to stadialism.[85] As we will see in Chapter Two, the discourse of tolerance on which Millar's abolitionism implicitly depends is not unproblematic. Yet to the extent that Western modernity remains the product of habits of mind produced by the Enlightenment, it is worth remembering that thinkers like Hume, Smith, Kames, and Millar—however much we may now find fault with their methods and conclusions—earnestly believed their schema would help bring about a more cohesive sense of global humanity.

KANT'S GLOBALISM

This belief is shared by the Romantic-era philosopher whose ideas arguably had the greatest impact on subsequent centuries of thought: Immanuel Kant. I want to conclude this chapter, then, by briefly considering the global dynamic of Kant's political writings. The Scottish Enlightenment's influence on the philosopher from Königsberg is well known; by Kant's own admission, he was awakened from his "dogmatic slumbers" by Hume's skepticism, especially his "attack on causality," the answer to which Kant would provide with the Transcendental Analytic in his *Critique of Pure Reason* (1781; 2nd ed. 1787).[86] The connections between Kant and the literati, however, extend well beyond this crucial point of contact. Especially in light of the accessibility of German translations of *Wealth of Nations* (which Kant somewhat inaccurately quotes in the section "What Is Money?" in *The Metaphysics of Morals* [1797]), *Distinction of Ranks,* and other foundational Scottish Enlightenment texts, Fania Oz-Salzburger argues convincingly that Hume, Smith, and Kant all share "the legalist conviction ... that a good political society is one governed by laws monitored by reason, upheld by subjects enjoying their rights and observing their duties, and vouchsafed by stable institutions."[87] The influence of the Scots thinkers' historical methodology is apparent in the titles of such early Kantian essays as "Idea for a Universal History with a Cosmopolitan Aim" (1784) and "Conjectural Beginning of Human History" (1786). Kant clearly sympathized with their desire to extrapolate from Hume's "science of man" a science of society that would embrace not only the nation-state but also the globe as a whole.

These sympathies are displayed most prominently in "Toward Perpetual Peace" (1795) and the sections on the "right of nations" and "cosmopolitan right" in *The Metaphysics of Morals*. For Kant, both a "league of nations" and the idea of cosmopolitan right are essential components of any condition of lasting world peace, which is necessary to bring about if humans are to be fully free. (War, even merely as a potential, is a threat to individual freedom since "war is, after all, only the regrettable expedient for asserting one's right by force in a state of nature. . . . "[88]) Kant was aware of coming slightly late to such prospects; in "Toward Perpetual Peace" he credits both the Abbé de Saint Pierre and Rousseau with having published previous accounts of the steps that could be taken to secure a lasting world peace. Kant even structures his essay like the Abbé's, in the form of a satirical treaty divided into "preliminary" and "definitive" articles.[89] Where the Abbé limited himself to proposing a European union of Christian nations, however, Kant maintains no such inherent limitations, instead calling for "*a pacific league*" open to all republican nations "[that] seeks to end *all war* forever" (327).[90] Seyla Benhabib observes that the requirement that participating states have republican constitutions points away from an older, Westphalian understanding of international relations—in which each nation is independently sovereign and "relations with other sovereigns are voluntary and contingent and limited in kind and scope"—to a more modern conception of liberal internationalism in which "the formal equality of states is increasingly dependent upon their subscribing to common values and principles," like equal representation and the division of governmental branches.[91]

Furthermore, Kant imagines his league's development in terms that implicitly echo the incremental logic of the Scottish Enlighteners' stadial theory:

> In accordance with reason there is only one way that states in relation with one another can leave the lawless condition, which involves nothing but war; it is that, like individual human beings, they give up their savage (lawless) freedom, accommodate themselves to public coercive laws, and so form an (always growing) *state of nations* (*civitas gentium*) that would finally encompass all the nations of the earth. (328)

For Kant, the desired outcome of his league of nations is the establishment of a permanent peace, not just in Europe but across the globe.[92] Granted, in *Metaphysics of Morals* Kant hedges that by "league of nations" he means "a voluntary coalition of different states which can be *dissolved* at any time, not a federation" (488); nevertheless, Pauline Kleingeld plausibly suggests Kant made this distinction as a nod to practicability despite believing that "an international federation of states with the authority to coercively enforce a common federal law" is the only legitimate goal of global politics.[93]

Kant's commitment to lasting peace via a transnational deliberative framework would bear legitimate, albeit imperfect fruit in the early twentieth century with the formation of the League of Nations and then the United Nations. Equally important to Kant's theoretical global blueprint is his concept of "cosmopolitan right." An international union of nation-states, he recognized, would be hobbled without a concomitant doctrine designed to regulate relations between individuals and nations. Comprising the third and final definitive article of "Toward Perpetual Peace," cosmopolitan right is defined as "the right of a foreigner not to be treated with hostility because he has arrived on the land of another" (329). As Kant makes clear, this principle of "universal *hospitality*" (328) does not mean that foreigners must be accepted into nations other than their own, but rather that they must be allowed to apply for such acceptance (with the all-important exception that one cannot be turned away if it will likely result in one's death). Kant's notion of hospitality—a concept to which I return in Chapter Five—is thus less robust than some commentators, like Benhabib, would prefer. His rationale is derived from humanity's common use of the Earth: as Kant elaborates in *Metaphysics*, "since possession of the land, on which an inhabitant of the earth can live, can be thought only as possession of a part in a determinate whole . . . it follows that all nations stand *originally* in a community of land" (489). Accordingly, the offer by one person (or nation) "*to engage in commerce* with any other" (489) should never be treated by the other party with knee-jerk belligerence. In this way, says Kant, "distant parts of the world can enter peaceably into relations with one another, which can eventually become publicly lawful and so finally bring the human race ever closer to a cosmopolitan constitution" (329).

Most striking about Kant's conception of "cosmopolitan right"—which, despite its relative brevity, is now frequently considered the most important concept in "Perpetual Peace"—is how it both presupposes and helps materialize a recognizably "interdependent world"[94] in which, as the Scottish Enlighteners already foresaw, all actors are both imbricated and implicated. At the same time, Kant seems to recognize that perpetual peace is an aspirational rather than an actually attainable goal; he not only writes "Toward Perpetual Peace" "under the sign of failure," as Peter Fenves has argued,[95] but also admits in *Metaphysics of Morals* that "*perpetual peace*, the ultimate goal of the whole right of nations, is indeed an unachievable idea" (487). One works to bring about world peace, less because one believes it is actually achievable than because doing so helps shape the legal and ethical contours of individuals, nations, and international institutions in ways most conducive to its approximation.[96]

This brief discussion of Kant's proposals for the institutional and ethical implementation of global governance is not meant to suggest that the Scottish Enlighteners who preceded him necessarily would have endorsed Kant's propositions; his republicanism alone would have made his political views unpalatable to the more conservative literati.[97] I hope, however, to have suggested how their theories of economic and historical global development, refracted through Kant's own brand of philosophical idealism, created a progressive, egalitarian vision that continues to inspire many today. As Robert Holton asserts, "the cosmopolitan legacy to the contemporary world urges that universal or global commitments to all should, in some sense, override though not necessarily deny or negate local and particular loyalties of kinship, place and nation."[98] For his part, Kant retained his basic faith in the republican ideals of the French Revolution even as it morphed into the Terror and began to consume itself. For the British writers who followed the main body of the Scottish Enlighteners, however, the global perspective and cosmopolitan ideals of the Enlightenment would come to seem both more radical, and more potentially emancipatory, than Hume, Smith, and their peers likely imagined. My next chapter turns primarily to Ann Radcliffe's extraordinarily popular Gothic novels to examine the ways in which they unexpectedly carry forward significant elements of the literati's globalism.

CHAPTER TWO

The Global Gothic

SYMPATHY, COSMOPOLITANISM, AND TOLERANCE IN RADCLIFFE'S ROMANCES

*W*ITH the notable exception of Hume's *Treatise*, the writings of the Scottish Enlightenment mostly enjoyed large and attentive audiences, first in Britain and America, and then in Europe.[1] Nonetheless, critics have generally assumed that the most popular fictional genre of the early Romantic era, the Gothic novel, essentially rejected the Enlightened rationalism that was otherwise becoming a mainstay of late-eighteenth-century culture. Where the Scottish literari had attempted to dispel superstition—in Horkheimer and Adorno's well-known phrase, they shared the broad Enlightened goal of "the disenchantment of the world"[2]—Gothic romances appeared to want to send men (and, supposedly in even larger numbers, women) running fearfully back toward it. Gothic authors themselves tended to claim something similar; in the original introduction to the novella that initiated the genre, Horace Walpole presents *The Castle of Otranto* (1764) as penned by an "artful priest" hoping to stem the tide of secularism by "avail[ing] himself of his abilities as an author to confirm the populace in their ancient errors and superstitions."[3] So there is plenty of evidence supporting Deidre Lynch's assertion that the Gothic genre from its inception provided ways for "an educated populace, weaned from superstition, schooled in the empiricist protocols of the Scientific Revolution," to become "reacquainted . . . with the perverse pleasures of *un*certainty."[4]

Nevertheless, as in Gothic novels themselves, things are not always what they seem. Lynch subsequently observes that through the repetition of certain common techniques of plot (the twist, the deferral, the digression, the revelation), setting (haunted or labyrinthine castles, ruined abbeys, caverns), and characterization (the fainting heroine, the chivalrous hero, the lecherous villain), even as they promote uncertainty, Gothic fictions simultaneously create a shared horizon of readerly expectation.[5] This double-sided understanding of the Gothic novel's generic DNA—it produces effects of surprise and even terror that, taken together, become highly predictable—is similar in form to the argument I make in this chapter concerning the fundamentally global orientation of Radcliffe's major novels. Contrary to appearances, Radcliffe's Gothic novels are much closer to the Enlightened tradition of globalism than has generally been recognized. In fact, in the years surrounding the French Revolution, Radcliffe's romances presented British readers with some of their best opportunities to observe and absorb the workings of sympathy, a key discursive register of emerging globalism.

ENLIGHTENED ROMANTICISM

In recent decades, a number of critics have challenged the once widely accepted idea that Romanticism was predicated on the wholesale rejection of eighteenth-century principles and worldviews; by contrast, many Romantic-era writers now appear deeply influenced by their Enlightened predecessors.[6] Particularly important for my concept of Romantic globalism is the extent to which the Scottish literati's ideas were absorbed into the popular literature of the Romantic era. In this regard, much convincing work has already been done on Scott's Waverley Novels, which for all their superficial investments in folk tales and boyish adventures are heavily indebted to Scottish Enlightenment stadial history.[7] But imprints of Hume's and Smith's theories show up even earlier, in the Gothic fictions of the later eighteenth century. Here, one finds not only repeated treatments of the transition from feudal to bourgeois economies, but also the reappearance of Smith's famous economic invisible hand in the ghostly hands that literally intervene in so many Gothic scenes.[8]

The Gothic's well-known investment in the virtues of tempered sensibility—the heroes and heroines of Walpole, Clara Reeve, Radcliffe, and many others are almost uniformly exemplary in their emotional and aesthetic sensitivities—draws on yet another important component of Scottish Enlightenment thinking: sympathy. Although they differ in some details, both Hume and Smith agree that sympathy—the ability of people to feel each other's feelings—forms the affective bedrock of modern civil society. Significantly, there is little evidence that either thought of sympathy as a potentially global force; as I have described elsewhere, both Humean and Smithian sympathies frequently have trouble bridging intra-national divides, much less international ones.[9] This is not to deny that sympathy was a major force behind eighteenth-century abolitionism, which clearly encouraged Britons to think—and, perhaps more importantly, to feel—across racial and ethnic divides.[10] Yet with a few exceptions (for example, Millar on slavery), the Scottish literati appear to have spent little time considering how their sympathetic theories might be deployed in conjunction with their increasingly global understandings of economic, historical, and sociological phenomena.

Nevertheless, Radcliffe works toward realizing precisely this conjunction in her major Gothic romances.[11] At first blush, this argument may seem improbable; as we will see, it certainly cuts against the grain of most current readings of her oeuvre. Radcliffe's earliest readers, however, were well aware of the fundamentally Enlightened cast of her novels. Scott was among the first to recognize that Radcliffe's "major technical signature" was "the revelation of the spectral as simulacra," that is, the quintessentially Enlightened exposure of seemingly supernatural phenomena as effects of merely human, even quotidian causes.[12] Although relatively little is known about Radcliffe's personal reading habits, internal evidence suggests she was familiar with a number of Enlightened concepts, including not only Edmund Burke's ideas on the sublime and beautiful, but also the literati's theories regarding stadial development.[13] To be sure, E. J. Clery argues that Radcliffe's technique of the "explained supernatural" is less about rational disenchantment than about symbolic displacement: "When supposed phantoms are detected so are systems of lawlessness and cruelty which secretly coexist with the 'natural' economies of legitimate profit-making, or of familial affection."[14] Either way, Radcliffe's substitutive strategy notably reaffirms Hume's and especially Smith's convictions regarding the common circulatory nature of money and feelings.[15] Although in what follows I focus more on Radcliffe's use of sympathetic than economic discourses, I do not mean to imply that her treatment of them is mutually exclusive.[16] On the contrary, my argument concerning Radcliffe's major novels—that she supplements the globalism of Hume and Smith by extending their sympathetic theories to include international relations—may differ from recent readings of her fiction, but it supports the growing consensus that the Romantics used a wide variety of Enlightened theories to make sense of the developing world-system of the later eighteenth century.

THE SECRET LIVES OF GOTHIC NOVELISTS

Before moving directly to Radcliffe's novels, a few matters of context and biography need attention. Despite the profusion of new work deconstructing old barriers between Enlightened and Romantic worldviews, Radcliffe herself has yet to figure greatly in these discussions. This may be due in part to the fact that both during her lifetime and well into the second half of the twentieth century, "Mrs. Radcliffe" (as she was patronizingly called) was represented as primarily a purveyor of sensational tales. Whether her novels were seen as innocently amusing, as they're portrayed in Coleridge's and John Keats' letters, or dangerously stimulating, as in the fulminations of some contemporaneous critics, they were generally regarded as containing little of intrinsic value. By the 1860s, William Thackeray was able to write with mock-sincere nostalgia, "Inquire at Mudie's, or the London Library, who asks for the *Mysteries of Udolpho* now?"[17] Almost a century later, Ian Watt's *The Rise of the Novel*, which helped establish the contemporary academic study of the history of the novel along sociological lines, makes no mention whatsoever of Radcliffe.[18] Her subsequent rediscovery, at least in scholarly circles, as a writer of merit can be traced in large part to Ellen Moers' *Literary Women*, which made Radcliffe the foundational writer of what Moers influentially calls "the Female Gothic": novels written by and primarily for women that use Gothic conventions and settings to represent dramatically the oppressions and anxieties negotiated by women in a bourgeois, patriarchal society. Even as Moers put Radcliffe back in the critical spotlight, however, she reproduced the disparaging truism that Radcliffe "was the most popular writer of her day, and, in her moral views, among the most conventional."[19]

Such assumptions regarding Radcliffe's supposed conservatism have persisted ever since.[20] In his 1994 article "Techniques of Terror, Technologies of Nationality: Ann Radcliffe's *The Italian*," Cannon Schmitt rang a new variation on an old theme by asserting that whatever other ambiguities or contradictions her novels might contain, Radcliffe's fictional oeuvre in general, and *The Italian* in particular, systematically promote English superiority:

> *The Italian*, like the rest of Radcliffe's work, belongs to a period of particular importance in the formation of the English nation and the elaboration of a concept of English national identity. The text presents in its heroine an incarnation of Englishness. In addition, it employs a device enabled by eighteenth-century travel writing but nonetheless specifically attributable to the Gothic: the fictional presentation of foreign landscapes and foreign villains as anti-types, exempla of otherness.[21]

This is such a strong reading that it has subsequently become a largely foregone conclusion.[22] Toni Wein's reconsideration of Radcliffe's oeuvre, for example, begins by insisting that "accusations that Radcliffe painted black-and-white portraits . . . overstate the case," but nonetheless confirms that *The Italian* ends with a final cry that "ring[s] with the optimism of Britain triumphant, at home and abroad."[23] To her credit, Wein recognizes that it was "Britishness," at least as much "Englishness," which was at stake in Romantic-era representations of national identity.[24] Yet like most literary historians who write about Radcliffe as an ardent nationalist, Wein overlooks the obvious fact that *The Italian*'s ultimate shout of triumph is made by an *Italian* character, using an *Italian* expression that is reproduced, untranslated, by Radcliffe ("O giorno felice!"). This provides, I want to suggest, the opening for a new interpretation of Radcliffe's politics—one that finds in her novels not paranoid invocations of foreign lands and peoples in the service of fear-mongering nationalism, but mostly moderate and reasoned representations of Continental nations and creeds, inhabited and traversed by characters who at their best demonstrate highly ethical forms of sympathy, cosmopolitanism, and tolerance in the face of suffering and fear.

For a long time, little was known about the personal life of Ann Ward beyond her marriage in 1787 to the journalist William Radcliffe; she famously avoided the spotlight during her lifetime, kept no journals or correspondence, stopped publishing at the height of her popularity, and led such a reclusive retirement that even before her death in 1823 rumors circulated that her novels had gone to her head and driven her mad. Her first biography was a brief account attached to the posthumous publication of her final novel (a historical romance, *Gaston de Blondeville,* which features the sole "real" ghost of her fiction); in the 1880s, Christina Rossetti abandoned her account of Radcliffe's life due to the scarcity of primary sources. The few biographies that appeared over the next century added little to the known facts, generally assuming that Radcliffe lived the life of a typical middle-class English housewife, only writing novels because she was childless and had too much time on her hands.

But especially following Robert Miles' 1995 book-length study of her major novels, which established "that Radcliffe's texts possess aesthetic depth" and "develop in interesting 'intentional' ways,"[25] the stage was set for Rictor Norton's 1999 biography, *Mistress of Udolpho: The Life of Ann Radcliffe*. Norton set out to prove, in his own words, that "Ann Radcliffe was fully aware of the radical politics of her time and sympathized with them." The conclusion of his preface is worth reading in full:

> Contrary to the received image of Ann Radcliffe as a privileged, well-educated, refined gentlewoman, I hope to make it clear that she emerged from a radical Unitarian, rather than a conventional Anglican, background, and that she fully merits consideration as part of that circle of radical Dissenters that included Anna Laetitia Barbauld, Elizabeth Inchbald, Mary Hays and Mary Wollstonecraft. She was indeed one of the "unsex'd revolutionaries" of her time.[26]

Norton argues that Radcliffe was undoubtedly acquainted with and likely supported many of her era's most radical thinkers, including men in the famously progressive Unitarian church like her maternal grand-uncle, Dr. John Jebb, and her uncle through marriage, Thomas Bentley.[27] Through them, Radcliffe appears to have had substantial contact with one of the most controversial radicals of her day, Joseph Priestley, and developed friendly relations with another, William Godwin.[28] Norton also shows that Radcliffe's husband, William, not only became the proprietor and co-editor of the progressive *English Chronicle* (a thrice-weekly newspaper he bought in 1796), but also began his career working for an openly republican paper, *The Gazetteer*.[29] Taken together, these biographical facts—which were not widely available until the late 1990s—invite skepticism regarding the traditional assumption of Radcliffe's conservatism.

Radcliffe came of age in a political atmosphere that was markedly, albeit evanescently, optimistic. Especially in radical British circles, the fall of the Bastille and the early successes of the French Revolution were met with enthusiasm, even elation. As Wordsworth famously recalls in *The Prelude* (1805), "Bliss was it in that dawn to be alive, / But to be young was very heaven!"[30] Several lines later, he asserts that the republican and egalitarian ideals of the French Revolution were not to be realized on

> . . . some secreted Island, Heaven knows where—
> But in the very world which is the world
> Of all of us, the place in which, in the end,
> We find our happiness, or not at all. (X.725–28)

Superficially, the descriptive clause "the very world *which is the world / Of all of us*" (my italics) seems redundant—of course the world is *our* world, "the place in which . . . / *We* find our happiness" (my italics). Commentators have usually focused on the radical implications of Wordsworth's suggestion that, as far as his younger self was concerned, salvation was an earthly and not a heavenly prospect. Equally striking, however, is his Kant-like insistence on the shared nature of the world we inhabit together.[31] Revolutionary ideals were not only to be realized in the here and now, but were to be actualized everywhere, not just in France. And while a given "spirit of the age" is certainly capable of producing its opposite—indeed, anti-Jacobin sentiment ran increasingly strong as the decade of the 1790s wore on—the facts of Radcliffe's biography, along with the Revolutionary fervor around her, strongly support a more liberal reading of her politics than has previously been the norm.

SYMPATHY AND HUMANITY IN *THE ROMANCE OF THE FOREST*

At first glance there is little in Radcliffe's initial novels—two slim volumes published in quick succession in 1789 and 1790—to suggest much interest in Revolutionary events, or in the generally turbulent politics of the Romantic era. *The Castles of Athlin and Dunbayne* is something of a false start: set in Scotland during the Middle Ages, it left little impression on the critics of her day.[32] *A Sicilian Romance*, her next fiction, was better received, and contains more hallmarks of Radcliffe's mature works: the persecuted, fainting, but ultimately triumphant heroine; the valiant, sensitive hero; the ambitious, aristocratic antagonist who desires the heroine as much (if not more) for the property she stands to inherit as for her person; and of course the explained supernatural. In this case, the apparent haunting of the abandoned wing of the Mazzini mansion, from which strange lights and noises regularly emanate nocturnally, turns out to be caused by the secret captivity of the heroine's long-presumed-dead mother.

The presence of these conventions, upon which Radcliffe would work numerous variations in her subsequent fictions, in *A Sicilian Romance* is well known. Far less attention, however, has been paid to the nascent globalism that informs it. The novel is set entirely in Italy, a country Radcliffe hadn't visited but nevertheless describes—presumably drawing on others' firsthand accounts—in great and affectionate detail as her characters travel through it, often at breakneck speed. Many critics have noted that the ability to observe and take pleasure in landscapes is a key attribute of Radcliffe's protagonists, endowing them with a tasteful sensibility that indexes their inner virtue and marks them as implicitly modern and bourgeois, no matter the facts of their births. Yet it was likely the sheer foreignness of the geographies depicted that most impressed Radcliffe's original readers, who were becoming habituated to experiencing the picturesque as a domesticating mode either by imbuing

British landscapes with the softening touches of Claude Lorrain, or by moderating the threat of the foreign with the chiaroscuro of Salvator Rosa.[33] Radcliffe was not, of course, the first British novelist to choose European settings for her major novels, but she was largely responsible for popularizing them with British readers—a fact made more notable given the increasing tension and then, after Louis XVI's execution in January 1793, outright hostility between Britain and France. George Dekker remarks that Radcliffe "may well have been the author most responsible for fixing the name 'romance' on the kind of novel that combines psychological realism with extraordinary events in settings that are 'far and strange.'"[34] Beginning with *A Sicilian Romance*, Radcliffe not only depicts Continental landscapes and exciting situations that would have been literally foreign to her British readers, but also populates them with exotic-born protagonists who nevertheless were understandable, even familiar, from a theory-of-mind perspective to her readers.[35] As a result, I will argue, British readers could learn to appreciate what was distinctive about European geography and culture, while simultaneously coming to recognize that, in many respects, their European counterparts were not so different from themselves.

The Romance of the Forest signals Radcliffe's increasing authorial sophistication. Her contemporaries were quick to pick up on its significance; the *Critical Review* declared that "this lady . . . has greatly exceeded her first work," and the *Monthly Review* confirmed that "[W]e have seldom met with a fiction which has more forcibly fixed the attention, or more agreeably interested the feelings, throughout the whole narrative."[36] Much of the novel's interest stems from Radcliffe's consistent encouragement of readers to identify with the plight of its virtuous heroine. *The Romance of the Forest* can thus be read as an early female bildungsroman, in which Adeline—initially depicted as helpless, vulnerable, and isolated—is tempered and strengthened by a series of trials and persecutions that ultimately leads to a happy marriage and financial security. But this reading perhaps overstates Adeline's character development, since she is practically perfect from the start; more importantly for my purposes, it neglects the extent to which her successes are heavily mediated by—indeed, utterly dependent upon—her constant sympathetic relations with other characters. In *The Romance of the Forest*, Adeline's eventual triumph depends chiefly on the combination of her ability to elicit sympathy from others and to respond in like manner to others' plights.

Adeline's aptitude for eliciting sympathy is evident from the novel's opening pages, which depict the flight of M. de La Motte, his wife, and their small retinue from Paris into the French countryside to escape La Motte's mounting debts. Adeline's first appearance in the novel is also characterized by a kind of dislocation: she is quite literally in no man's land, passed from one set of (male) hands to another, when she is thrust at gunpoint into La Motte's care. The latter is hardly the most generous or courageous person, yet he is immediately moved by Adeline's situation: "She sunk at his feet, and with supplicating eyes, that streamed with tears, implored him to have pity on her. Notwithstanding his present agitation, he found it impossible to contemplate the beauty and distress of the object before him with indifference."[37] Here and elsewhere, Radcliffe draws on Burke's well-known maxim that "beauty in distress is much the most affecting beauty."[38] Indeed, the longer La Motte looks at Adeline's beautiful anguish—such that the voyeuristic pleasure of observing another's pain is intimated but immediately displaced[39]—the more "interested" he becomes, until he almost involuntarily begins "to comfort her, and his sense of compassion was too sincere to be misunderstood. [Adeline's] terror gradually subsided into gratitude and grief" (7). Shortly thereafter, Radcliffe uses almost identical language to describe how La Motte's wife experiences the same involuntary awakening of sympathy, informing us that Adeline's "deep convulsive sighs frequently drew the attention of Mme. La Motte, whose compassion became gradually interested in her behalf, and who now endeavored to tranquilize her spirits" (8).

Adeline obtains such sympathy, moreover, in the almost total absence of her speech. Up to this point in the novel, in fact, she speaks only one line each of direct and indirect dialogue: both are generic pleas directed at La Motte. Her near-muteness indicates that sympathy—and here Radcliffe follows the theoretical footsteps of the Scottish Enlightenment, as well as the sentimental tradition of earlier eighteenth-century novelists like Samuel Richardson and Laurence Sterne—is first and foremost an extra-linguistic form of emotional communication, signified by somatic responses like shared blushes and tears, whose primary effect is to establish inter-personal bonds. Even after Adeline finds her voice, sympathy continues to function this way. Once the La Motte party arrives at the abandoned manor in the novel's titular forest, Adeline becomes entirely attentive to Mme. de La Motte's frequent depressive moods. When the older woman weeps at the prospect of having to spend another night in the forest, for example, we learn that "Adeline's heart was as mournful as Madame's, but she rallied her drooping spirits, and gave the first instance of her kindness by endeavouring to revive those of her friend" (25–26). Such sympathetic displays initially do not affect La Motte's self-interest enough to prevent him from effectively trafficking Adeline to the lascivious Marquis de Montalt. But when the Marquis discovers that Adeline is actually his niece— a vital piece of information withheld from both Adeline and the reader until the novel's conclusion—and subsequently employs La Motte to murder her, the latter finds he cannot commit this violence, and instead facilitates her escape with his servant Peter. Notably, Radcliffe declines to provide an explicit rationale for La Motte's change of heart: Adeline's cry, "O save me—save me from the Marquis!" is followed immediately, with no narrative commentary, by La Motte's declaration, "Rise then . . . and dress yourself quickly—I shall be back again in a few moments" (231). The instant of La Motte's decision, to put it in loosely Derridean terms, is simultaneously and necessarily an act of madness, a break with the past and a leap into an unknown, profoundly unknowable future.[40] But its ethical dimension—La Motte's overcoming of his own self-interest to promote Adeline's survival[41]—is evidently catalyzed by the involuntary sympathy he feels at Adeline's distress.

Her narrow escape from the treacherous Marquis leads Adeline to an idyllic village in the tiny Duchy of Savoy, where she is protected by a benevolent pastor, La Luc, who reinforces everything Adeline has already experienced regarding the beneficial, community-building effects of sympathetic interaction. Radcliffe explains that "[c]alamity [had] taught [La Luc] to feel with peculiar sympathy the distresses of others" (245). He is thus well positioned, not only to extend to Adeline the consolations of sympathy, but also to envelop the entire village in his sympathetic goodwill: "The chearfulness [sic] and harmony that reigned within the chateau was delightful, but the philanthropy which, flowing from the heart of the pastor, was diffused through the whole village, and united the inhabitants in the sweet and firm bonds of social compact, was divine" (277). Immediately preceding this description of La Luc's benevolent influence, moreover, we are told he unites "the strength of philosophy" with "the finest tenderness of humanity" (277). From the novel's start, in fact, "humanity" and "sympathy" are twinned, with the former acting as both the agent and the ultimate expression of the latter. "Humanity" is also the only term of approbation that appears more frequently (sixteen times) than "sympathy" (thirteen times) in *The Romance of the Forest* to describe a character's motivations. When La Motte, who has just escaped with Adeline from the house where they had both been detained, pauses to recollect what has transpired and to consider his options, Radcliffe explains that "[t]he present charge, and the chance of future trouble brought upon him by this adventure, occasioned some dissatisfaction; but the beauty and seeming innocence of Adeline, *united with the pleadings of humanity in her favour*, and he determined to protect her" (8; my italics). "The *pleadings* of humanity" explicitly denotes how the core of Adeline's person hails what is similarly human in La Motte, awakening his sympathy and triggering his altruistic instincts. Adeline's beauty in distress certainly doesn't hurt her chances here—just as it helps La Luc's daughter, Clara, when she is saved from plunging over an

Alpine ravine by a stranger who afterward "begged that he might be spared the pain of receiving thanks for having followed only an impulse of common humanity" (267). Nevertheless, in such scenes Radcliffe clearly indicates that what I will shortly call sympathetic cosmopolitanism establishes extrafamilial bonds of compassion that are theoretically extendable to all humanity.

Schmitt and others have noted that Radcliffe frequently imbues her characters with explicitly nationalistic sentiments, especially a fondness for the landscapes of their birthplaces. Yet such preferences, expressed most strongly and frequently by Radcliffe's servants and peasants, are implicitly framed as amusingly naive. When Peter returns with Adeline to his native Savoy, for instance, we are told that "[w]hen he came within sight of his native mountains, his extravagant joy often burst forth into frequent exclamations, and he would often ask Adeline if she had ever seen such *hills* in France. 'No, no,' said he, the hills there are very well for French hills, but they are not to be named on the same day with ours'" (240). Such sentiments clearly should be taken by readers with a grain of salt, like similar expressions in *The Italian* uttered by the servant Vivaldi when he volubly prefers the mountains of his native Naples above all others.[42] Nevertheless, by the decade's end Wordsworth would be publishing eventual classics of the "greater Romantic lyric" like "Lines Written a Few Miles above Tintern Abbey," explicitly set on "the banks of the WYE," which begins by using pointed deictics to praise "*[t]hese* waters" and "*these* steep and lofty cliffs. . . ."[43] I am suggesting neither that we equate Radcliffe's and Wordsworth's descriptive strategies, nor that we overlook how Wordsworth infuses his poem's Welsh landscape with personal significance that goes well beyond the clichéd appreciations of Radcliffe's bumptious servants. I do mean to suggest, however, that Radcliffe's servants participate in a tradition of national landscape appreciation that within a few years would become a staple of canonical Romantic poetry. Seen in this light, we can easily imagine that Radcliffe's representations helped her British readers understand that Europeans were just as attached to their Alpine (or Neapolitan, or otherwise) landscapes as Britons were—or at least were becoming, as the Romantic era evolved—to the various locales of their own "green and pleasant land."[44] Such attachments certainly took local and specific forms; the predilection for forming them, however, is recognized and promoted by Radcliffe as a universal human tendency. For some critics, this tendency is explained by her frequent recourse to the "natural theology" locatable in her religiously infused landscape depictions.[45] But in a more earthly context, it should also be aligned with Susan Buck-Morss' recent observation, with regard to the insufficiency of the trendy slogan "Think Global—Act Local," that "[w]e need to find ways through the *local* specificities of our own traditions toward a conceptual orientation that can inform *global* action."⁴⁶ The sympathetic cosmopolitanism promoted by Radcliffe—both through her characters' compassionate interactions with each other, and through the ways she encourages British readers to sympathize with the patriotic sentiments of her European characters—enacts one form of the strategy Buck-Morss describes.

Of course, *Romance of the Forest* is hardly devoid of the national stereotypes common in Romantic-era Britain. Together, for example, La Luc and Verneuil (Clara's rescuer and eventual husband) contrast the sobriety and seriousness of most Englishmen with the "sparkling, but sophistical discourse, frivolous occupations, and . . . folly" of Frenchmen (268–69). Such clichéd generalizations do not invalidate Radcliffe's sympathetic cosmopolitanism as much as throw into relief its surprising modernity. For Kwame Anthony Appiah, "there are two strands that intertwine in the notion of cosmopolitanism. One is the idea that we have obligations to others," and "[t]he other is that we take seriously the value not just of human life but of particular human lives, which means taking an interest in the practices and beliefs that lend them significance."⁴⁷ The former, which Appiah calls "universal concern," is clearly consonant with the operations of sympathetic cosmopolitanism I have located in *The Romance of the Forest*. The latter, which Appiah summarizes as "respect for legitimate difference," is arguably what Radcliffe broaches in the aforementioned conversation between La Luc and Verneuil. Stereotypes of the dour Englishman and the frolicsome Frenchman will always be more or less reactionary generalizations, but in Radcliffe's hands they demonstrate at least the potential to be transformed into appreciation for cultural variety.

Before leaving *The Romance of the Forest* to track these ideas' development in Radcliffe's later novels, I want to clarify that even in 1791, the form of globalism Radcliffe promotes was never identical to the overly sophisticated, cerebral cosmopolitanism British conservatives would increasingly condemn. The most conventionally cosmopolitan speech of the novel is given by the villainous Marquis de Montalt. Bracing La Motte to murder Adeline in her sleep, Montalt explains that "[n]ature, uncontaminated by false refinement . . . every where acts alike in the great occurrences of life," before using examples of revenge-killings by "[t]he Indian . . . the wild Asiatic . . . the Turk . . . [and] [e]ven the polished Italian" to justify Adeline's destruction. He ends by claiming that "[i]t is the first proof of a superior mind to liberate itself from prejudices of country, or of education" (222). The obvious self-interest of Montalt's motivations, combined with the deadly violence he licenses, indicate that readers are not meant to condone his perspective;

moreover, as described earlier, although La Motte appears to accept Montalt's logic, when he is actually faced with the prospect of stabbing Adeline in her sleep, he cannot bring himself to do it. (The same sympathetic instinct seizes the ruffians whom Montalt originally hires to murder Adeline, when they secretly give her to La Motte instead.) In this way, a bloodless—or in Montalt's case, an overly sanguinary—cosmopolitanism is rejected in favor of a humane, sympathetically motivated one that makes room for both local attachments *and* the formation of affective bonds extending not only beyond families, but also well beyond the borders of nation-states.

Consequently, the conclusion of *The Romance of the Forest* dissipates the horrors of exile, a term both M. and Mme. de La Motte use repeatedly to describe their initial flight from Paris. Adeline, who eventually marries La Luc's son Theodore, is happily transplanted to the village of Leloncourt "on the beautiful banks of the lake of Geneva" (362). Having forfeited Montalt's offer of restoration to her former Parisian glory (and with the evil aristocrat himself already dead by his own hand to avoid jail), La Motte's death sentence is commuted to banishment thanks to Adeline's intercession, and he and his wife once again leave Paris with a "design to settle" in England. This time, however, there is no talk of "exile"; instead, now that his character has "gradually recovered the hue which it would probably always have worn had he never been exposed to the tempting dissipations of Paris" (354), it appears that M. and Mme. de La Motte will happily and successfully integrate themselves into British life. Such is Radcliffe's ultimate delineation of sympathetic cosmopolitanism in *The Romance of the Forest*: the ability to feel at home no matter where one actually resides.

SYMPATHETIC COSMOPOLITANISM IN *THE MYSTERIES OF UDOLPHO* AND *THE ITALIAN*

Radcliffe's next novels extend and expand the discourse of sympathetic cosmopolitanism. *The Mysteries of Udolpho* was met with almost universal applause; *The Monthly Review* even cautioned readers against skipping its lengthy landscape passages, warning that "[i]f the reader, in the eagerness of curiosity, should be tempted to pass over any of them for the sake of proceeding more rapidly with the story, he will do both himself and the author injustice."[48] Other original readers were less happy with its protracted length, especially given the increasing predictability of Radcliffe's happy endings and penultimate revelations; as one American critic complained, "It appears the labour of a Mountain, to bring forth a mouse."[49] Some of the most illuminating recent interpretations of *Udolpho* have read the novel's bagginess as a mechanism for generating both suspense and a sense of suspension, temporal as well as intellectual, in readers.[50] By once more focusing on the counter-Enlightened elements of *Udolpho*, however, these interpretations risk missing how Radcliffe's most sustained novel works hard to awaken its British readers from their dogmatic national slumbers.

With particular reference to *Udolpho*, Samuel Baker argues that "[t]he gothic was, in short, a genre for and about political emotions."[51] Following his lead, I find in *Udolpho* more evidence of Radcliffe's ongoing commitment to mobilizing sympathy in the service of cosmopolitanism. The novel's heroine, Emily St. Aubert, begins life in rural French contentment with her parents; she is subsequently orphaned and transported to the gloomy titular castle of the greedy Signor Montoni, but eventually escapes to happiness with her longtime admirer, Valancourt. If such plots were already familiar to Radcliffe's readers, then so were *Udolpho*'s main themes: terms like "sympathy" and "humanity" again frequently characterize the actions of characters with whom Radcliffe encourages the reader to identify, and local affections once more promote an overarching cosmopolitan outlook. Emily's father, for example, is simultaneously highly attached to the Gascony countryside in which he was raised and a model of benevolent paternalism even on his deathbed. Furthermore, an avaricious aristocrat again becomes the primary example of bad behavior in the novel, marrying Emily's aunt to facilitate inheriting St. Aubert's estates, and actively neglecting the unfortunate Signora (even unto her feverish death) upon realizing he must turn his attentions to Emily in order inherit St. Aubert's property.

Emily's ensuing sufferings are more intellectual and emotional than physical. They are also frequently self-inflicted, as when she famously believes she has glimpsed the preserved corpse of Udolpho's previous mistress in a castle alcove, only to discover at novel's end that what she actually saw was a wax dummy. Her long imprisonment in Montoni's castle effectively isolates Emily, cutting her off from the sympathetic community that originally sustained her; her aunt becomes depressed and withdrawn as she realizes she has been duped, while Montoni exults in the power he now exercises over both women.[52] Ingrid Horrocks notes that Emily's isolation during this period extends to the novels' narrative structure itself, which almost completely lacks either the extra-textual quotations or the original poetry which Radcliffe liberally interweaves into *Udolpho*'s other sections.[53] Throughout her lengthy confinement, Emily draws comfort only from the occasional snatches of music of her native Gascony she hears through her window, the source of which is eventually revealed to be another prisoner named DuPont. Their escape leads to a prolonged third act in which Emily, DuPont, and two faithful servants make their way back to France, meeting up along the way with another nobleman and his daughter who welcome Emily into their family and thereby reconstitute a sympathetic community.

The ending of *Udolpho* initially appears in line with nationalist readings: reunited and in full possession of all their property, Emily and Valancourt retire to her father's original country house in "the beloved landscapes of their native country" (672). Yet previous to this final homecoming, Radcliffe has already seriously compromised the notion of a pure national identity or heritage. In an apparently digressive subplot that echoes similar scenes in earlier Gothic novels like Reeve's *The Old English Baron* (1778), one of *Udolpho*'s faithful servants performs a nighttime vigil in a supposedly haunted wing of the Count de Villeroi's chateau. Trying to stay awake, Ludovico opens an old book, retrieved from "an obscure corner of the Marquis' library" (551) and begins to read its Provençal legends. When readers *inside* Gothic novels do their own reading, however, the results are frequently unpredictable.[54] In this case, the local legends that Ludovico reads are explicitly glossed as cultural hybrids, "whether drawn from the Arabian legends, brought by the Saracens into Spain, or recounting the chivalric exploits performed by the crusaders" (551). Here, in microcosm, we see the inextricability of local sentiments and global dynamics in Radcliffe's novels; even the most apparently local tales turn out to draw on sources that defy regional or national borders, and testify instead to the long tradition of global, cross-cultural exchange.

A similar revelation is staged a few chapters later when the Count and his followers, making their way across the Pyrenees (a cross-border mountain range that Radcliffe consistently contrasts with the nationally contained isolation of the Apennines in which the terrifying castle of *Udolpho* is situated), come across a band of "French and Spanish peasants" who, we are informed, are "the inhabitants of a neighbouring hamlet" (597). This mixed group is a prime example of what April Alliston calls the "[u]topian sympathetic communities" that frequently feature in Romantic fictions, especially in "spaces that are liminal to the nation-states, both culturally and geographically."[55] It makes sense, then, that Radcliffe's hybrid band of peasants are "performing a sprightly dance, the women with castanets in their hands, to the sounds of a lute and a tambourine, till, from the brisk melody of France, the music softened into a slow movement, to which two female peasants danced a Spanish Pavan" (597). If Emily and Valancourt's final retirement in the French countryside expresses the universality of national attachment, the Franco-Spanish peasants of the Pyrenees embody the cosmopolitan spirit that equally informs *The Mysteries of Udolpho*.

When *Udolpho* was published in the summer of 1794, Britain and France had already been at war for approximately a year and a half. Keeping this in mind, we can appreciate both Radcliffe's achievement in writing a bestseller whose protagonists all hail from an "enemy nation," and the rapidity with which her favored generic vehicle—the Gothic romance—was hijacked for less cosmopolitan ends. I allude to the 1795 publication of *The Monk* by Matthew Lewis, a professed admirer of Radcliffe who nevertheless tellingly admitted in a letter to his mother that he found all the parts of *Udolpho* before Emily's captivity to be "uncommonly dull."[56] While still a teenager, Lewis set out to write a novel combining the intricate plotting of a Radcliffean romance with the supernatural horrors of the German *Schauer-Romantik* tradition which he had discovered while in Europe.[57] It's a nice irony, then, that his fiercely xenophobic novel—a much better example of so-called Gothic nationalism than anything Radcliffe wrote—is itself an inter-national hybrid, generically speaking.

The Monk thoroughly explores and exposes what Slavoj Žižek might call the "obscene underside" of the Radcliffean romance:[58] its scandalous success hinges on Lewis' ability to turn Radcliffe's well-mannered Gothic romances into apparent expressions of the most primal and vicious human urges.[59] Yet the novel's "political unconscious," to borrow Jameson's well-known phrase, is surprisingly near its surface, where graphic scenes of anarchic, indiscriminately destructive mobs none too subtly echo contemporary British depictions of French Revolutionary crowds run amok.[60] Lewis was not alone in using the Gothic as a vehicle for patriotic sentiments—James Watt has shown that an entire subgenre of "loyalist Gothic" was simultaneously being published[61]—but the young author showed a singular affinity for exaggeration that resonated with an anxious British nation. Madrid, standing in for Paris, is described as "a city where superstition reigns with . . . despotic sway" (7); international travel is condoned primarily as way for young noblemen to learn how best to manage their future tenants (96); and exile is bemoaned—in one of the many crudely written poems that Lewis inserts into his narrative—as a hideous fate (215–17). In fact, Lewis' own life was markedly cosmopolitan, with stays in Paris, Weimar, and the Hague already in his past, and a relatively liberal estate-master's life (and death, from yellow fever) in Jamaica in his future. But little in the novel reflects its author's own worldliness, instead anticipating the kind of patriotic demagoguery mobilized by authors like Hannah More in her *Cheap Repository Tracts* of the later

1790s. Thus despite *The Monk*'s reception by its own era's critics as "Jacobinical, pornographic, and morbidly continental-influenced," I agree with Peter Mortensen's conclusion that it is "a profoundly and self-consciously English book" in the narrowest sense.[62]

Radcliffe seems to have recognized that *The Monk* represented not only an aesthetic affront to what Yael Shapira calls her "delicate Gothic," but also an ideological challenge to her sympathetic cosmopolitanism.[63] *The Italian, or the Confessional of the Black Penitents* was the final novel published in Radcliffe's lifetime, and its additional subtitle, "A Romance," seems to emphasize her determination to reclaim the genre. Once again the setting is Italy, but this time the action takes place only forty-odd years in the past, underscoring its relevance to contemporary affairs while nevertheless affording Radcliffe the license of historical (as well as geographical) distance. A brief but fascinating prefatory narrative takes place even more recently, "About 1764," and sets up an explicitly international situation as it follows a party of English tourists visiting Naples.[64] This framing device introduces the confessional box that plays a key role in the main narrative, and allows Radcliffe to present the novel as a "found manuscript" given to one of the travelers by an Italian friend. Its main interest, however, is to explore the unnamed Englishman's response to the sight of a suspicious-looking man lurking within the church being toured. When the former learns that the reclusive figure is an assassin seeking asylum, his incredulity provokes the following dialogue:

> "He has sought sanctuary here," replied the friar; "within these walls he may not be hurt." "Do your altars, then, protect the murderer?" said the Englishman. "He could find shelter no where else," answered the friar meekly. "This is astonishing!" said the Englishman; "of what avail are your laws, if the most atrocious criminal may thus find shelter from them? But how does he contrive to exist here! He is, at least, in danger of being starved?" (2)

This exchange is typically understood as immediately establishing an essential link between the foreign and the dangerous.[65] Yet such an interpretation misses the absurdity of the Englishman's final question, which seems seriously to propose that it would be both just and ethical purposefully to starve a man to death after allowing him sanctuary. If Radcliffe intended by this to confirm the superiority of English morality, she could have created a more convincing mouthpiece. Instead, the novel's frame effectively destabilizes any spurious opposition between English civility and Italian barbarity, first by bringing the two cultures (and by extension, Britishness and all its myriad "others") into intimate contact with each other, then by implying that the Englishman, despite his supposed superiority, is sadly deficient in tolerance not only of criminals but also of other cultures' laws and customs.

The theme of tolerance runs throughout *The Italian*. The noun itself, which initially primarily denoted the ability to withstand pain or hardship, had only recently acquired its modern meanings of "the disposition to be patient with or indulgent to the opinions or practices of others" and "freedom from bigotry"; the *Oxford English Dictionary* dates the first usage in these latter senses to 1765. Interestingly, the specific reference appears in one of Robert Lowth's public letters to his fellow critic, high churchman, and frequent rival William Warburton, in which the Oxford professor and future Bishop of London complains that Warburton's biblical interpretations admit of "no tolerance, no intercommunity of spirits, not the least difference of opinion."[66] Given her Dissenting background, Radcliffe may have been familiar with Lowth's letters; in any case, *The Italian* is full of praise for open-mindedness and acceptance of cultural and national differences. When the heroic Vivaldi is somewhat faulted for his pride of birth, for example, we are immediately reassured that "a high sense of honor rendered him no more jealous of offence, than a delicate humanity made him ready for reconciliation" (8). For her part, the novel's apparently low-born heroine, Ellena, conceals the fact that she embroiders to support herself and her aunt "to protect herself from . . . the narrow prejudices of the world around her" (9). By contrast, Radcliffe characterizes Vivaldi's mother, with her implacable resistance to her son's marriage to Ellena, as motivated by a deadly combination of "prejudice and pride" (122).[67] The main plot, in which the Marchesa first arranges for Ellena to be kidnapped and spirited away, then condones her attempted murder, is thus catalyzed by a status-based version of the same intolerance that all Radcliffe's major novels condemn.

Although the Marchesa and her accomplice, the wily priest Schedoni, embody the worst stereotypes of Italian mendacity and ruthlessness, their vices are more than balanced by the virtues of Vivaldi, Ellena, and Vivaldi's faithful servant Paulo. Cannon Schmitt asserts that Radcliffe's foreign-born protagonists, especially her heroines, are mere ciphers of Englishness, and when they finally celebrate their marriage at the novel's conclusion, Vivaldi and Ellena indeed retire to a Neapolitan villa characterized as having English-style gardens.[68] Yet Radcliffe's consistent blurring of the lines between English and Italian does not merely universalize the former at the expense of the latter. In the preface to her single work of non-fiction published in her lifetime, *A Journey Made in the Summer of 1794* (1795), Radcliffe defends against precisely this misunderstanding:

> With respect to the book itself . . . [I] will venture to defend a practice adopted in the following pages, that has been sometimes blamed for its apparent nationality, by writers of the most respected authority. The references to England, which frequently occur during the foreign part of the tour, are made because it has seemed that one of the best modes of describing to any class of readers what they may not know, is by comparing it with what they do.[69]

Radcliffe was clearly well aware of her frequent allusions to English phenomena when describing foreign people and places; even more clearly, these were intended neither to denigrate the foreign nor to establish Englishness as the norm, but rather to facilitate precisely the kind of sympathetic cosmopolitanism ("intercommunity of spirits") necessary for the establishment of cross-cultural comprehension.[70]

Like her previous major novels, *The Italian* functions in part as a virtual travelogue, allowing British readers to engage in the kind of armchair travel that was the safest kind of Continental exploration available by the later 1790s. Admiring descriptions of various Italian landscapes, which Katarina Gephardt notes are more greatly differentiated in *The Italian* than in Radcliffe's earlier (pre-*Journey*) novels, once again fill many pages.[71] Schmitt argues that Radcliffe mocks the local prejudices displayed by Paulo when, following his master across the country, he denigrates every new sight in favor of its counterpart in his native Naples. His provincial predilections seem to contrast starkly with Vivaldi's and Ellena's more sophisticated appreciations of the varied landscapes of Italy as, respectively, sublime and beautiful phenomena.[72] As in *The Romance of the Forest*, however, the effusive praise Radcliffe's European characters lavish on their native landscapes is in keeping with the similar feelings of national and local pride with which Britons were likewise learning to view their own countryside in the Romantic era. Moreover, Schmitt's claim that Paulo's local attachments contrast poorly with the nationalism Radcliffe is supposedly naturalizing is markedly anachronistic; since the political unification of the Italian peninsula did not begin until after 1815, it would indeed be strange for Paulo to profess loyalty to a national entity that did not yet exist. It makes more sense to see Paulo's attachment to his native Naples as primarily stemming from his intense devotion to his Neapolitan master; this also explains why, later in the novel, he prefers to be taken to Rome to face the Inquisition alongside Vivaldi rather than remain free to return to his beloved Naples.

Just as she exposes the fallacy of her British readers' cultural superiority in *The Italian*'s preface and challenges their prejudices throughout the main narrative, Radcliffe uses its climactic Inquisition scenes to unfold the ethical implications of a tolerant worldview. Romantic-era representations of the Inquisition tend to conflate it with underground or extra-legal organizations like the Illuminati (or, as we shall see in Chapter Five, the Germanic Vehme Gericht) that were blamed for fomenting unrest in France and elsewhere. In Britain, the Inquisition was a particular lightning rod for those wishing to condemn the tyrannical powers of the Catholic Church; this is precisely how it features in *The Monk*.

At first, *The Italian* seems to follow this pattern. Vivaldi, ignorant of the charges against him, initially fails to impress the Inquisitors with his innocence because, as Radcliffe explains, "the simplicity and energy of truth failed to impress conviction on minds, which, no longer possessing the virtue themselves, were not competent to understand the symptoms of it in others" (305). But as the court's proceedings are increasingly disrupted by the presence of a mysterious monk who knows Schedoni's past crimes, its attitude of grim-faced authority is transformed. The trial's grand-vicar slowly commits to revealing Schedoni's criminal history, questioning him and his accuser alike with a "candour" that initially surprises Vivaldi and eventually reduces him to tears of joy (351–52). Mark Canuel remarks that "[t]he task of *The Italian* . . . is to make the Inquisition work, paradoxically, against the traditional confessional mechanisms of the Inquisition itself";[73] I would add that in doing so, Radcliffe upends her British readers' expectations regarding the perfidy of foreign institutions and Catholics alike. The ending of *The Italian* plainly demonstrates that all people, including southern Europeans and Catholics, are more than capable of compassionate, ethical behavior.

These were particularly important goals for Radcliffe to achieve, because *The Monk* had already demonstrated that Radcliffe's previous Gothic villains were all too easily converted into vehicles for expressing the irredeemably *foreign* nature of evil. Lewis makes plain on numerous occasions that Ambrosio's pride, vanity, and lust are directly caused by his Spanish heritage and Catholic upbringing.[74] By contrast, Radcliffe presents her last major Gothic villain as someone whose villainy derives largely from his inability to sympathize with others. Manipulative, ambitious, and cruel, one of Schedoni's most alarming powers is his ability to *appear* to sympathize with others: "he could adapt himself to the tempers and passions of persons, whom he wishes to conciliate, with astonishing facility, and generally with complete triumph" (35). Yet this is self-interested mimicry rather than true sympathy, and although it worrisomely resurrects the connection between selfishness and altruism earlier explored by Mandeville, Radcliffe clearly differentiates it from the real emotional communication Ellena shares with the virtuous nun Olivia in the convent of San Stefano. It is also distinct from the authentic emotions finally experienced by Schedoni when, having removed Ellena to a remote cottage on the shores of the Adriatic, he prepares to murder the sleeping heroine, only to catch sight of his own features in the miniature she wears around her neck. Believing that he has been about to kill his own daughter, Schedoni's emotional reaction surprises Ellena and the narrator alike:

> Ellena's terror began to yield to astonishment, and this emotion increased, when, Schedoni approaching her, she perceived tears swell in his eyes, which were fixt on her's, and his countenance soften from the wild disorder that had marked it. Still he could not speak. At length he yielded to the fullness of his heart, and Schedoni, the stern Schedoni, wept and sighed! (236)

In *The Monk*, Ambrosio realizes his victims are his long-lost mother and sister only after he has done them mortal harm (including raping the latter); here, Radcliffe ensures her villain does not repeat the same tragic, sensational mistake. By allowing Schedoni to feel and express the full effects of his mingled terror and relief, Radcliffe simultaneously complicates and humanizes her Gothic antagonist. His reactions are neither caused nor even influenced by his doubly foreign identity as an Italian Catholic; rather, they transcend national differences and become universally human. Schedoni's newfound emotional openness does not finally save him. Nevertheless, Radcliffe makes every attempt to erase or at least ease Lewis' strong association of Gothic villainy with absolute, incomprehensible foreignness. Fittingly, the novel concludes with Paulo's happy and repeated cries of "*O! giorno felice! O! giorno felice!*" being taken up, in an enactment of the sympathetic communication of shared feelings, by Ellena, Vivaldi, their wedding party, and all the revelers.

ON THE LIMITS OF TOLERANCE

Radcliffe's novels deserve to be reread under the conjoined signs of sympathetic cosmopolitanism and tolerance. Nevertheless, I want to conclude this chapter with some thoughts on this approach's limitations. To begin historically, despite Radcliffe's best efforts to humanize Schedoni in *The Italian*, Lewis was not the only early reader impressed by the apparently irredeemable otherness of her villains. Anna Laetitia Barbauld (whose own poetry could be highly ambivalent with regard to nationalism, as I discuss in Chapter Three), in her introduction to Radcliffe's works for the 1810 *British Novelists* collection, flatly characterizes the older novelist's villains as "dark, singular, atrocious. They are not of English growth. . . ."[75] More famously, the Gothic-obsessed heroine of Austen's *Northanger Abbey* (1818), who has just finished reading *Udolpho*, is disabused of her conspiracy theories regarding Mrs. Tilney's death by being advised to "[r]emember the country and the age in which we live. Remember that we are English, that we are Christians."[76] Regardless of whether Austen herself believed this—and there are good reasons to believe she didn't[77]—such sentiments indicate the extent to which many of Radcliffe's earliest readers remained most comfortable reading Gothic villains as embodiments of foreignness.

Along more contemporary lines, each of the normatively positive qualities I have argued Radcliffe promotes in her novels has lately been productively problematized. With regard to tolerance, for example, Žižek contends that as an inter-subjective practice it is so hedged with restrictions and qualifications, especially the implicit requirement that the Other remain unthreatening to the Self's identity, as to be essentially reactionary. Even worse from his perspective is the coopting of tolerance discourse by socially sanctioned multiculturalism, which to the extent that it masks or displaces vertical social antagonisms is for Žižek a pure example of contemporary, "post-political" ideological mystification.[78] Likewise, Wendy Brown questions the "conventional story" of tolerance's ascent to the pinnacle of Western political values, arguing that we need to pay more attention to its frequent deployments by individuals and especially nation-states in order to foreclose alternative, more politically radical modes of social relations.[79]

Similarly, cosmopolitanism has come under attack from both ends of the political spectrum. Timothy Brennan, speaking from the Left, labels cosmopolitanism a "fundamentally ambivalent phenomenon" both for its inevitable rootedness in local and national interests[80]—such that different definitions or forms of cosmopolitanism are promoted in various contexts for various agendas—and for the ways in which it frequently "function[s] as a relay for the center's values, sublimating differences on grounds of understanding by way of a motive to export ideological products made to the measure of the world of saleable things."[81] This last point has also been taken up by Žižek, who neatly exposes the collusion of cosmopolitanism with neoliberalism when he writes, apropos of local resentments against contemporary capitalist epiphenomena like outsourcing, that "it is global capital which is inherently multicultural and tolerant."[82] For these theorists, such points of contact and homologies between the fluid, multi-national, amoral dynamics of the modern world-system and the West's avowedly humanistic values of tolerance and cosmopolitanism primarily provide occasions for critique, both of the latter's hypocrisy and of the Anglo-European Left's inability to realize viable alternatives to either. Nonetheless, their concerns corroborate my argument that Radcliffe's repeated deployments of discourses of sympathetic cosmopolitanism and tolerance are essential components of early Romantic globalism. For the Romantic globalists, in contrast to today's leftist critics of globalization, the similar itineraries of feelings and money, the circulatory routes of sympathy and progress-bearing capital, and the parallel developments of "worldwideification" and a potentially egalitarian modern world order, were as likely to appear causes for optimism as for pessimism.

For evidence of this difference of perspective, we need only return to Radcliffe's historico-political context. Here, it quickly becomes clear that cosmopolitanism and tolerance, however vexed they may appear today, were perceived as threats to Britain's internal stability and external status by the era's conservatives and anti-Jacobins. Burke's rage in his *Reflections on the Revolution in France* against the "speculatists," for example, to whom "it is vain to talk . . . of the practice of their ancestors, the fundamental laws of their country" once they have seized upon "the rights of men" as their rallying cry, is an early strike against those who would call for the universality of unqualified human rights over and above the citizenship rights granted by individual, sovereign states.[83] Such calls are not without their own critics, in turn, who hear in them yet another reduction of individuals to the figure that Giorgio Agamben calls "bare life" (whose place in the structure of modern world order I consider in greater detail in Chapter Five).[84] Nevertheless, if this book's guiding hypothesis is correct—that is, if our contemporary global situation indeed inherits dynamics and dispositions from processes and worldviews that stretch back to the Romantics—then the sympathetic, community-oriented globalism delineated in Radcliffe's novels should hold significant interest for those still (or newly) seeking alternatives to the hegemony of today's competitive, neoliberal dogma.

Despite their extraordinary popularity during her lifetime and immediately afterward, Radcliffe's Gothic romances did not retain either their readership or their prestige for long. Many causes facilitated their swift decline, including the proliferation of second-rate Gothic romance imitators, the withering satires of Gothic conventions by writers like Thomas Love Peacock, and the ascension of new prose fiction subgenres, including Austen's domestic fictions and Scott's historical novels. Set against the increasingly strident patriotism that the wartime governments of Romantic-era Britain both encouraged and required, moreover, the globalism of novels like *The Romance of the Forest* and *The Italian* likely appeared increasingly out of sync with the national mood. Especially after Napoleon's rise, many Britons seem to have had neither the patience nor the appetite for sympathetic cosmopolitanism; instead, they were increasingly eager to consume narratives of British power and global dominance.[85] In my next chapter, I examine how several poets of the Napoleonic era responded to and represented the global conflicts that monopolized Britons' attentions in the early years of the nineteenth century. Cosmopolitanism and tolerance may have seemed like relics of a bygone era; thinking globally, however, was more crucial than ever.

CHAPTER THREE

Fighting Words

BRITISH POETRY AND
THE NAPOLEONIC WARS

*H*AVING returned home a wealthy man during the "false peace" of 1814, Captain Frederick Wentworth is certain that a woman's place is not in the midst of war. Speaking out against the Navy's practice of giving unofficial passage to female travelers, Wentworth opines that "I hate to hear of women on board, or to see them on board; and no ship, under my command, shall ever convey a family of ladies any where, if I can help it."[1] As with much else in *Persuasion* (1817), Austen may not have been entirely serious when she wrote this—the seafaring Mrs. Croft is subsequently given ample opportunity to refute Wentworth—but the general sentiment certainly rang true: British women were officially restricted from taking part in any of the manifold theaters of war during the entire period of conflict with Revolutionary and then Napoleonic France.[2]

If women were not allowed to fight, however, they were still allowed to voice their opinions in print. As Ann Mellor has demonstrated, "women participated fully in the discursive public sphere and in the formation of public opinion in Britain by the late eighteenth century," although not without encountering varying degrees of resistance.[3] With texts like Helen Maria Williams' *Letters Written in France* (1790) and Hannah More's *Village Politics* (1792), women initially took up a variety of public perspectives on how Britons ought to respond to events taking place across the Channel. Yet after war was declared following Louis XVI's execution in January of 1793, the stakes of writing about the widening hostilities were raised considerably. Government repression was partly to blame for this new state of affairs, but so was an increasingly pervasive sense that questioning the motives or methods of the war effort was essentially treasonous. According to Stephen Behrendt, in this atmosphere "[e]ven those whose associations with radical and antiwar associations [were] known tended to be circumspect and indirect in their approach to the subject," preferring to draw sentimental attention to the costs of combat in general rather than to criticize the war effort directly and thereby open themselves to attack by the largely conservative press.[4] This strategy was adopted even by a generally fearless writer like Byron, whose stanzas on the Peninsular War at the end of the first canto of *Childe Harold's Pilgrimage* (1812) stick largely to rhetorical platitudes like "Flows there a tear of pity for the dead?"[5]

Despite this muting of criticism, many writers—including a number of women—used what freedom of the press still remained to publicize their views on the growing conflict. This chapter explores texts by several of the best-known wartime poets—Felicia Hemans, Anna Laetitia Barbauld, and Walter Scott—along with a substantial poem by one of their lesser-known contemporaries, Anne Grant. Throughout, I calibrate my interpretations to the Napoleonic era's many dramatic turning points, the better to emphasize how the various wartime perspectives these poets offer are highly attuned to the changing nature of events themselves. Notwithstanding the attention I pay to their political and ideological as well as gender differences, however, I also claim that they are unified by a set of common attitudes to wartime. First, they all share an ambivalent relationship to the globalism of the Scottish Enlightenment and the sympathetic cosmopolitanism of the Radcliffean romance. Although these poets generally accept the globalizing premises of the former—indeed, even a pessimistic poem like *Eighteen Hundred and Eleven* assumes the necessity of adopting a global framework for understanding Britain's national status and destiny—they are able to offer only intermittent glimpses of a cosmopolitan perspective amidst the increasingly dense fog of war. Second, each of them participates in the modern construction of war as an all-pervasive phenomenon, rendered real and urgent even for those not directly participating in it through a variety of technological and literary mediations. Here, I build on Mary Favret's insight that questions of mediation—of how war becomes *wartime* via its representations in literature and art—are central to our understanding of how British Romanticism "established forms for how we continue to think and feel about war at a distance."[6] Combined with the fact that the Napoleonic Wars arguably introduced the phenomenon of "total war," both geographically and in terms of its scope and scale,[7] the conversion of war into wartime undertaken by each of the poets I consider made the experience of the Napoleonic Wars comprehensible to Britain as a whole. By rendering war expressible in the same spatio-temporal terms that the Scottish Enlighteners developed a generation earlier, Hemans, Barbauld, Grant, and Scott all implicitly encourage their readers to think of war as an unavoidable, indeed perhaps necessary, stage of development of modern world order. And while each ultimately proposes that a version of Kantian "perpetual peace" will obtain following Napoleon's defeat, each has difficulty imagining the end of conflict as anything less than the end of history itself.

GOING TO WAR (IMAGINATIVELY) WITH HEMANS

Felicia Hemans' *England and Spain; or, Valour and Patriotism* is a singular accomplishment for a fourteen-year-old poet. Her later reputation as a consummate domestic poetess is belied by this early, highly political work directly inspired by an older brother's service in Spain under Sir John Moore. It was initially greeted with critical approval: in 1808 the *Poetical Register* lauded *England and Spain* for its "polished" verse and "genuinely poetical language," and even the highly conservative *British Critic,* although taken aback by the author's gender and youth (which would likely have been public knowledge by 1810, when the review was published), praised Hemans for her "fine words and smooth verses."[8] Yet despite this favorable reception, as well as the recent critical resuscitation of Hemans as a poet who, in Marlon Ross' words, was "central in helping to define the national taste of Britain and Anglophone America during the nineteenth century," *England and Spain* remains largely overlooked.[9]

Compared to Hemans' later, more nuanced works, at first glance this early production seems embarrassingly naïve, full of youthful idealism and unsophisticated enthusiasm in its defense of a muscular, militaristic Britain. Regardless of—or perhaps because of—these qualities, *England and Spain* offers a valuable window onto the way the vicissitudes of the ongoing conflict with France were felt by Britons at home. If, as Stuart Curran has suggested, Hemans can be thought of as "a Regency laureate manqué,"[10] then we would do well to pay closer attention to her earliest long meditation on Britain's geopolitical position in the midst of the Napoleonic Wars. Whatever we might think of the prospect of war today, the majority of Britons in Hemans' day (Whig and Tory alike) strongly supported the war against Napoleon, and Hemans clearly speaks on their behalf. In her efforts to establish the inevitability of freedom's progress around the globe, however, she paradoxically ends up praising the destruction of previous civilizations. More troubling still, in her enthusiasm for the Spaniards' patriotism during the Peninsular War, Hemans ultimately promotes a vision of warfare that would prove deadly in future conflicts.

England and Spain begins with an epigraph from Pope's translation of Homer's *Iliad*: "His sword the brave man draws / and asks no omen but his country's cause." It is a fitting epigraph both in terms of content and style, as Hemans' neoclassical choice reflects her early affiliations with the poetry of the previous century, and reminds us just how familiar the Romantic poets were with the past century's traditions.[11] As Behrendt indicates, Hemans' advertisement of her neoclassicism also likely garnered legitimacy in the eyes of a male critical establishment that equated classical learning with authority.[12] The opening of Hemans' poem closely resembles in mood and orientation Alexander Pope's "Windsor Forest" (1713), written nearly a century earlier. Where Pope celebrates "[t]hy forests, Windsor! and thy green retreats" as symbols of England's late-Stuart prosperity, however, Hemans sets a much larger stage for her poem: "Too long have Tyranny and Power combin'd, / To sway, with iron scepter, o'er mankind; / Long has Oppression worn th'imperial robe, / And rapine's sword has wasted half the globe!"[13] Clearly, there is no longer any question of the British poet assuming the borders of the nation as the limits of her poetry. Of course, Pope already knew that Britain's growing prosperity was due in significant part to its "lofty Woods, / Where tow'ring Oaks their spreading Honours rear, / And future Navies on thy [the Thames'] bank appear" (ll. 218–20), but such international considerations do not explicitly enter his poem until it is well under way.[14] By contrast, Hemans makes clear from the start her interest in what Nanora Sweet aptly calls "the glories and geopolitics of the Peninsular War."[15] Her use of the phrase "half the globe" reminds readers that France was currently in possession, if not of half the world, then at least of enough territory to make Britain and its European allies extremely anxious. As Hemans states in the lines immediately following, "O'er Europe's cultur'd realms, and climes afar, / Triumphant Gaul has pour'd the tide of war" (5–6). The Latinate term "Gaul" not only underscores that she is thinking in distinctly neoclassical terms, but also expresses Hemans' concern over Napoleon's imperial ambitions. At the same time, her division of France's conquered territories into the cultured (Europe) and the merely geographical ("foreign climes") bespeaks Hemans' own assumptions about the centrality of Europe—and adjacent to it, Britain—to the developing world system.

When *England and Spain* was published in 1808, Britain's future still looked relatively uncertain. As Hemans notes in her opening stanzas, Napoleon's recent victories over his European antagonists had been nearly total. Prussia's decision to go to war independently of its other allies except Russia, which was too distant to provide much help, led to disastrous simultaneous defeats at Jena and Auerstedt on 14 October 1806, and Napoleon entered Berlin some two weeks later. In Hemans' view, Prussia represented a model of how *not* to respond to Napoleon's power; in the wake of defeat, "drooping o'er her hero's [the Duke of Brunswick's] grave," who died of wounds received at Auerstedt, Prussia is rendered femininely helpless (17). Prussia's fate, in turn, appears to anticipate that of the rest of Europe; taking full advantage of personification, Hemans relates how "[t]hy blast, oh Ruin! On tremendous wing, / Has proudly swept o'er empires, nations, kings" (23–24). Diego Saglia notes that throughout her career, Hemans maintained an "ambivalent attitude . . . towards military conflict as a destructive, yet also glorious, enterprise," and there is a clear note of excitement in the poet's voice as she compares Napoleon's power to "the wild hurricane's impetuous force," which "[w]ith dark destruction marks its whelming course" (25–26).[16]

With the Battle of Trafalgar, which put to rest Napoleon's plans to invade Britain, already several years in the past, Britons were no longer seriously worried about their safety at home. The Continental Blockade instituted in November 1806 nevertheless continued to isolate them, and only Britain's powerful navy and emerging industry kept it from economic ruin during these years. Militarily, the British could do little more than watch as Napoleon subsequently drove the Russians out of Poland, obliged the Czar to sign the treaty of Tilsit, and forced the Swedes to give up the region of Pomerania on the southern Baltic coast. When France invaded Spain in late 1807 and early 1808 as part of its plan to force Portugal's participation in the embargo against Britain, however, the latter was afforded a fresh opportunity to stand up to Napoleon—an opportunity that the young Hemans, along with many more conservative Tories, did not wish to see squandered:

> Rise, Freedom, rise! And breaking from thy trance,
> Wave the dread banner, seize the glitt'ring lance!
> With arm of might assert thy sacred cause,
> And call thy champions to defend thy laws! (29–32)

Borrowing from the idiom of chivalric romance newly repopularized by Scott's *Lay of the Last Minstrel* (1805) and *Marmion* (1808), Hemans figures Freedom as a feudal knight who, having been entranced, now revives to brandish his instruments of war and lead his forces into battle.[17] But such confidently martial imagery is undercut by the questions—perhaps rhetorical, but nevertheless unsettling—which end the stanza: "How long shall tyrant power her throne maintain? / How long shall despots and usurpers reign?" (33–34). Gesturing indignantly at Napoleon's policy of replacing conquered monarchs with his own relations, Hemans cannot help but remind readers that, thus far, Napoleon has been quite successful at maintaining his grip on Europe.

Much later in the poem, Hemans enthusiastically imagines Napoleon tortured by his own mind into regretting his sanguinary actions: "Oh! When accusing conscience wakes thy soul, / With awful terrors, and with dread controul / . . . Is then thy cheek with guilt and horror pale?" (415–16, 423).[18] To reach this point, however, the poet first must prophesize that Britain and Spain will together successfully confront Napoleon, which in turn involves rehearsing great swaths of each country's history. Like an essayist laying out her argument in accordance with the key terms of her title, Hemans subsequently reinforces the links between English history, the English character, and a general cultural spirit of bravery and industriousness. Hence her liberal use of apostrophe:

> Hail, ALBION! Hail, thou land of freedom's birth!
> Pride of the main, and Phoenix of the earth!
> Thou second Rome, where mercy, justice, dwell,
> Whose sons in wisdom as in arms excel! (69–72)

Seemingly unworried by explicitly comparing Britain to Rome—as famous in the Romantic period for its decline and fall as for its eminence—Hemans invokes the latter as the guarantor of Britain's morality as well as power.[19] Clearly, she has not yet adopted the more sophisticated stance that Sweet calls her "Mediterranean aesthetics of the beautiful whose instability and productivity work against the sublimity of monument and empire, whether these are associated with Paris, Rome, Athens, or London";[20] instead, the young poet confidently announces that England not only rivals but surpasses ancient Rome in terms of trade and commerce.[21] Moreover, she freely admits that Britain's global trade networks are made possible primarily by force, or at least its threat: "For this thy noble sons have spread alarms, / And bade the zones resound with BRITAIN'S arms!" (101–2). With its naval might felt round the world, "the conquering isle" has done well for itself, and its battle-hardened sons have "made the BRITISH FLAG" a sign of renown worldwide (106, 134). In a rhetorical move that anticipates the poem's later complications,

British valor is even likened to "the Samiel-blast of war," a reference to Arabian sandstorms. A few stanzas later, Hemans will use another notably Orientalist image when she compares Britain's position of privilege in the world to that of "the pyramid [which] indignant rears / Its awful head, and mocks the waste of years" (147–48).[22] In the ensuing verses, Hemans softens her tone only somewhat as she relates her country's cultural accomplishments in conjunction with its historical progress.

Having completed her celebration of Britain's martial prowess (with last-minute praise for Shakespeare, Ossian, and Milton adumbrating Britain's literary tradition [177–96]), Hemans turns to address Spain. The Spanish, she immediately notes, are motivated by something in addition to the sheer love of freedom and valor that supposedly animates all Britons: patriotism. Again making plentiful use of anaphora, Hemans asserts that the Spanish fight from pure love of country:

> Not to secure dominion's boundless reign,
> Ye wave the flag of conquest o'er the slain;
> No cruel rapine leads you to the war,
> Nor mad ambition, whirl'd in crimson car;
> No, brave Castilians! your's a nobler end,
> Your land, your laws, your monarch to defend! (201–6)

Seemingly unconcerned that she is undermining her former praise of Britain's imperial ambitions, Hemans marks the defense of country as the most just cause of war. Readers were not meant to impugn Britain's motives for getting involved in the Peninsular War; indeed, Britain's military strategy was frequently defended on the simple grounds that it was better to fight the French on the Peninsula than closer to home. Still, Hemans sounds frankly relieved to be on moral ground firmly removed from the exigencies of geopolitical strategizing. Only much later, and only once, does she acknowledge that Spain had its own imperial ambitions in the not-too-distant past—ambitions that drove it directly into conflict with Britain (see 391–96). Instead, at this critical historical juncture Hemans is eager to depict the Spaniards as patriotic heroes, even martyrs. Hence her inclusion of a long, dramatic scene describing in excruciating detail a Spanish fighter's death: "He bleeds! he falls! his death-bed is the field! / His dirge the trumpet, and his bier the shield" (217–18).

Earlier in the poem, Hemans takes a quick tour through English history to remind her readers of the valor of their past leaders. When it comes time to do something similar with Spanish history, however, Hemans slows her pace considerably, perhaps assuming a degree of ignorance among her English readers on the subject, or more likely (as Rebecca Cole Heinowitz argues) to facilitate Britons' "shift from enmity to identification" with one of their long-standing European rivals for trade routes and naval dominance.[23] Although Spain's feudal glory days are over, its qualities remain embodied in present-day Spaniards: "Yet though thy transient pageantries are gone, / Like fairy visions, bright, yet swiftly flown; / Genius of chivalry! Thy noble train, / Thy firm, exalted virtues yet remain!" (321–24). After bringing the reader quickly through Spain's Middle Ages, Hemans settles on its Islamic era to exemplify how the Spanish managed to throw off the yoke of foreign oppression in the past, and can therefore vanquish Napoleon now.

At this juncture, however, the poet runs into an unexpected difficulty. As Hemans likely knew thanks to her educated upbringing, the period of Islamic settlement in Spain and Gibraltar brought about an unprecedented cultural flowering alongside increased religious harmony between Jews, Christians, and Muslims. (Such at least was the nineteenth-century viewpoint; contemporary scholars continue to debate this claim.[24]) Although Hemans ends this section by celebrating the repatriation of the kingdom of Granada under the reign of Ferdinand and Isabella, in the middle she pays tribute to the grandeur of Al-Andalus, the Arabic term for the territories of the Iberian Peninsula occupied by Islamic forces between 711 and 1492. The so-called golden age of the Caliphate of Cordoba, which began in 929, receives particular praise:

> When Moorish bands their suffering lands possest
> And fierce oppression rear'd her giant crest;
> The wealthy caliphs on Cordova's throne,
> In eastern gems and purple splendour shone;
> Theirs was the proud magnificence, that vied
> With stately Bagdat's oriental pride;
> Their's were the courts in regal pomp array'd,
> Where arts and luxury their charms display'd [. . .] (339–46)

Although this passage starts out by condemning the Muslim occupation, it quickly takes on an admiring tone as Hemans lists the many accomplishments and achievements facilitated by the infusion of Eastern culture and knowledge. Such compliments become particularly noteworthy near the stanza's end: "All that a poet's dream could picture bright, / One sweet Elysium, charm's the wond'ring sight! / Too fair, too rich, for work of mortal hand, / It seem'd an Eden from Armida's wand!" (351–54). At first, Hemans' logic is unclear: why should the Moorish occupation be too good to be true? The allusion in the last line suggests the direction she will go to resolve this paradox: just as Armida, the enchantress of Tasso's *Jerusalem Delivered* (1581), cannot be trusted to create a real paradise, so too the hybrid culture of Al-Andalus, built on an unusual-seeming combination of foreign occupation and intellectual flowering, could not be entirely substantial either. Instead, in Hemans' telling, the successive kingdoms established in Islam's name were bound to collapse: "Yet vain their pride, their wealth, and radiant state, / When freedom wav'd on high the sword of fate!" (355–56). That freedom should lead to the ruin of a great civilization is a second paradox upon which Hemans does not dwell for long—certainly not long enough to unearth any more parallels between imperial Rome and Britain. Instead, freedom's course, somewhat like the movement of Genius in Barbauld's *Eighteen-Hundred and Eleven* (as we will see shortly), is represented as both predetermined and infallible. Trumping every other consideration, Hemans must imagine freedom as the ultimate good in order to justify the collapse of Moorish Spain.

All of the above sits awkwardly with the poem's conclusion several hundred lines later. Here, the reader initially encounters little more than a recapitulation of Hemans' earlier rhetoric, as she builds a mighty exhortation out of yet another catalogue of historical English victories:

> Oh! by the shades of Cressy's martial dead,
> By warrior-bands, at Agincourt who bled; [. . .]
> By ALBION's thousand, thousand deeds sublime,
> Renowned from zone to zone, from clime to clime,
> Ye BRITISH heroes! May your trophies raise,
> A deathless monument to future days! (451–52, 457–60)

Utilizing enough anaphora to satisfy the most ardent neoclassicist, Hemans combines another primer on British military history with a national call for more bloodshed and sacrifice. Again emphasizing the global reach of Britain's military ("from zone to zone, from clime to clime"), the poet gestures toward "future days" and victories that will in turn become the subjects of future encomiums. From this perspective, armed conflict remains the primary vehicle of Britain's global progress. The "deathless monument" that Hemans imagines being raised, however, not only contrasts baldly with the many human deaths that will have made it possible, but also figures this future in a peculiarly static image, as if the only way Hemans can foresee a conflict-free future is to imagine it reified, frozen in time. The realization of

Hemans' global vision of Britain triumphant, in other words, simultaneously requires unprecedented violence and participates in the "traumatized sense of history" that Favret argues is characteristic of the Napoleonic era (and perhaps our own).[25]

Immediately following this passage, Hemans takes a final, unexpected turn. Still cheering her fellow Britons to victory overseas, she stops mid-sentence as the goal of all this interminable fighting suddenly becomes clear: "The reign of Freedom let your arms restore, / And bid oppression fall—to rise no more!" (465–66). Still speaking to the British soldiers in question, Hemans imagines what they will do after finally achieving this aim:

> Then, soon returning to your native isle,
> May love and beauty hail you with their smile; [. . .]
> Thy smile of heav'n shall ev'ry muse inspire,
> To thee the bard shall strike the silver lyre. (467–68, 491–92)

Such sentiments are hardly novel; the soldier's return to his fields, like the poet's transition from songs of war to paeans of peace, is thoroughly classical in origin. The problem in this case is that, having previously lauded Britain's and Spain's military prowess, and also having argued that Al-Andalus' downfall was necessary for freedom's realization, Hemans' last-minute assertion that violence need not forever characterize world order is less than convincing. The unstoppable march of Freedom celebrated earlier in the poem awkwardly becomes precisely what now must be stopped. Just what will happen afterward—once history effectively comes to a close—Hemans does not, or more likely cannot say. (The *pax Britannica* of the nineteenth century would provide a highly imperfect answer.[26]) Accordingly, the poem ends with a fervent but vague plea directed to the "[o]mnipotent Supreme!: [. . .] Oh! Send on earth thy consecrated dove, / To bear the sacred olive from above" (519–20).

England and Spain is ultimately at odds with itself. Intermittently aware of the new opportunities and challenges afforded by an increasingly linked global community of nations, it is nevertheless still largely in thrall to the neoclassical, monological expansionism articulated by earlier poems like Pope's "Windsor Forest." In its suspension between these worldviews, it thus joins those eighteenth-century texts that John Barrell and Harriet Guest have taught us to recognize as productively confused: "poems which enabled disparate discourses to be assembled into an aesthetic whole may have been performing the function of *enabling* contradictions to be uttered."[27] The imaginary resolution of real contradictions is of course a classic Marxian definition of ideology; whether Hemans intended her poem to have this effect, or crafted it unconscious of its paradoxes, is largely irrelevant. Either way, and somewhat ironically, events on the ground would bear out her prophetic vision, although likely not as she imagined. The signing of the controversial Convention of Sintra (or Cintra) in August 1808—which provoked fierce responses in Wordsworth, Byron, and others—allowed the French a free withdrawal from Portugal, and subsequently paved the way for Napoleon's eventual return to the Peninsula with 200,000 additional troops.[28] From that point on, there would be no peace in the area until after Napoleon's abdication. Perhaps even more significant in the long term was the subsequent development in occupied Spain of new warfare tactics. Funded by the British, cells of Spanish irregulars, frequently wearing civilian clothing to blend in with ordinary citizens after an ambush, harried the French troops mercilessly. These Spanish patriots proved so successful that their "war of little wars"—*Guerra de guerrillas*—provided both the name and the method of modern guerilla warfare: a cellular form of unofficial combat that has been used worldwide with deadly results ever since. Hemans' encouragement of the Spaniards to rise up against the French thus can be said to have borne sanguinary fruit that even she could not have predicted.[29]

BARBAULD'S PESSIMISTIC PROPHECY

When Hemans first published *England and Spain,* most reviewers assumed, despite the name on the title page, that it was a man's work.[30] When Anna Laetitia Barbauld published *Eighteen Hundred and Eleven* under her own name four years later, reviewers were equally quick to chastise her for abandoning her proper feminine realm. Best known is John Wilson Croker's melodramatic response in the *Quarterly Review,* in which he complains not only that "she has wandered from the course in which she was respectable and useful, and miserably mistaken both her power and her duty," but also that "we had hoped, indeed, that the empire might have been saved without the intervention of a lady-author."[31] Fittingly, Barbauld's poem, written when the author was a mature sixty-eight years old, has in recent years attracted renewed attention for precisely the sorts of reasons that led critics like Croker to condemn it. William Keach describes *Eighteen Hundred and Eleven* as a prophecy that upset its earliest readers because it "marks a decisive break with the meliorist historical perspective" common to the progressive Dissenting discourse in which Barbauld was steeped.[32] Similarly, James Chandler uses Barbauld's poem as an example of the kind of ruminations on the "spirit of the age" that characterized the Romantic era.³³ From Chandler's perspective, *Eighteen Hundred and Eleven*'s harsh reception stemmed from the fact that male critics were protecting generic turf—articulations of the zeitgeist—understood as inherently masculine. But this raises a question: what exactly was so threatening about Barbauld's attempt to depict, in party-neutral language, Britain's geopolitical fate?

In 1811, British fortunes were at a crossroads. After the disastrous Welcheren Expedition of 1809, Britain stuck to using its naval superiority to wage hit-and-run operations against the French; not until Wellesley's victory at the Battle of Vitoria in June 1813 would they earn another meaningful victory on the Continent. (This was after Napoleon had practically destroyed his forces in Russia the previous year.) Meanwhile, however, the Anglo-Dutch Java War was turning in favor of the British, and the Continental blockade was proving less than fully effective. Events on the ground, in other words, were clearly open to interpretation; as a result, as Nicholas Birns points out, "the existing critical discourse on [*Eighteen Hundred and Eleven*] seems unable to decide whether Barbauld's fervor was animated by Britain's successes in the Napoleonic Wars or by its failures."³⁴ Without deciding entirely on this question, in this section I examine some of the ways Barbauld's poem acts as a counterstatement to the optimistic patriotism of a poet like the young Hemans. Combining elements of Keach's and Chandler's arguments, I argue that the disquieting aspects of *Eighteen Hundred and Eleven* stem precisely from its combination of the two perspectives, that is, from its synthesis of an inherently female-centered viewpoint with a world-spanning scope.³⁵ Combining these two elements, the poem firmly situates Britain in a global narrative, but ultimately refuses to give its readers the comfort either of a happy ending for the nascent British Empire, or of a discrete temporality to the time of war.

Whereas Hemans' *England and Spain* opens with the statement, part intuition and part hopeful prophecy, that the war has already been going on "too long," *Eighteen Hundred and Eleven* immediately registers the seeming interminability of the conflict: "STILL the loud death drum, thundering from afar, / O'er the vexed nations pours the storm of war."³⁶ Making at least as liberal use of personification as Hemans, Barbauld continues: "Colossal Power with overwhelming force / Bears down each fort of Freedom in its course" (7–8). But several aspects distinguish this opening litany of defeat from the much younger poet's earlier chronicle of Europe's tribulations. First, Barbauld makes no references or allusions to specific battles, people, or events, and this lack of identifying detail makes her descriptions of war's many terrors more abstract and timeless; the situation is one of endless, relentless calamity, rather than of individual, historically specific events. "Freedom" is borne down by varieties of "Colossal Power" repeatedly in the course of the poem, as Marlon Ross has noted, and the reader soon feels these events represent war's eternal destructiveness.[37] What Croker calls the poem's major fault—"we very confidently assert that there is not a topic in 'Eighteen Hundred and Eleven' which is not quite as applicable to 1810 or 1812"[38]—is in fact one of its principal strengths, as Barbauld's lack of specificity allows her to compose situations exemplifying the never-ending costs of war without becoming ensnared in their details.

At the same time, Barbauld is highly sensitive to war's impact on the everyday lives of Britons at home. Although (like Hemans) she eventually allows her imaginative vision to range freely over time and space, Barbauld's poetic perspective is initially aligned most closely with the narrative perspective Favret calls "everyday war." With the conflict with France entering its second decade and no end in sight, Favret writes, "Romantic writers found it nearly impossible to imagine any space or time free from the pains . . . of warfare."[39] In Barbauld's poem, this experiential alteration is evident from the first stanza, where we learn that all citizens, not just those who fight, feel "the alternate hope and fear" of wartime. Nevertheless, she subsequently presents war primarily as a disruption rather than a continuation of everyday life across Europe: "And where the Soldier gleans the scant supply, / The helpless Peasant but retires to die; / No laws his hut from licensed outrage shield, / And war's least horror is the ensanguined field" (19–22). In passages like this, Barbauld's vision of wartime as implicitly unnatural effectively problematizes any incorporation of war into the linear temporality favored by the Scottish Enlighteners and other proponents of global progress.

Barbauld soon makes clear that war is hellish not only for those on the battlefield or caught in the crossfire, but also for those whose lives are intimately touched by devastation and loss even as they experience the fighting primarily through the mediation of print. As Barbauld explains,

> Oft o'er the daily page some soft-one bends
> To learn the fate of husband, brothers, friends,
> Or the spread map with anxious eye explores,
> Its dotted boundaries and penciled shores,
> Asks *where* the spot that wrecked her bliss is found,
> And learns its name but to detest the sound. (33–38)

In this scene of female reading, newspapers and maps provide the main sources of knowledge about the fate of loved ones across the Channel.

Although the "boundaries" and "shores" of Europe exist for the spouse at home primarily as virtual rather than concrete entities, the pain experienced upon learning the exact location of a husband's death is nonetheless entirely real. As a result, the technology of print capitalism, which according to Benedict Anderson's well-known formulation unifies a national readership, in this case arguably performs the opposite function, leaving each new widow isolated in her grief.[40] Newspapers and maps may give women a wider window onto contemporary geopolitics, but not greater powers of worldly intervention.

The end of Hemans' poem pictures a world renewed and revitalized by the coming of peace, however asymptotic that arrival might be. By contrast, Barbauld is quick to point out that humans have a tendency to mar happy endings: "Man calls to Famine, nor invokes in vain, / Disease and rapine follow in her train" (15–16). Against Hemans' neo-Enlightened belief in man's perfectibility, Barbauld deploys unapologetic pessimism. As opposed to the "flatterers" (45) who try to convince the reading public that Britain's island geography and naval superiority will keep it eternally free from invasion, Barbauld knows better: "Thou who hast shared the guilt must share the woe" she intones cryptically, likely with specific reference to Britain's participation in the slave trade and, more generally, to its imbrications in world affairs (46). For Barbauld, the writing is on the wall: Britain's decline is inevitable.[41] Furthermore, she represents this decline in terms of the very quality—Britain's commercial power—that Hemans and the Scottish Enlighteners celebrate. Addressing her country, Barbauld claims that "[t]hy baseless wealth dissolves in air away, / Like mists that melt before the morning ray . . . Yes, thou must droop; thy Midas dream is o'er; / The golden tide of Commerce leaves thy shore" (53–54, 61–62).[42] Hitting her middle-class readers where it hurts most, Barbauld proclaims that the end of Britain's financial strength, and thus its continued ability to function under the Continental Blockade, is near.

She inverts another typical source of national pride by prophesizing that Britain's developing global ambitions are already becoming unsustainable. Working under the assumption (to which I will return in a moment) that its glory days are numbered, Barbauld sees Britain's expansionistic tendencies as signs of weakness rather than strength:

> If westward streams the light that leaves thy shores,
> Still from thy lamp the streaming radiance pours.
> Wide spreads thy race from Ganges to the pole,
> O'er half the western world thy accents roll. (79–82)

Other nations will first become like Britain and then supersede it, until "England, the seat of arts, be only known / By the gray ruin and the mouldering stone" (123–24). This perspective is a kind of future anterior; as Emily Rohrbach indicates, *Eighteen Hundred and Eleven* "presents a history of the future, a historical explanation for a specific future that proleptically casts a dark shadow" over a present already riven with uncertainty.[43] Accordingly, Barbauld's crime, at least from her critics' implicit perspective, is to take the Whig narrative of progress—a legacy of the Scottish Enlightenment's stadialism—to its logical extreme. Where the literati propose that all societies pass through the same evolutionary stages, Barbauld imagines progress as a personified force unbounded by national borders. Once it has finished its work in Britain, the "Spirit" will move elsewhere—in Barbauld's opinion, to the Americas—leaving only ruin and desolation behind:

> There walks a Spirit o'er the peopled earth,
> Secret his progress is, unknown his birth;
> Moody and viewless as the changing wind,
> No force arrests his foot, no chains can bind; (215–18)

This Spirit's movement is simultaneously foreseeable and unpredictable: it follows a steady course from East to West, thus reproducing the standard Enlightened narrative of European triumphalism, but precisely *when* it will decamp from one civilization to another is unknown; statements like "[t]he Genius now forsakes the favored shore, / And hates, capricious, what he loved before" (241–42) profoundly undercut any regular and therefore reassuring pattern of spatio-temporal change.

Late in the poem, Barbauld returns to the more predictable, albeit pessimistic logic of an Enlightener like Adam Ferguson when she declares, "Arts, arms and wealth destroy the fruits they bring; / Commerce, like beauty, knows no second spring" (315–16). Here, in a fashion akin to what Derrida calls "autoimmunity"—"that strange behavior where a living being, in quasi-*suicidal* fashion, 'itself' works to destroy its own protection, to immunize itself against its 'own' immunity"[44]—Britain's past and current successes are seen to contain the seeds of their own destruction. All British accomplishments will be reduced inevitably to mere traces, remembered primarily for their influences on future civilizations. No matter how vainly they struggle, Barbauld insinuates, Britons cannot avoid eventually shrinking to a few lines in history's chronicle; in a vein Percy Shelley mines a few years later in "Ozymandias" (1818), she predicts that future visitors to a ruined London "shall own with humbled pride the lesson just / By Time's slow finger written in the dust" (214–15).

We can now appreciate more fully why critics like Croker reacted so venomously to *Eighteen Hundred and Eleven*. Barbauld's poem is not disturbing because it prophesizes that Britain will be defeated by France, which it never says explicitly in any case, but because it predicts that Britain is doomed to destruction *regardless* of the outcome of the Napoleonic Wars. In global terms, Barbauld correctly predicts that the modern world-system Britain has been helping create, whose center it would indeed occupy in the decades following Waterloo, will ultimately overwhelm it. Accordingly, whereas Hemans' poem concludes by imagining the future renovation of the world in the illuminating light of perpetual peace, Barbauld can only imagine such a future for the New World. When the "Genius" of progress decisively and ultimately "turns from Europe's desolated shores," the result is freedom and rejuvenation not for Britain, but rather for South America: "Thy world, Columbus, shall be free" (321–22, 334).[45] For its part, Britain will be kept alive in memory only as a sort of theme park which other world-citizens will visit to remind themselves of their nearly forgotten origins.

ANNE GRANT STRIKES BACK

Among those upset by Barbauld's vision of Britain reduced to the margins of the world picture, Anne Grant—known to readers of her day as "Mrs. Grant of Laggan"—deserves special mention. The author of several previous works of poetry and prose, including *Essays on the Superstitions of the Highlands of Scotland* (1811), whose influence Scott acknowledges at the end of *Waverley; or 'Tis Sixty Years Since* (1814), Grant was a well-established "exponent of the Highland romance" but an unlikely candidate for public controversy.[46] Her decision to respond publicly to Barbauld appears motivated primarily by a desire to defend Britain's reputation against a seemingly treacherous attack from within. As a poetic riposte to *Eighteen Hundred and Eleven*, Grant's *Eighteen Hundred and Thirteen* seems designed to refute or replace the earlier poem's every facet, beginning with its title. At almost three thousand lines, Grant's poem is more than eight times longer than Barbauld's; where the latter shies away from referencing contemporary events, the former inserts frequent allusions to specific battles and figures both ancient and contemporary. Even as she superficially replicates Felicia Hemans' strategy of temporally integrating wartime into world history (at least until the traumatically idealistic end of *England and Spain*), however, Grant also manipulates chronology and even geography, repeatedly remapping battles and conflating historical figures to suit her conservative agenda.

Britain's situation improved dramatically in the months following *Eighteen Hundred and Eleven*'s publication. Napoleon's disastrous invasion of Russia marked a turning point for the Allies, who thereafter enjoyed an almost constant numerical advantage. Despite victories at Lutzen, Bautzen, and Dresden between May and August of 1813, Napoleon's armies were steadily forced to give ground, and in October the French forces, outnumbered almost two to one, were soundly defeated at the Battle of Leipzig. Although Napoleon would continue to win battles, including during his long retreat back to France, the tide of war had permanently turned against him. This change is reflected in Grant's choice of epigraph, taken from Milton's *Samson Agonistes* (1671): "O how comely it is, and how reviving / To the spirit of just men long oppressed, / When God into the hand of their deliverer / Puts invincible might." It also affects her narrative perspective: whereas Barbauld anticipates a ruinous future in order to cast doubt on the present state of things, Grant looks backward, the better to appreciate the present: "Yet more the glorious present to enhance, / Let us cast back a retrospective glance."[47]

Nevertheless, in some respects Grant's vision is not that different from Barbauld's. Like the latter, Grant sees Britain betrayed by America, whose treachery is worsened because the former colony owes its very existence to Britain: "Our language, lineage, faith, are still the same, / The torch that kindled Freedom's holy flame / To light the western world, from British altars came" (I.71–73). But Grant is certain that despite the ongoing war (later known as the War of 1812), harmony will eventually be restored between these two natural allies (I.114–17). Such thoughts lead her, via the tenuous associational logic characterizing most of her poem, to take up the same theme that occupies Hemans, and present the Peninsular War as evidence of Britain's eternal valor: "Who has not heard the applauding world's acclaim / Of Britain's generous aid, and Wellesley's deathless name[?]" (136–37). Grant follows this rhetorical question with a diatribe against pessimistic prognostication, implicitly condemning Barbauld for joining those who

> . . . with presumptuous pride elate
> Anticipate the dark decrees of Fate,
> Or calculate, on this terrestrial ball,
> How high the strong may rise, how low the proud *must* fall;
> Nor bow the heart, nor lift the awful eye,
> To own the Omnipresent Deity,

Whose potent will confounds their airy schemes,
As day's effulgence scatters morning dreams. (I.138–45)

Grant excoriates Barbauld for daring to foretell Britain's eventual downfall. By evoking a pagan version of Fate, a likely allusion to *Eighteen Hundred and Eleven*'s "Genius" or "Spirit," the poet implies that Barbauld has failed to take God—who must, after all, be on the side of the British—into account. In place of Barbauld's pessimism, Grant substitutes a providential account of Britain's destiny in which the repeated adjective "propitious" signals the divine engine of history. In a wartime context, such transcendent references ultimately have the same effect Favret finds in much British war poetry of the period: "Warfare, despite all its strategies and tactics, is thus placed outside human agency."[48]

The idea that only God can foretell the future becomes the thematic linchpin of Grant's case against Barbauld. With unmistakable echoes of Pope's *Essay on Man* (1734), she repeatedly stresses the impossibility of knowing heaven's will: "Ah! Who to wonder-working wisdom blind, / Can scan the counsels of th'Almighty mind?" (I.182–83). The poet's task, Grant implies, is not to predict what will happen but rather to celebrate what has already happened, the better to prepare readers for an even more glorious future. After retelling the story of Napoleon's ill-fated Russian invasion—"[t]o ruin urged thy blind, impetuous way," she gloats (I.276)—Grant expects that Russia's repulse of the French will invariably lead to a cultural revitalization (modeled, it turns out, on the British Enlightenment) in which poets will play a key role:

The Bard inspired by Heaven, and he alone,
Can shed a lasting luster around the throne;
The noble deeds, sung to the immortal lyre,
The souls of future bards and heroes fire: (I.342–45)

For Grant, the poet's role is to uphold the current order and prepare the way for later generations, who will perform yet more great acts for future poets to memorialize. This poetic calling is later reinvoked in spiritual terms: "When Speculation wings its upward flight, / Say not it misses profit or delight; / When its strong pinion takes its utmost scope, / It meets an angel form, and calls it Hope" (II.1297–1300). Defending her prerogative to write about the loftiest themes, Grant asserts that poets have every right to engage in such conjectures, as long as they are ultimately subordinated to God's all-powerful authority.

Part I of *Eighteen Hundred and Thirteen* is primarily restricted to retelling current events, including but not limited to the Peninsular War. In Part II, Grant digressively sets out her larger argument that Britain is the destined savior not just of Spain but of all Europe and even beyond. Comparing Britain to a merciful Biblical rain cloud, she writes:

> Like that arising from the sea it spread,
> And wide o'er all its freshening influence shed;
> And when the term of punishment was past,
> From Britain Mercy's rays diverged at last. (II.160–65)

When Napoleon's domination of Europe ("the term of punishment") is broken by the British, their "freshening influence" can envelop the other Allied nations. In a striking expansion of traditional "body politic" imagery, Grant opens Part II by asserting that Britain is already the heart of the world's body:

> Turn, wearied Muse, to Britain speed thy flight . . .
> This heart from which the genial currents flow,
> That general energy and life bestow,
> Then, circling glad through every distant vein,
> Return to cheer their genial source again. (II.10, 14–17)

In contrast to Barbauld's prophesy that Britain will inevitably be marginalized by the global system it is helping create, Grant describes a nation energized and revitalized by the circulation of "genial currents" of goods, money, people, and information between the British center and its world-system peripheries. Later, she even evokes an "after-wartime," when its global ambitions will be entirely satisfied:

> And when the wild, disastrous form of war
> No longer threatens from his iron car;
> O'er the wide world when desolations cease,
> And virtues flourish in the soil of peace,
> Then shall Britannia with auspicious toil
> The olive plant in Afric's fertile soil. (II.408–13)

Drawing again on naturalizing, organic imagery, Grant imagines that Britain will put its post-war influence to good use; her vocabulary here looks forward to the *pax Britannica* of the later nineteenth century.

The rhetoric of Britain as a salvific global force intensifies as Grant's poem approaches its oft-delayed conclusion. Recalling Barbauld's pessimistic prognostication that Britain will be remembered only by those nations that supplant it, Grant replaces her one-way movement of the Spirit or Genius with a vision of multi-directional cultural expansion. After a Dryden-like invocation of 1813 as another *annus mirabilis* (II.1869), Grant declares that everyone will be amazed by Britain's accomplishments: "On every faithful soul, and generous breast, / This glorious era shall be deep imprest" (II.1881–82). Her conclusion first recalls Hemans' final ode to Peace, then looks forward to Britain's inevitable assumption of its providential global mantle:

> Invoked by Britain in serener skies,
> With mildest beams the Star of Peace shall rise;
> Once more her hand that balance shall sustain,
> That bids Germania be herself again;
> To Europe all its wonted bounds restores,
> And gives to liberal Commerce all its shores; (II.1893–98)

Anticipating the restitution of Europe's pre-Napoleonic borders, as well as the end of the Continental Blockade, Grant correctly foresees a nineteenth-century future in which Britain's geopolitical star will rise. Her final lines aggressively turn back Barbauld's dark prophecy, and predict instead British global hegemony:

> O'er every land her energetic tongue
> Conveys the lays her lofty bards have sung:
> Her children spread o'er Earth's remote extremes,
> Or by Columbia's lakes, or Ganges' streams,
> Whether they serve, or suffer, or command,
> Led by the Genius of their native land,
> Shall at their country's hallow'd altars bend,
> And truth and freedom o'er the world extend. (II.1923–30)

Superimposing religious and nationalistic vocabularies, Grant imagines Britons participating in settler colonialism while paying heartfelt homage to their native country. As one of the most explicitly imperialist poets of the Romantic era, Grant bends the spatio-temporal grid of emerging globalism to her purposes, such that Britain becomes simultaneously a transhistorical force and a transnational power.

On closer inspection, however, Grant's ambitious vision turns out to be less than fully convincing. The poet manipulates her representations of time and space throughout *Eighteen Hundred and Thirteen,* and taken together these moments of spatio-temporal warping introduce considerable noise into her superficially triumphant signal. Penny Fielding observes that in Grant's zeal to give Britain a privileged status in the war against France, she credits Wellington and the British with facilitating the Allied victory at Leipzig, even though they were not present at it (see I.215–39).[49] Perhaps to avoid enflaming old Anglo-Scottish wounds regarding the royal succession, Grant also takes advantage of identical surnames to conflate Thomas Graham, a British commander who helped restore the Prince of Orange to the Netherlandish throne, and James Graham, Earl of Montrose, who commanded the Royalist faction in Scotland during the Civil War. Accordingly, although the poem strives to end on a purely sweet note—repudiating Barbauld's concluding vista of a New World free from the constraints of the Old, Grant even adds a final forecast that "[Britain's] offspring stretch'd along the western main, / Deceived a while by alien foes in vain, / Again shall with rekindled filial love, / Within her sphere of mild attraction move" (II.1931–34)—*Eighteen Hundred and Thirteen* is at least partially soured by such acts of geopolitical legerdemain.

Despite its idiosyncrasies and obsolete sentiments, Grant's prophecy of a world remade by Anglo-American hegemony proved prescient. Assessing whether Hemans, Barbauld, or Grant is the most accurate concerning Britain's future, however, depends on the time scale invoked. In the short term, Hemans was correct to predict British and Spanish victory in the Peninsular War; in the medium term, Grant was right to see that Britain would emerge from the Napoleonic Wars in many respects more powerful than ever. As for Barbauld, in the Victorian era and the first half of the twentieth century, her predictions of Britain's imminent dissolution must have seemed wildly off the mark, yet in the context of waning British global power and influence after World War II, it now seems more prescient than ever.

Yet beyond their differences in tone, perspective, and disposition, what is perhaps most striking about these poems today—especially when reread in dialogue with one another, as I have tried to do here, and as the British public initially would have received them—is their shared commitment to helping readers conceptualize their changing global position. Each poem challenges readers to think of Britain, not as existing in splendid isolation vis-à-vis the rest of the world, but as part of an interlocking web of nations making up the evolving world order. Of course, global concerns were an important element of British literature well before Romanticism: "the interplay of imperial ambitions, provincial anxieties, and national self-assertion" was informing

British poetry since at least Dryden's time.[50] Nevertheless, in the years immediately preceding Britain's great victory of 1815—"a victory that would forever alter British attitudes towards the rest of the world"[51]—the poetry of Hemans, Barbauld, and Grant strongly registers the increased self-consciousness with which Britons were approaching their expanded role on the world stage. These poems, oscillating between optimism and pessimism with regard to Britain's ability to bestride the ever-less-narrow world, bear witness to the evolution of Romantic globalism as it took shape during the war years. And although Captain Wentworth might not have approved, they confirm that women's public voices on war, wartime, and "worldwideification" were here to stay.

SCOTT'S POETRY OF TOTAL WAR

Even as female poets continued to make an impact on the reading public—Hemans' *Records of Women* (1828), for example, would sell more copies than any of her previous titles—Walter Scott remained by a wide margin the most influential British poet of the Napoleonic era.[52] Certainly, there was no lack of authors ready and able to publish during the period.[53] Nevertheless, for sheer popularity as well as influence, nobody came close to Scott, at least not until the first canto of Byron's *Childe Harold's Pilgrimage* in 1812. Scott's trio of Scottish "metrical romances" from the first decade of the nineteenth century—*The Lay of the Last Minstrel*, *Marmion*, and *The Lady of the Lake* (1810)—not only established him as the period's best-selling poet, but also cemented his ability "to assert a wider British patriotism" through the use of bardic and other Celtic motifs.[54]

By utilizing tales from the chivalric past to inspire the present, Scott's wartime poetry helped both drive and satisfy the national desire for martial vigor and political unity during a time of conflict. Despite setting all of his major early poems in the quasi-feudal past, Scott experimented with representing present concerns more directly; each canto of *Marmion*, for example, begins with an introductory verse epistle celebrating the most important British political and military figures of the day.[55] In this section, I focus on the two poems by Scott that immediately followed *The Lady of the Lake*: *The Vision of Don Roderick* and *The Field of Waterloo*. While neither achieved as much popularity as the earlier Scottish verse romances, each not only extends the contemporary thrust of *Marmion*'s introductory epistles, but also amplifies the global concerns of Hemans, Barbauld, and Grant in telling ways. *The Vision* attempts to make sense of Britain's involvement in the Peninsular War, while *The Field* tries to set an optimistic course for Britain's post-Napoleonic future.

It was not until *The Vision of Don Roderick* that Scott decided the time was right to extend his poetic reach beyond Britain's borders. Like many Tories, he was a keen observer of the Peninsular campaign, following events on the ground in the newspapers and even keeping track of the battles on a personal map.[56] Perhaps as a result, in *The Vision*'s opening stanzas Scott declares he is tired of chronicling "feuds obscure, and Border ravaging."[57] After reviewing several possible poetic settings that adumbrate the scope of Britain's global ambitions from equatorial Africa to the plains of North America, Scott—perhaps thinking of Hemans' *England and Spain,* and certainly with the Peninsular War in mind—eventually focuses on the "Barbaric monuments" of Islamic Spain (I.10.4). Invoking first the famous Alhambra palace, he then describes the medieval city of Toledo,

> . . . where the banners of more ruthless foes
> Than the fierce Moor, float o'er Toledo's fane,
> From whose tall towers even now the patriot throws
> An anxious glance, to spy upon the plain
> The blended ranks of England, Portugal, and Spain. (I.10.5–9)

Past and present are superimposed as the banners of medieval invaders morph into those of Napoleon's forces, compressing centuries of warfare into a single, all-encompassing conflict. The result, in Philip Shaw's words, is "a poem that would seek to restore a sense of national unity and purpose" through a synthesis of romance and history, past and present.[58]

As Scott explains in an introduction to the work's characteristically voluminous notes, *Vision* consists of a series of historical visions granted to Don Roderick, the last Gothic king of Spain, before the eighth-century Islamic invasion. The first pair—of the invasion itself, and of the zenith of the Spanish and Portuguese empires—occupies much of the poem's middle section, but the final stanzas of the second canto are of more interest for my purposes. Here, Scott opens with several passages of invective directed at Napoleon—described as "burst[ing] . . . honour's oath, and friendship's ties" in order to clutch at "fair Spain his prize" with a "vulture-grasp" (II.37.8–9)—before (again like Hemans) enthusiastically describing the Spanish guerillas:

> By day the Invaders ravaged hill and dale,
> But, with the darkness, the Guerilla band

> Came like night's tempest, and avenged the land,
> And claim'd for blood the retribution due,
> Probed the hard heart, and lopp'd the murderous hand.
> And Dawn, when o'er the scene her beams she threw
> Midst ruins they had made, the spoilers' corpses knew. (II.49.3–9)

The cold-bloodedness of these lines is notable, but with the conflict still raging, Scott appears comfortable deploying graphic imagery to arouse readers' passions. Its "eye for an eye" logic finds a counterpart in a later depiction of French cruelty:

> The peasant butcher'd in his ruin'd cot,
> The hoary priest even at the altar shot,
> Childhood and age given o'er to sword and flame,
> Women to infamy—no crime forgot,
> By which inventive demons might proclaim
> Immortal hate to man, and scorn of God's great name! (III.6.4–9)

Here, Scott plainly crosses the line between stirring poetry and dehumanizing rhetoric, representing the enemies of the British not as misguided but as irredeemably evil. As John Sutherland suggests, the scenes of warfare in *The Vision* are almost entirely "in the spirit of the propaganda newsreel."[59] Although this approach is unusual for Scott, who generally shows much more empathy for both sides of a given conflict in his Waverley Novels, it typifies the thinking that David A. Bell argues characterizes the "total war" phenomenon brought to fruition by the Napoleonic Wars.[60]

Scott paints the arrival of the allied forces on the Peninsula with clichéd but undeniable effectiveness: "It was a dread, yet spirit-stirring sight! / The billows foam'd beneath a thousand oars, / Fast as they land the red-cross ranks unite, / Legions on legions bright'ning all the shores" (II.56.1–4). As befits a Scotsman, he carefully lists the specific intra-nationalities of the British expeditionary force: "A various host—from kindred realms they came, / Brethren in arms, but rivals in renown" (II.58.1–2). Once again, Scott's talent for bringing the nation together in the crucible of war is on display. Less obvious is his thorough white-washing of the actual events of the first Peninsular campaign, in which the British were forced to evacuate hastily from Corunna in January 1809. To avoid recalling this humiliation, Scott omits any mention of the martyred British hero of that battle, Sir John Moore, dwelling instead on the deaths of more obscure military heroes in other actions, and making the Peninsular War sound like an unbroken string of British triumphs rather than the see-sawing, costly engagement it actually was. Like Grant's manipulations of wartime details of *Eighteen Hundred and Thirteen,* Scott's revisionist history in *The Vision of Don Roderick* quietly speaks to the fragility of Britain's global standing during the Napoleonic era, even as it loudly tries to bolster it.

Whereas *The Vision* attempts to provide clarity of purpose for British readers in the midst of war's fogginess, *The Field of Waterloo* celebrates the successful conclusion of a conflict that had left the nation simultaneously jubilant and exhausted. Scott knew the latter poem did not rank with his best work; in his brief introduction he claims to regret its hurried composition, noting that "[i]t may be some apology for the imperfections of this poem, that it was composed hastily, and during a short tour upon the Continent . . . but its best apology is that it was written for the purpose of assisting the Waterloo Subscription."[61] As Scott highlights the charitable impulse behind the poem, he also gives it an air of authenticity: this is the work of an eyewitness to the scene of battle, albeit not to the battle itself.[62]

Although Waterloo was later considered a relatively easy victory for the Allies, the enormous number of casualties (approximately 50,000 in a single day) meant it was initially "viewed by many writers as a Pyrrhic victory."[63] To counter this perception, Scott tries to provide a seemingly unmediated perspective on the field of battle. He begins by leading readers to the site where the fighting occurred:

> Yet one mile on—yon shatter'd hedge
> Crests the soft hill whose long smooth ridge
>   Looks on the field below,
> And sinks so gently on the dale,
> That not the folds of Beauty's veil,
>   In easier curves can flow . . .
> Now, see'st thou aught in this lone scene
> Can tell of that which late hath been? (3.7–12, 4.1–2)

The concluding question, which also opens a new section, is simultaneously straightforward and rhetorical. Scott knows his readers can easily guess what site he is describing, thanks to the poem's giveaway title, but asking it establishes his authority to inform readers about what is no longer apparent to the naked eye of the beholder. Scott has fashioned himself, in other words, into the poet of past national glories for whom Hemans called in *England and France.*

Having already broadly hinted at what has transpired, Scott moves rapidly to represent the battle itself. As Simon Bainbridge notes, in his earlier poetry

Scott distinctly prefers to represent combat on the personal level rather than en masse, a choice that seems to have had aesthetic as well as historical motivations: individual combat was not only easier and more dramatic to describe, but also accorded better with Scott's frequent idealization of warfare as primarily consisting of "heroic" and "picturesque" actions.[64] In *The Field*, by contrast, Scott opts for a full-on retelling of the entire battle, writing more than a dozen stanzas of cavalry charges, artillery barrages, and so forth. Although modern readers may still find these descriptions highly idealized, in many instances Scott seems determined to delineate the horrors of battle in markedly realistic terms. Describing the fateful day as "ten long hours of doubt and dread" (8.11), for example, he repeatedly draws attention to the terrible loss of life which ensued, including allusions to the "promiscuous carnage" and "ghastly sights" of the battlefield (8.3, 9.5), as well as descriptions of the "mangled" bodies of the wounded as they are dragged from the field (9.7).

Such examples of war's atrocities are nonetheless outnumbered by numerous stanzas depicting the bravery and fortitude of the British and their allies as they withstand waves of French attack before rallying under Wellington's courageous leadership. If *The Field*'s battle scenes seemed familiar to Scott's readers, this was not only because many of them already would have read non-fiction accounts of Waterloo's events, but also because Scott leans heavily on his own previous writings for many of *The Field*'s set-piece descriptions.[65] Bainbridge implicitly imputes this quasi-self-plagiarism to waning creativity on Scott's part, yet such repetition, inadvertent or not, effectively positions Waterloo as simultaneously the culmination and conclusion of all previous battles fought by British forces. Scott makes this point explicit when, taking poetical leave of the field, he recognizes the world-historical importance of what he has just versified:

> Yes, Agincourt may be forgot,
> And Cressy be an unknown spot,
>   And Blenheim's name be new;
> But still in story and in song,
> For many an age remembered long,
> Shall live the towers of Hougomont,
>   And field of Waterloo. (23.15–21)

The most recognizable cognitive hallmark of globalization, time/space compression, is on display here via the superimposition of multiple, historic British military victories into a continuous national memory, with Waterloo as its most recent impression.

Yet *The Field* does not end on this wholly triumphant note. Instead, switching from octosyllabic verse to the Spenserian stanzas of *The Vision*, Scott adds a final framing stanza that blends triumphalism with caution. Here, he addresses all Britons in a Barbauld-like voice of the poet-prophet:

> Yet 'mid the confidence of just renown,
> Renown dear-bought, but dearest thus acquired,
> Write, Britain, write the moral lesson down:
> 'Tis not alone the heart with valour fired,
> The discipline so dreaded and admired,
> In many a field of bloody conquest known;
> Such may by fame be lured, by gold be hired;
> 'Tis constancy in the good cause alone,
> Best justifies the meed thy valiant sons have won. (Conclusion; unnumbered)

The chivalric archaism of "meed" should not obscure these lines' proleptic quality. Standing on the far side of the Napoleonic Wars, Scott chooses to look forward rather than back, intuiting that Britain is entering a new era rife with danger as well as opportunity. If he hopes that over the course of the new century "valour" and "discipline" will become synonymous with British expansionism, he also sees that any imperial project must be motivated by something (a "good cause") more than mere geo-political ambition. Otherwise, the Romantic globalism he and his fellow wartime poets variously promote and interrogate will become little more than the pretext for future rounds of bloody fighting.

Despite Scott's efforts, *The Field of Waterloo* was not a great success. Although it sold respectably, *The Critical Review* called it Scott's "poorest, dullest, least interesting composition"—a judgment that may have hastened Scott's decision to give up poems almost altogether.[66] Yet if Scott's pre-Waterloo monopoly on the poetry market was ending, his post-Waterloo dominance of the novel market was just beginning. In Chapter Five, I consider several of Scott's influential late novels, which narrate how European modernity constituted itself along proto-global lines; in the next chapter, however, I explore some of the post-Napoleonic literature by Scott and Byron concerned with making sense of Britain's increasing expansion eastward. We have seen that poetry written during the Napoleonic Wars and its immediate aftermath demonstrates ever more awareness of the high stakes of Britain's foreign engagements. Those stakes were raised yet again in a post-Napoleonic world in which Britain now occupied the very center of the global stage.

CHAPTER FOUR

The Clash of Civilizations and Its Discontents

BYRON, SCOTT, AND THE EAST

*F*RANCIS JEFFREY published two influential pieces on Byron's Eastern Tales in *The Edinburgh Review*: a short but favorable blurb in July 1813 on *The Giaour* (1813), and a longer, equally positive account of *The Bride of Abydos* (1813) and *The Corsair* (1814) the next year. The latter review attempts a general explanation of Byron's popularity. According to Jeffrey, Byron's diction, versification, and descriptions are all laudable, but it is "to his pictures of the stronger passions, that he is indebted for the fullness of his fame."[1] The influential critic speculates that the extraordinary popularity of Byron's Eastern Tales—*The Bride* sold six thousand copies in its first month of publication, and *The Corsair* sold ten thousand copies on its first *day*— may also be due to the poet's fortunate historical moment. Outlining a stadial theory of social evolution clearly indebted to the Scottish Enlightenment, Jeffrey hypothesizes that when a society reaches the zenith of its development, a certain degree of emotional regression inevitably ensues:

> When the pleasures of security are no longer new, and the dangers of excessive or intemperate vehemence cease to be thought of in the upper ranks of society, it is natural that the utility of the precautions which had been taken against them should be brought into question, and their severity in a great measure relaxed.... This is the stage of society in which fanaticism has its second birth, and political enthusiasm its first true development—

when plans of visionary reform and schemes of boundless ambition are conceived, and almost realized by the energy with which they are pursued—the era of revolutions and of projects—of vast performances, and infinite expectations. (55)

Jeffrey seems of two minds here. As Marilyn Butler points out, phrases like "vast performances" and "infinite expectations" suggest approval of these social developments.[2] At the same time, readers could hardly fail to catch Jeffrey's allusions to the Revolutionary and Napoleonic wars, those "plans of visionary reform" and "schemes of boundless ambition," from which Britain had only recently seemed to emerge. (Jeffrey of course could not foresee that Napoleon's imprisonment on Elba was temporary.) Either way, Britain now occupied the center of the world order about to be mandated by the Congress of Vienna, which began a few months after the publication of Jeffrey's second review, and the major question facing it was how to manage its newfound global primacy.

Returning to more narrowly literary matters, Jeffrey subsequently asserts that where history goes, poetry follows; accordingly, the poems of this new era will necessarily be "more enthusiastic, authoritative, and impassioned" than previous ones. To find fit subjects, the contemporary poet has two choices: write about the past, "when strong passions were indulged, or at least displayed without controul," or take up the "savages and barbarians that are still to be found in the world, [and] are, no doubt, very exact likenesses of those whom civilization has driven out of it" (57). Following the Scottish literati's globalizing schema, Jeffrey equates geographic marginality (from a Eurocentric point of view) with asynchronous temporality. But he knows, too, that most contemporary poets—Jeffrey mentions Robert Southey and Scott as well as Byron—do not write purely about the past, or even about the past in the present; instead, in a shrewd ploy to gain readers, they generally try to combine atavistic passions with contemporary manners (59). What sets Byron apart, and largely exempts him from the charge of inauthenticity that Jeffrey levels at Southey especially, is thus more a matter of degree than of kind: it is the superior "force and energy of [Byron's] sentiments and expressions," combined with "the novelty of his situations" (60). Nevertheless, Jeffrey finally admits that he cannot entirely penetrate the mystery of Byron's success: "How he has managed it, we do not yet exactly understand" (60).

Today, some critics claim to have solved the riddle of Byron's early popularity through simple deduction: "The popularity of Byron's . . . Tales was in their appeal to stereotypical fantasies."[3] There is undoubtedly some truth to this, as well as to the argument that the Byronic cult of personality quickly played a large role in magnifying his fame. These well-known perspectives, however, can be productively supplemented through recourse to a sufficiently global perspective. In this chapter, I investigate some of the ways that several of Byron's Eastern poems and plays not only tap a deep public wellspring of interest regarding Britain's increasingly expansive geopolitical reach following Napoleon's defeat(s), but also complicate readers' likely assumptions regarding such exotic encounters.

I start from the premise that Byron's verse plays on the British public's simultaneous fascination with and fear of the possibility of "turning Turk" or "going native" as the result of extended contact with or immersion in foreign cultures. This trope has a long history in British literature, of course, but Byron's updating of it says a lot about the historically specific ways that Britons were learning to think globally in the Romantic era. The first two cantos of *Childe Harold's Pilgrimage* and the early Eastern Tales were written while the outcome of war with France was still unknown. Perhaps as a result, in them Byron consistently paints portraits of Western heroes finding (or losing) their ways in Eastern locales.[4] By contrast, his later Eastern Tales—the focus of this chapter's initial sections—reverse this pattern: *Lara* and *The Siege of Corinth* feature protagonists who, like soldiers coming home from war, have returned to the West bearing with them unmistakable traces of their Eastern experiences. I read them as embodiments of the process Aravamudan calls levantinization: "a creative response to orientalisms as a plural rather than singular category and the specifically dynamic interactions of European culture with Islamic ones that go back at least to the Crusades."[5] In the wake of Napoleon's unconditional abdication (6 April 1814), Britain began to grapple with the possible repercussions of its newfound global authority. Byron's final two major Eastern Tales reflect upon this profound shift by providing British readers with narratives that highlight both the desirability and the difficulty of maintaining dual subject positions simultaneously. Try as they might, neither Lara nor Alp can successfully inhabit his levantinized subject positions for long. Whereas other critics read their demises as indexing Byron's pessimism regarding the commingling of East and West, I argue their deaths are the result, not of the inherent untenability of their hybridized subjectivities, but rather of their respective societies' inability or unwillingness to abandon a "clash of civilizations" mentality: a dangerously simplified and antagonistic globalism that makes levantinization appear untenable. Subsequently, I turn to *Sardanapalus* to see how questions of sexuality and nationality are dealt with in Byron's most mature "Orientalist" production. Finally, I consider

Scott's popular novel *The Talisman* as a Romantic-era vision of how the clash of civilizations, properly understood—which is to say, thoroughly deconstructed—need not end in bloodshed and ruin.

DISPUTING "THE CLASH"

To clarify the stakes of my argument, I want briefly to review the contemporary history of the concept of the clash of civilizations. Although the phrase did not originate with him, it was popularized by the political scientist Samuel P. Huntington when he used it as the title of a 1993 article that he subsequently expanded into a monograph.[6] (The original title phrase contained a question mark that was significantly left off the book.) His central premise is "that culture and cultural identities, which at the broadest level are civilizational identities, are shaping the patterns of cohesion, disintegration, and conflict in the post-Cold War world" (20). Emphasizing in good neoliberal fashion the inevitability of global competition over cooperation, moreover, Huntington rather eagerly predicts a future of planetary conflict:

> In this new world the most pervasive, important, and dangerous conflicts will not be between social classes, rich and poor, or other economically defined groups, but between people belonging to different cultural entities. Tribal wars and ethnic conflicts will occur within civilizations. Violence between states and groups from different civilizations, however, carries with it the potential for escalation as other states and groups from these civilizations rally to the support of their "kin countries." (28)

At first, Huntington's work attracted attention primarily from other academics and international policy experts.[7] After September 11, 2001, however, it began to be invoked as both the cause and at least implicitly the justification for global conflicts.

As it grew in popularity and policy-making influence, however, Huntington's clash of civilizations thesis was quickly questioned on a number of grounds. Edward Said, for example, publicly censured Huntington for numerous errors, including ignoring "the internal dynamics and plurality of every civilization," claiming "to survey the entire world from a perch outside all ordinary attachments and hidden loyalties," and promulgating the "basic paradigm of 'the West versus the rest' (the cold war opposition reformulated)."[8] In fact, despite his putatively unbiased tone, Huntington makes little pretense to objectivity: his opening chapter states, "The West is and will remain for years to come the most powerful civilization" (29), and one of its maps is bluntly titled "The West and the Rest" (22–23). More damaging is Said's observation that Huntington fundamentally oversimplifies both the long-durational history *and* the current reality of globalization. As Amartya Sen also noted at the time, the clash of civilizations paradigm not only ignores "diversity *within* distinct civilizations," but also implicitly denies "major global interactions in science, technology, mathematics, and literature over millennia," which are "made to disappear so as to construct a parochial view of the uniqueness of Western civilization."[9] Additionally, Buck-Morss has recently argued that Huntington's basic view of civilizations as culturally distinct entities is highly problematic inasmuch as "[c]ultures—always borrowing, always being borrowed—belong exclusively to no civilization, and therefore cannot define 'civilization' or produce a clash between them."[10] In other words, Huntington mistakes effects for causes: far from causing civilizational frictions, cultural differences are in fact produced by the very conflicts he tries to explain and justify through them. By turning Huntington's thesis on its head, Buck-Morss exposes its serious limitations and indicates its unintentional value: the paradigm of civilizational clash may be highly misleading for policy-oriented attempts to navigate global configurations and conflicts, but viewed critically may be a useful framework for seeing how the West has systematically misunderstood its relation to the rest of the world.

In what follows, then, I invoke the clash of civilizations not as an accurate way to describe the global situations of the Romantics' era (much less our own), but rather as a shorthand for the all-too-typical oversimplification of globality—including the frequent denial of the possibility of mutually productive or cooperative global interchanges—by the modern West. That neither Byron's nor Scott's texts fit such a reductive paradigm, I will argue, and moreover that each author in fact challenges or problematizes it—Byron with increasingly bitter irony, Scott with imaginative historicity—underscores the timeliness of revisiting their literary interventions into Britain's post-Napoleonic worldview.[11]

LOOKING FOR OTHERNESS IN *LARA*

Although it features differently named characters, critics generally treat *Lara* as an imaginative extension of *The Corsair*, and with good reason. Byron's manuscript subtitle straightforwardly calls *Lara* a sequel to that earlier poem, and in the Advertisement to the initial anonymous edition he declares that "although the situations of the characters are changed, the stories are in some measure connected. The countenance is nearly the same—but with a different expression."[12] Further, in a letter to John Murray, Byron refers to *Lara* as "complet[ing] the series [of *The Giaour, The Bride of Abydos,* and *The Corsair*], and its very likeness renders it necessary to the others."[13] Nevertheless, I am less interested in treating *Lara* as the capstone of that earlier sequence of poems than in considering it as the first of a pair (with *The Siege of Corinth*) in which levantinized protagonists struggle to re-adapt to Western milieus. As *Lara* struggles to reclaim his place in the European environment he left behind years before, he finds no way to retain his new identity and simultaneously reconcile himself to the Western status quo. The poem's pathos is generated by Lara's ultimately unsuccessful attempts to reform his environment to accommodate his hybridized subjectivity.

Lara opens with an immediate display of the difficulties of cross-cultural translation. With their local nobleman returned home, we are told that "[t]he Serfs are glad through Lara's wide domain, / And Slavery half forgets her feudal chain," to which Byron immediately appends the following note:

> The reader is apprised, that the name Lara being Spanish, and no circumstances of local and natural description fixing the scene or hero of the poem to any country or age, the word 'Serf,' which could not be correctly applied to the lower classes in Spain, who were never vassals of the soil, has nevertheless been employed to designate the followers of our fictitious chieftain.[14]

This passage not only sets the poem in an intentionally vague European space, but also explicitly recognizes that calling Lara's followers "serfs" is an inaccurate translation into Westernized terms of a medieval peasantry that (thanks to the legacy of Islamic rule in Spain, discussed in the previous chapter) was not bound by formal vassalage. From the start, then, Lara's reappearance after years of absence threatens to scramble the normal terms of Western social operation.

As Jerome Christensen pithily puts it, "*Lara* brings the Byronic hero home."[15] The details of where Lara has been, how long he was away, and what he did during his years abroad are kept deliberately elusive, enveloping him in mystery. The plot turns precisely on Lara's unwillingness (or inability) to disclose the details of his foreign travels. Even his motivations for having gone abroad are kept under wraps: "The chief of Lara is return'd again: / And why had Lara cross'd the bounding main?" (I.11–12). From a basic psychoanalytic perspective, Lara's *wanderlust* could be ascribed to his childhood lack of a strong father figure; if they are not taken as a mere non sequitur, the next lines invite this explanation by suggesting that Lara was "[l]eft by his sire, too young such loss to know, / Lord of himself" (I.13–14).[16] Similarly, Peter J. Manning has described Lara as a "failed adult" who returns home to compensate for "the collapse of his independence."[17] As with Ezzelin's later allegation that Lara has done terrible deeds in the East, however, the text provides little evidence for this position. On the contrary, in this case the narrator expressly observes that Lara seems more, not less, mature upon his homecoming: "Ambition, glory, love, the common aim, / That some can conquer, and that all would claim, / Within his breast appear'd no more to strive" (I.79–81). We also learn that Lara now "did not share, / The common pleasure or the general care / . . . Nor shadowy honour, nor substantial gain, / Nor beauty's preference, and the rival's pain" (I.101–2, 105–6). If Lara's Eastern sojourn has helped him master his passions and retire his ambitions, this newfound quiescence arguably signals emotional maturation, not arrested development.

This is not to deny that Byron drops several enticing suggestions regarding Lara's unusual past; Nigel Leask notes that "[a]n air of macabre mystery hangs over the orphaned Lara's activities 'out east.'"[18] The perspective from which those Eastern "activities" appear sinister, however, is implicitly Western. Since Lara says nothing regarding his past experiences abroad, it is primarily the narrator's and other characters' insinuations that cast them in a malevolent light. Although the narrator claims that "'tis quickly seen, / Whate'er he be, 'twas not what he had been" (I.65–66), the poem itself provides scant proof of this. Lara's retainers and dependents are of course free to speculate: "Why slept he not when others were at rest? / Why heard no music, and received no guest? / All was not well, they deem'd—but where the wrong?" (I.147/–149). As the final question emphasizes, however, nothing is necessarily amiss; Lara's behavior simply fails to conform to Western norms and expectations. To the extent that he seems unusually melancholy following his return from abroad, his state of mind may be explained by Judith Butler's insight that "[t]he violence of social regulation is not to be found in its unilateral action, but in the circuitous route by which the psyche accuses itself of its own worthlessness."[19] Butler's writings on the constitutive, albeit not wholly determining roles played by social norms in the formation of individual subjectivities can help unpack the psychic makeup of the Byronic persona.[20] If Lara is unhappy, this is arguably due in no small part to the fact that he no longer easily fits in with his Westernized followers and peers, and this isolation is the cause at least as much as the effect of his alienated behavior.

Likewise, Lara's levantinized psychology, at least as much as his air of guilt, is what makes him so prototypically Byronic.[21] Again, although Byron drops many hints that Lara experienced tragedy in the Orient, he provides no confirming details. When we are told, for example, that Lara cannot enjoy a beautiful evening because "[s]uch scene reminded him of other days . . . a night like this / A night of beauty, mock'd such breast as his" (I.175, I.179–80), we learn little beyond Lara's nebulous nostalgia for the East. Unless we assume that *The Corsair*'s plot provides Lara's backstory, we can only speculate on his past. Such speculation, moreover, is both encouraged through Byron's artful scattering of dark hints and ridiculed, as when he writes that "history's pen its praise or blame supplies, / And lies like truth, and still most truly lies" (I.189–90). The strategy here is similar to what Emily A. Bernhard Jackson identifies in *Manfred* (1817) in which, she argues, Byron enjoys "thrust[ing] the burden of definition onto the reader, who, given only a series of most general clues, must shape the protagonist's character and motivation according to her own extrapolations and assumptions."[22]

The darkest clue that Byron plants regarding Lara's Eastern sojourn is the nightmare he seemingly experiences during the above-mentioned "night of beauty." Upon awakening, his first words are incomprehensible, "strung / In terms that seem not of his native tongue; / Distinct but strange, enough they understand / To deem them accents of another land" (I.229–32). Still in a semi-somnolent state, Lara apparently speaks the foreign language of the country or region in which he previously dwelt, using words "meant to meet an ear / That hears him not—alas! that cannot hear!" (I.233–34). But at least one person present both understands and responds: Kaled, Lara's "page," who "alone appear'd / To know the import of the words they heard" (I.235–36). Kaled's decision not to translate Lara's wild, foreign speech appears intended to keep his master's secrets, such that in typical Byronic fashion, past crimes are suggested but not confirmed. This pattern, as Tom Mole observes, can certainly be understood as part of Byron's strategy to fan the flames of his celebrity.[23] Yet the assumption that Lara is hiding something rests specifically on the foreignness of his feverish speech. Linguistic incomprehensibility as a sign of the exotic was not, of course, Byron's own invention; Wordsworth's "The Solitary Reaper" (1803), for example, takes advantage of the poet's inability to understand a highland peasant's Gaelic song to augment its affective power (allowing it, significantly, to evoke an image of "Arabian sands" for him).[24] In Lara's case, such conventionality turns sour as the imputation of wrongdoing becomes inextricable from his followers' incomprehension and inability to translate his words into a Western idiom.

Lara's encounter with Ezzelin in Otho's castle proceeds similarly. Once more, the imputation of transgression or crime belies the impossibility of knowing exactly what Lara did during his time in the East; a vague reference to a female to whom Lara owes a "debt / Eternity forbids thee to forget" (I.441–42) is the closest Ezzelin comes to a full accusation. Alleging ignorance of what the knight speaks—indeed, claiming not to know him at all—Lara scorns Ezzelin's pretensions to judgment: "I shun no question, and I wear no mask . . . Whate'er I be, / Words wild as these, accusers like to thee / I list no further" (I.436, I.455–57). Whether this is calculated bluster or authentic outrage, the reader is again left to decide. The challenge, I think, is precisely *not* to assume Lara's guilt merely because he has been broadly accused of some Eastern impropriety. Although Ezzelin counts on such prejudice to sway the court of public opinion, Otho demands evidence: "If thou, Sir Ezzelin, hast aught to show / Which it befits Count Lara's ear to know, / To-morrow, here, or elsewhere, as may best / Beseem your mutual judgment, speak the rest" (I.467–70). By appealing to the "mutual judgment" of Lara and Ezzelin, Otho affirms his faith in both parties' abilities to negotiate their differences in a proto-Habermasian spirit of rational exchange.[25] For a moment, it seems that Lara may even find a sympathetic soul in this process, since Ezzelin too is "now return'd alone / From other lands, almost a stranger grown" (I.472–73).

No such meeting of minds, however, is possible in *Lara*'s world. After Ezzelin fails to appear at the arranged meeting, Otho repeats his pledge to stand for the missing knight, and is subsequently defeated in single combat by Lara. In this context, Lara's "freeing" of his "serfs" conveniently provides the rationale Otho needs to seek revenge under cover of defending the feudal status quo. Like everything else in the poem, Lara's motivations for his act of emancipation are murky at best, and critics have generally focused on the lines "What cared he for the freedom of the crowd? / He raised the humble but to bend the proud" (II.252–54) to suggest that it is primarily "self-aggrandizing."[26] Nevertheless, early in the poem Byron intimates that Lara's willingness to challenge the feudal system is at least partially precipitated by his previous Eastern experiences: "But that long absence from his native clime / Had left him stainless of oppression's crime" (II.170–71). Lara is literally guiltless of benefiting from feudalism during the years he was abroad; by association, it is precisely his levantinized sensibility that fundamentally facilitates his "freeing" of his followers. This imaginative license has less to do with the actual, historical East that Lara might have experienced than with Byron's sense of the Orient as, in Makdisi's words, "not only a refuge from modernity—that is, a space from which to flee modernity—but also a space from which to critique modernity and the West itself."[27] Lara can imagine alternatives to feudalism because his Eastern sojourn has presumably exposed him to social systems other than Western ones. It is this exposure, and the alternative to feudalism's hegemony it represents, that makes him dangerous to his Western peers, and allows Otho to rally them against the rogue nobleman.

Shot in the side as he rallies his troops, Lara dies attended only by Kaled. On his deathbed, his ties to the East are again highlighted as he once more speaks only "in that other tongue" (II.444); his final gestures are to point wordlessly "to the East" (II.467) and to refuse Christian rituals when they are offered (II.477–81). Although this stanza ends with the narrator piously explaining that "[i]mmortality" is available "[t]o none, save them whose faith in Christ is sure" (II.488–89), Byron tacitly approves of Lara's final refusal to apologize for his levantinization, making his gestures of defiance far more moving than the boilerplate theology with which the stanza concludes. The discovery of multiple scars disfiguring Lara's corpse does not dispel the mystery of his Eastern sojourn as much as reinforce it; they are quite literally the undecipherable marks of his past experience.[28]

The poem's penultimate revelation—that Kaled is actually a woman, and therefore likely Lara's Eastern lover (often identified as Gulnare from *The Corsair*)—functions similarly: driven insane with melancholy, Kaled's last recorded action is to "trace strange characters along the sand" (625). Even the final disclosure that she likely orchestrated Ezzelin's disappearance—possibly in order to protect Lara's reputation, or possibly out of jealousy—merely underscores, rather than condemns, the foreign nature of the crime. Echoing Leila's drowning by Hassan in *The Giaour*, Kaled's disposal of Ezzelin's body in the river may implicitly evoke stereotypes of "oriental" secrecy and skullduggery,[29] but such associations—as well as the assumption that it was indeed Ezzelin's corpse dumped in the water (the text at this point contains two "if" clauses)—are generated by the reader as much as by the text itself. The true victim of *Lara* is not Ezzelin (who after all made his initial accusations with a "haughty sneer" [I.425]) but rather the possibility of a hybridized East–West sensibility. In a society that bans any mingling of supposedly mutually exclusive cultures in the name of a de facto clash of civilizations mentality, Lara's and Kaled's lives (and deaths) are fierce indictments of this worldview's systemic violence. The note of desolation on which the poem ends is Byron's condemnation of a society that can make no space in itself for otherness.

EXPLODING MULTICULTURALISM IN *THE SIEGE OF CORINTH*

The Siege of Corinth is not usually given equal consideration with Byron's earlier Eastern Tales, especially since the poet himself said *Lara* "completes the series" begun with the earlier works. Nevertheless, Byron thought enough of *The Siege* to dedicate it to his good friend and traveling companion John Cam Hobhouse. Although unpopular with critics, who especially objected to its nearly apocalyptic denouement, *The Siege* went through four editions by 1818.[30] (When considering the falling-off of the sales of Byron's Eastern Tales following *The Corsair*, it's good to remember that "Scott and Byron sold more poems in a normal afternoon than Shelley and Keats did during the whole of their lives."[31]) It is notable not only for its more precise historical setting than previous Eastern Tales, but also for its even more unrepentantly levantinized hero. Usually considered one of Byron's most nihilistic protagonists, Alp is also his most radically hybridized one. Although he and several of *The Siege*'s other characters reflect the global situation that post-Waterloo Britain was negotiating, they all remain tragically unable either to think beyond the limits of their own identities or to imagine alternatives to civilizational conflict.

The Siege was Byron's first attempt to base an entire Tale on historical events.[32] His headnote provides factual details of the actual battle for Corinth, in which peace talks between leaders of the besieged city and the attacking Turks were disrupted by an accidental explosion in the Turkish camp that killed between six and seven hundred men. In Byron's version the explosion is purposeful and it levels the entire city. The historical episode clearly appealed to his keen sense of irony, especially given Corinth's long, hybridic history. Situated on a narrow stretch of land joining the Peloponnesus peninsula to mainland Greece, since classical times Corinth had been an important trading and port city. Conquered by the Turks in 1458, it was eventually captured by the Venetians in 1687, formally coming under the Republic of Venice's control in 1699. Retaken by the Ottomans in 1715 in the action that forms *The Siege*'s basis, the city was subsequently decimated during the Greek War of Independence, and not officially freed from Ottoman rule until 1832.

Byron's poem opens with two stanzas spoken by an unnamed narrator who asks, "Stranger—wilt thou follow now, / And sit with me on Acro-Corinth's brow?"[33] Readers then learn details about the men with whom the narrator used to traverse the region: "We were of all tongues and creeds;— / Some were those who counted beads, / Some of mosque, and some of church, / And some, or I mis-say, of neither" (18–21). Apparently, this former company was an assortment of Christians, Muslims, and non-believers whose heterogeneity made the narrator proud: "Yet through the wide world might ye search, / Nor find a motlier crew nor blither" (22–23). This otherwise superfluous introduction establishes the possibility of multicultural, supra-national concord, and throws into relief the subsequent failure of the main narrative's characters to achieve anything resembling this ideal state of affairs.

The central narrative pits the Christian Venetians and Greeks inside the city walls against the Ottoman Muslims without. Richard Maxwell notes that representations of sieges in historical novel frequently allow "that rare commodity, a forthrightly collective protagonist," to take center stage.[34] Perhaps not surprisingly for a poet whose popularity rested in large part on his outsized personality, however, Byron's poetic narrative partially violates this pattern. His description of the besieging army, for example, begins by glossing its apparent homogeneity—"And far and wide as eye can reach / The turban'd cohorts throng the beach" (2.34–35)—but soon draws attention to its actual variety: "And there the Arab's camel kneels, / And there his steed the Tartar wheels; The Turcoman hath left his herd, / The saber round his loins to gird" (2.36–39). Instead of depicting the Muslim attackers as an undifferentiated horde, Byron prompts readers to recognize the diversity of the Ottoman Empire's peoples. Yet the poem does not sustain this initial attention to this internal diversity; as the siege progresses, such individualizing—and thus humanizing—gestures become fewer, so that as its literally explosive conclusion nears, the narrator more regularly falls back on generalizations like "the turban'd host" versus "the Christians" (29.877, 29.882). Such oversimplified dichotomies demonstrate the difficulty of maintaining respect for difference in the heat of conflict. In his discussion of Saint Paul, Alain Badiou notes that "[d]ifferences can be transcended only if benevolence with regard to customs and opinions presents itself as *an indifference that tolerates differences.*"[35] It is precisely this kind of universalizing indifference that proves impossible to sustain in *The Siege of Corinth*.

Byron exploits the irony that, in his retelling at least, the leader of the Ottoman forces is a former Venetian. The story of Alp's transformation from Christian to Muslim is given in fragments: forbidden to marry the daughter of the man, Minotti, who will eventually become Corinth's governor, and having subsequently fled into the Ottoman Empire to avoid being tried for characteristically unnamed crimes (of which the narrator implies Alp may be innocent), Alp has returned to Corinth's walls to fight his former colleagues. As a convert, his commitment to his new religious identity is perhaps stronger than if he had been born a Muslim: "To Greece and Venice equal foes, / He stood a foe, with all the zeal / Which young and fiery converts feel" (4.79–81).[36] Byron's repetition of "foe" underscores the enmity Alp now feels towards his former brethren. In a poetic version of free indirect style, the stanza's final couplet suggests Alp has long harbored a clash of civilizations mindset: the years following his conversion to Islam have passed "in strife / That taught his land how great her loss / In him who triumph'd o'er the Cross, / 'Gainst which he rear'd the Crescent high, / And battled to avenge or die"

(4.91–95). Yet when Alp is unable to sleep after the day's battle, we are told that

> [h]e stood alone among the host;
> Not his the loud fanatic boast
> To plant the crescent o'er the cross,
> Or risk a life with little loss,
> Secure in paradise to be
> By Houris loved immortally. (12.251–56)

The repetition of symbols is striking, but this time their meaning is reversed, for as we soon learn, Alp does not wish to triumph "o'er the cross" as much as to use the current conflict as cover under which to claim his beloved Francesca's hand. As these thoughts occur, Alp finds that "[t]he turban on his hot brow press'd" with ever greater weight (13.293)—his new identity has become as burdensome as his old once was. Thus although Susan Oliver wittily calls Alp "a cultural cross-dress[er]" and implies that he merely "poses as a Muslim invader," her descriptions imply a fluidity of identity that Alp neither enjoys nor possesses.[37]

The contours of Alp's symbolic resignification are further delineated when, wandering nocturnally outside Corinth's battered walls, he is confronted by a vision of Francesca. His first response is telling: "His trembling hands refused to sign / The cross he deem'd no more divine: He had resumed it in that hour, / But conscience wrung away the power" (20.493–96). Startled, Alp almost reverts to a Christian gesture. Further, his re-conversion is precisely what the spectral Francesca demands as a precondition of their reunion: "Thou hast done a fearful deed / In falling away from thy father's creed: / But dash that turban to the earth, and sign / The sign of the cross, and for ever be mine" (221.530–33). Caroline Franklin notes that this request neatly reverses the usual *femme fatale* pattern, in which a figure like Keats' Belle Dame sans Merci tempts the Christian male with pagan sexuality.[38] The further twist here, which Alp does not discover until the next day, is that Francesca is already dead; thus the ironic "temptation" of reconversion that she offers him is, in Franklin's words, "a sign used by the Christian powers to try to secure the potential revolutionary's sentimental assent to patriotic, religious, and imperial orthodoxy."[39] Since Francesca's ghost has not literally been sent by Minotti or his Christian comrades, however, it seems more accurate to say that her spectral appearance indexes Alp's guilt over his conversion to Islam.[40] Either way, her posthumous appearance clearly signals Alp's confusion concerning his adopted identity, and the future he has foreclosed as a result of his choices.

Faced with Francesca's ghostly ultimatum, Alp's Byronic self-importance leads him astray: "His heart was swollen, and turn'd aside / By deep interminable pride. . . . And thus he spake—'Whate'er my fate, I am no changeling— 'tis too late'" (21.608–9, 622–23). This logic is obviously flawed, since Alp has changed religions once before, and when he claims that "[w]hat Venice made me, I must be, / Her foe in all, save love to thee" (22.626), his evasion of responsibility for his prior decisions becomes all too clear. Nonetheless, his unwillingness to reconvert to Christianity indicates a certain kind of psychic persistence that, according to Butler, implicitly acknowledges the power others have over us: "The desire to persist in one's own being requires submitting to a world of others that is not fundamentally one's own (a submission that does not take place at a later date, but which frames and makes possible the desire to be)."[41] Caught between his own intransigence and the equally entrenched positions of the forces fighting over his allegiance—and here the external siege of the city becomes recognizable as the objective correlative of Alp's internal struggle—he can only refuse to make further accommodations to otherness.

Alp's intransigence is mirrored by Minotti's, who confronts him the following day after Corinth's walls have been breached, and gloatingly tells him of Francesca's death the previous night: "Nor weep I for her spirit's flight: / None of my pure race shall be / Slaves to Mahomet and thee" (27.817–19). Distracted, Alp is shot dead by a sniper, who significantly fires "[f]rom within the neighbouring porch / Of a long defended church" (27.826–27). With the larger battle lost, Minotti retreats to the altar of the church and ignites the store of gunpowder kept beneath it. The subsequent explosion instantaneously eliminates the differences between the combatants, as Byron points out with grisly gusto:

> Up to the sky like rockets go
> All that mingled there below:
> Many a tall and goodly man,
> Scorch'd and shrivell'd to a span, . . .
> Some fell on the shore, but, far away,
> Scatter'd o'er the isthmus lay;
> Christian or Moslem, which be they?
> Let their mothers see and say! . . .
> Not the matrons that them bore
> Could discern their offspring more; (33.985–88, 994–97, 1003–4)

With the combatants rendered indistinguishable by incineration, Byron ghoulishly suggests that the only way to overcome the fatal polarization of identity promoted by a clash of civilizations mentality may be to blow everyone up and start again. Although Byron's contemporaries were horrified by the poem's graphic and nihilistic ending, it has a darkly ironic justification. Even as he artificially transplants jackals from Asia to Greece to enhance the macabre mood of the final stanzas, Byron drives home the tragic consequences of being unable to think outside the moral and conceptual binarisms that constrain Christians and Muslims alike in *The Siege of Corinth*.

EASTERN (BROKEN) PROMISES: *SARDANAPALUS'* FATAL IRONIES

After *The Siege of Corinth*, Byron's interest in critiquing the repercussions of Romantic globalism's potential narrowing into a clash of civilizations paradigm seems to have waned.[42] Indeed, he presents a surprisingly optimistic vision of multicultural harmony in his late poem *The Island, or Christian and His Comrades* (1823). Placed in a veritable vacuum—the poem's situation is modeled on the famous 1789 mutiny on the Royal Navy ship *Bounty*—the British sailors and the natives with whom they settle come to an agreeably eroticized understanding: "The white man landed! need the rest be told? / The New World stretch'd its dusk hand to the Old; / Each was to each a marvel, and the tie / Of wonder warm'd to better sympathy."[43] The islanders' natural innocence—as Jonathan Lamb points out, by the mid-eighteenth century "[i]t was already agreed that the islanders of the South Seas were by and large children of nature"[44]—facilitates their freedom from all ideological constraint; instead, it is other Englishmen, with their "chains" and "menace" (IV.4.6), who attempt to disrupt this pleasant idyll. Oliver notes that "[t]he idealistic resolution of *The Island* leaves Torquil in a utopian location and in an apparently complete union with his South-Sea wife."[45] Moreover, the poem concludes with a near-admission of its fairy-tale-like status, as Torquil eludes recapture and returns to his island home to experience "peace and pleasure, perilously earn'd; / A night succeeded by such happy days / As only the yet infant world displays" (IV.15.18–20).

The Island stands as an exception to Byron's increasingly ironic—not to say cynical—worldview, whose fullest expression is to be found in his unfinished masterpiece *Don Juan* (1819–24). His mature play *Sardanapalus*, however, provides a more focused vision of the clash of civilizations' corrosive effects. Once relatively neglected, it is now generally hailed as Byron's best closet drama, despite (or perhaps because of) what Barbara Judson calls "its sly miscegenation of high and low, tragedy and burlesque, politics and pleasure."[46] Such slyness informs its sophisticated meditation on both the possibilities and the limitations of inter-cultural communication, sympathy, and hybridization.

Set in ancient Assyria, *Sardanapalus* depicts the final hours of its eponymous hero, a notably effeminate and hedonistic ruler who is belatedly roused to defend his kingdom. A commandingly idiosyncratic figure, Sardanapalus is a Byronic hero with a difference: his "effeminacy is an attempt to live by his own principles, even though Byron invites us to see them as somewhat self-indulgent," in Andrew Elfenbein's astute synopsis.[47] The character of Myrrha, a longtime favorite of Sardanapalus who has become a valued member of his court as well as his lover, plays a key role in his halting transformation. Along with Sardanapalus' loyal brother-in-law, Salemenes, Myrrha spends much of her time onstage attempting to spur the king to action. She is acutely aware of her doubly foreign status in the king's court, as she is not only a concubine but also a Greek. In this context, her first on-stage appearance with the king is worth quoting at some length:

> SAR.: Beautiful being!
> Thou dost almost anticipate my heart;
> It throbb'd for thee, and here thou comest: let me
> Deem that some unknown influence, some sweet oracle,
> Communicates between us, though unseen,
> In absence, and attracts us to each other.
> MYR.: There doth.
> SAR.: I know there doth, but not its name:
> What is it?
> MYR.: In my native land a God,
> And in my heart a feeling like a God's,
> Exalted; yet I own 'tis only mortal;
> For what I feel is humble, and yet happy—
> That is, it would be happy; but—
> [MYRRHA pauses]
> SAR.: There comes
> For ever something between us and what
> We deem our happiness: let me remove
> The barrier which that hesitating accent
> Proclaims to thine, and mine is sealed.[48]

This initial dialogue achieves several effects. First, it underscores the authentic bond between king and concubine; second, it leads directly to the revelation that, even before Sardanapalus' kingdom is threatened, Myrrha is unhappy with her lover's effeminate style of comportment and rule. Further, her reference to her "native land" confirms that this discomfort stems from her Grecian lineage.

Unexpectedly, Myrrha carries the play's mantle of a Westernized sensibility that is coded as masculine, militant, and thus apparently opposed to Sardanapalus' Eastern effeminacy and languor. Enjoining him not to speak of Greece—"when another speaks of Greece, it wounds me" (I.ii.524)—Myrrha nevertheless references her country of origin frequently when exhorting Sardanapalus to be a more effective leader.[49] Her repeated calls for him to take up properly his kingly responsibilities are a series of concerted efforts to occidentalize him. Other characters tend to see Sardanapalus as irredeemably Eastern; after being ordered to leave the palace, for example, the rebellious Arbaces comments that the king follows "the very policy of orient [sic] monarchs— / Pardon and poison—favours and a sword— / A distant voyage, and an eternal sleep" (II.430–32). By contrast, Myrrha believes she can help Sardanapalus change his seemingly culturally determined ways. Upon learning that he has merely banished Arbaces and his fellow conspirator Beleses, for instance, Myrrha exclaims that she would have had them executed, provoking the following exchange:

> SAR.: This is strange;
> The gentle and the austere are both against me,
> And urge me to revenge.
> MYR.: 'Tis a Greek virtue.
> SAR.: But not a kingly one—I'll none on't . . . (II.578–81)

Myrrha fails here to convince her lover to behave in a more Western fashion, but events justify her efforts as Sardanapalus' decision to show mercy to the conspirators early on leads to his later defeat by their forces.

With his multiple refusals of violence and his desire to be loved rather than feared, Sardanapalus can certainly be read as Byron's self-critique of his earlier heroes. This is Christensen's interpretation as well as Daniela Garofalo's, who argues that "*Sardanapalus* performs this desecration of the thing of beauty Byron has created in order to show the political consequences of hero worship."[50] Without denying this dynamic, we can also recognize the ways *Sardanapalus* extends and modifies rather than simply demolishes the patterns established in those earlier texts. I've argued that in Eastern Tales like *Lara* and *The Siege of Corinth*, Byron emphasizes how a ubiquitous clash of civilizations worldview prevents levantinized characters from re-integrating into their original socio-symbolic environments. But *Sardanapalus* entertains the possibility that true hybridity—more specifically, an authentic admixture of Western and Eastern subjectivities—is achievable. With the palace under attack, Sardanapalus finally dons his armor to lead his remaining troops into battle, and Myrrha begins to believe that perhaps the king can truly change:

> I almost wish now, what I never wish'd
> Before, that he [Sardanapalus] were Grecian. If Alcides
> Were shamed in wearing Lydian Omphale's
> She-garb, and wielding her vile distaff; surely
> He, who springs up a Hercules at once,
> Nursed in effeminate arts from youth to manhood,
> And rushes from the banquet to the battle,
> As though it were a bed of love, deserves
> That a Greek girl should be his paramour,
> And a Greek bard his minstrel, a Greek tomb
> His monument. (III.217–27)

Fired by the king's belated willingness to risk his life in active, spectacularly masculine leadership, Myrrha at last can envision him as Grecian in spirit if not birth.

But this transformation comes too late. Although he leads and fights bravely, Sardanapalus' last-minute shedding of his "despotic oriental voluptuousness"[51] in favor of a heroic, masculine, Westernized persona proves insufficient to turn the battle's tide. Cornered by their enemies in the palace hall, Sardanapalus and Myrrha recognize they are doomed. Refusing to leave her lover's side, Myrrha sees that their only recourse is to die nobly: there remains to them

> *one deed*—the last
> And greatest to all mortals; crowning act
> Of all that was—or is—or is to be—
> The only thing common to all mankind,
> So different in their births, tongues, sexes, natures,
> Hues, features, climes, times, feelings, intellects,
> Without one point of union save in this,
> To which we tend, for which we're born, and thread
> The labyrinth of mystery, call'd life. (V.228–36)

The nihilistic climax of *Sardanapalus* recalls the ironic, bloody conclusion of *The Siege of Corinth;* in a society structured both conceptually and institutionally by binarisms, civilizational differences can finally be overcome only by death. Myrrha's grimly punning allusion to Sardanapalus' royal status ("*crowning* act") merely emphasizes the extent to which, in her opinion at least, his newfound kingliness can now be consummated only through self-sacrifice.

The multiple ironies that subtend *Sardanapalus'* conclusion clearly reveal the tragic insufficiencies of identities, individual and communal alike, which depend on oppositional paradigms that ultimately promote little beyond confusion and conflict. Less clear, however, is whether Byron believes that the clash of civilizations-style worldview into which post-Napoleonic Britain was threatening to slide could be avoided or surmounted. His trademark rhetorical style, which Oliver fittingly calls "flamboyant,"[52] licenses him to magnify the emotions, positions, and conflicts of the developing world order in ways that readers—most of whom, of course, would never visit Byron's exotic locations in person—found engaging and provocative. But, at least in the Eastern Tales and *Sardanapalus,* it also magnifies rather than resolves Byron's apparent ambivalence regarding "worldwideification." The final irony of Byron's career may well be his untimely death at Missolonghi, which some have speculated was hastened by his insistence on continuing to conduct outdoors, British-style military drills throughout the wet Grecian winter. Byron's failure to account for what Alan Bewell has called "the pathogenic topography" of Missolonghi, in other words, suggests he was either unable or unwilling to adopt in life the virtues of subjective adaptability and psychic hybridity that he so brilliantly celebrated—frequently, I have argued, by ironically delineating their loss or lack—in his poetry.[53]

CROSS, CRESCENT, AND CHIASMUS IN *THE TALISMAN*

Byronic irony was not the only available response to the clash of civilizations paradigm that presented itself with particular urgency in the uncertain period following Napoleon's defeat. As the most popular author of his day, we should not be surprised that most of Scott's best-known novels focus on apparent examples of civilizational clashes, loosely understood: between Scots and English (*Waverley, Rob Roy* [1817], *The Heart of Mid-Lothian* [1818]), Normans and Saxons (*Ivanhoe* [1819]), Jacobites and Hanoverians (*Redgauntlet* [1824]), and even Whigs and Tories (*The Antiquary* [1816], *The Bride of Lammermoor* [1819]). A number of recent critical studies have highlighted the sophistication and subtlety with which Scott handles, and frequently dismantles, the seeming oppositions between these sorts of national, ethnic, political, and religious communities. Considerably less attention has been paid, however, to the explicitly international interests and dynamics of Scott's later Waverley Novels. Yet his fictional output was instrumental, not only in cementing a shared sense of Britishness among his Scottish and English readers,[54] but also in encouraging Britons to adopt a global perspective irreducible to the simple dualisms encouraged by clash-like perspectives. In his most complete account of East–West relations, *The Talisman*, Scott seizes upon a historical situation that invites treatment as a Byronic spectacle of ironic tragedy, and instead uses it to challenge his British readers' assumptions regarding not only their "civilizational" superiority, but also the very East–West opposition on which such assumptions depend.[55]

The Talisman begins with an archetypal image of West meeting East: a lone knight rides steadfastly along the shoreline of the Dead Sea. Armed and armored from top to toe, Sir Kenneth appears every inch the valiant Christian crusader in Scott's introductory tableau. He is soon confronted by his Muslim counterpart, also dressed in an appropriately native costume complete with turban and caftan. As they gallop towards each other, Scott writes as if he knows he is expected to portray the collision of two civilizations:

> The Saracen came on at the speedy gallop of an Arab horseman, managing his steed more by his limbs, and the inflection of his body, than by any use of the reins . . . so that he was enabled to wield the light round buckler . . . which he wore on his arm, swinging it as if he meant to oppose its slender circle to the formidable thrust of the Western lance.[56]

With the "Western lance" "thrust[ing]" toward its Eastern opponent's small round shield, Scott potently mobilizes stereotypes of a masculinized West and a feminized East that we saw deployed in Byron's *Sardanapalus*.

Even before describing how the above confrontation concludes, we can already see that the opening of Scott's novel appears to exemplify perfectly the clash of civilizations paradigm. On the basis of such appearances, his *Tales of the Crusaders* (comprising *The Talisman* and a single-volume companion, *The Betrothed* [1825]) has been blamed for perpetuating various stereotypes of Islamic culture: "vague and vacant notions about stallions, harems, deserts, and dervishes and some schoolbook legends about the Crusades," in Clifford Geertz's words.[57] Such clichés, however, are arguably Scott's targets rather than his assumptions.[58] Had he intended simply to confirm the West's superiority over the East, after all, Scott could have written about the First Crusade, in which Godfrey of Bouillon bloodily captured Jerusalem in 1098.[59] Instead, Scott chose to portray the much less successful Third Crusade at the end of the twelfth century. In his introduction to the *Talisman*'s *magnum opus* edition, Scott explains his decision: "The period relating more immediately to the Crusades, which I at last fixed upon, was that at which the war-like character of Richard I, wild and generous, a pattern of chivalry, with all its extravagant virtues, and its no less absurd errors, was opposed to that of Saladin. . . . "[60] At first glance, this appears to endorse a clash of civilizations scheme: Richard the Lionheart, gloriously chivalric, is arrayed against the primitive Muslim warlord. On closer examination, however, the events and main actors of the Third Crusade defy easy categorization.[61] The *Talisman* is set in the days prior to Richard's decision to abandon his quest to liberate Jerusalem, Scott explains, because this was a time "in which the Christian and English monarch showed all the cruelty and violence of an Eastern Sultan; and Saladin, on the other hand, displayed the deep policy and prudence of a European sovereign."[62] Scott not only sees the cultural and religious stereotypes surrounding his chosen historical characters, but also articulates a desire to challenge them by exchanging their usual attributions.

Scott's chiasmatic transposition of Eastern and Western qualities is only half the story, however, for as Derrida teaches, simply reversing binary terms leaves intact the overarching metaphysical scaffolding of opposition.[63] Similarly, were Scott merely to invert the clichés associated with European kings and Oriental despots, he would leave unchallenged the supposedly insurmountable divisions between the cultures in contact. This is the conclusion of David Simpson, who argues that although Scott shows considerable sympathy for his Semitic characters, he nonetheless relies on a conceptual framework by which "Arab and Jew . . . [become] structurally identical and interchangeable in the imagination of the west."[64] Simpson's reading focuses on Scott's famous portrayal of Rebecca in *Ivanhoe*, which is beyond the scope of my present argument.[65] Scott's ambitious portrayal of warring Muslims and Christians in *The Talisman*, however, shows a more complex understanding of the unpredictable effects produced by global contact.

As a historical fiction, the novel is not unbiased: Scott glosses over Richard's infamous slaughter of 2,700 Muslim prisoners following his sack of the city of Acre, and likewise avoids detailing the king's humiliating capture and ransom by the Holy Roman Emperor on his homeward journey through Europe. Nevertheless, he repeatedly highlights the Crusaders' weaknesses rather than their strengths. When *The Talisman* begins, the Christian forces are already in decline, and the provisional truce at the novel's opening signals the loss of all momentum on their quest to retake Jerusalem. Scott is also clear that many of the Crusaders lack both mettle and moral integrity. Although the other leaders' jealousy of Richard's "courage, hardihood, and military talents" is problematic, Scott lays equal blame for the Third Crusade's dysfunctional state on "the offence taken by them at the uncurbed haughtiness of the English monarch, and the contempt which he exhibited for the sovereigns, who [were] his equals in rank" (54). Like a medieval "coalition of the willing" fragmented by its leader's penchant for unilateralism and scornful treatment of so-called junior partners, Richard's fragile alliance is close to implosion. Eventually, both Conrad of Montesserat and his Templar co-conspirator meet much-deserved deaths, but not before the Crusade itself is dissolved, with the other Christian nobles "assigning, for their defection from the Cause of the Cross, the inordinate ambition and arbitrary domination of Richard of England" (247). The message for Scott's post-Waterloo audience—a message that should still resonate today—seems clear: no matter how influential and far-reaching, a single power cannot simultaneously invade foreign lands, alienate its allies, fail to plan for peace, and still expect to achieve some semblance of victory.

Furthermore, *The Talisman* repeatedly disrupts British readers' assumptions of their moral and theological superiority over their Muslim counterparts. To return to its opening scene: after several rounds of fighting, in which neither combatant gains the upper hand, the Muslim warrior calls for a truce that Sir Kenneth (eventually revealed as the Crown Prince of Scotland) warily accepts. After retiring to a nearby oasis, the two begin a protracted session of comparative debate and observation on the relative merits of their cultures and religions. Initially, their dialogue seems merely to yield yet another study in civilizational oppositions, with Scott noting that "[t]he Saracen Emir formed a marked and striking contrast with the northern crusader" (13). Yet this Muslim differs in important ways from the stereotype with which Scott's readers would have been familiar: although "[t]he countenance of the Saracen naturally bore a general national resemblance to the eastern tribe from whom he descended," Scott also declares that he "was as unlike as possible to the exaggerated terms in which the minstrels of the day were wont to represent the infidel champions, and the fabulous description which a sister art still presents upon old-fashioned sign-posts" (14).[66] If he cannot be considered precisely handsome, Scott concludes, this is due to "something of too much thinness and sharpness of feature, *or at least what seemed such in an European estimate of beauty*" (14; my italics). By drawing attention to the particularized origin of seemingly universal standards of beauty, Scott highlights both their cultural constructedness and their Eurocentrism. Furthermore, when Sir Kenneth defends the practice of courtly love against the Saracen's polygamy, Scott allows the other man to have the withering final word: "I have heard of this frenzy among the warriors of the west . . . and have ever accounted it one of the accompanying symptoms of that insanity, which brings you hither to obtain possession of an empty sepulchre" (17).

Significantly, this debate is prefaced by the suggestion that, appearances to the contrary, the Muslim and Christian sides of this conflict have more in common than they recognize. While setting the scene of the former combatants' mutual repose, Scott sketches their shared cultural history and orientation:

> The distinction of religions, nay, the fanatical zeal which animated the followers of the Cross and of the Crescent against each other, was much softened by a feeling so natural to generous combatants, and especially cherished by the spirit of chivalry. This last strong impulse extended itself gradually from the Christians to their mortal enemies the Saracens, both of Spain and of Palestine. The latter were indeed no longer the fanatical savages, who had burst from the centre of Arabian deserts, with the sabre in one hand, and the Koran in the other. . . . But in contending with the Western Christians, animated by a zeal as fiery as their own . . . the Saracens gradually caught a part of their manners, and especially of those chivalrous observances, which were so well calculated to charm the minds of a proud and conquering people. (9)

From our contemporary vantage point this passage contains several objectionable assertions, but they should not cause us to miss Scott's avowal of equal zealotry amongst both parties. Equally important is his assertion that prolonged contact between Western and Eastern antagonists spread the chivalric code from the former to the latter. Furthermore, although this early passage suggests that such transculturation moves only one way, Scott later presents a more flexible view in his depiction of the heterogeneity of Richard's camp:

> Indeed, the luxury and profligate indulgence of the Christian leaders had occasioned a motley concourse in their tents, of musicians, courtezans, Jewish merchants, Copts, Turks, and all the varied refuse of the Eastern nations; so that the caftan and turban, though to drive both from the Holy Land was the professed object of the expedition, were nevertheless neither an uncommon nor an alarming sight in the camp of the Crusaders. (191)

Again, with its derogatory denominations, this passage falls well short of the endorsement of cultural hybridity we might hope for from a contemporary text. Nevertheless, Scott is highly cognizant of the high volume of cross-cultural traffic between the Crusaders and their Middle Eastern counterparts.[67] As Margaret Bruzelius observes, Richard's camp is "the only space that represents the public, European world" in *The Talisman*.[68] The Crusader camp, in other words, serves as a displaced *mise en abyme* for the disavowed heterogeneity of European society in general, including its multiple historical debts to Arabic, Persian, and other Eastern cultures in the realms of medicine, mathematics, and the sciences.

In addition to these moments of representational sophistication, the novel's overall narrative structure reflects Scott's resistance to reifying the British global ambitions of his historical moment. Readers might expect that, given the opportunity to portray an iconic national hero like Richard the Lionhearted, Scott would not hesitate to lionize him (pun intended). But despite his bluster, Richard spends much of the novel sick in his tent. Moreover, when the skills of the European physicians fail to save their sovereign, it is left to a humble Muslim physician, El Hakim (literally, "the doctor"), to cure Richard. El Hakim is initially viewed with suspicion and contempt by Richard's attendants, but his medical powers—aided by the novel's titular talisman[69]—soon win him both respect and trust. Once healthy again, Richard is easily able to quash the rebellions brewing among his allies, but the revelation that El Hakim is none other than Saladin himself adds to the growing sense that it is the Muslim leader, not the Christian one, who is the primary agent of both narrative and historical progress throughout the novel.

As several critics have noted, from start to finish Saladin is essentially the prime mover of *The Talisman*'s plot.[70] Able to appear and disappear seemingly at will, Saladin—still actively regarded by many Muslims as a hero[71]—turns out to be not only the wise and generous El Hakim, but also the implacable Saracen warrior with whom Sir Kenneth clashes in the novel's opening. When the latter's life is forfeited for allowing the English banner to be stolen while he stands guard, it is El Hakim who saves him, convincing Richard to commute the unfortunate knight's death sentence to enslavement. If this decision seems fantastic, it is explained by the "faith, and honor, and generosity" that even Saladin's most prejudiced European foes are forced to grant him (95); as Richard exclaims when Saladin refuses payment for his services, "I tell thee that this Moor, in his independence, might set an example to them who account themselves the flower of knighthood" (109). Clearly, it is Saladin, not Richard, who most embodies the chivalric code whose eastward spread Scott has previously explained.[72] Furthermore, the crowning moment of this unexpected translation of values—when Saladin formally invites Richard into his desert pavilion near the novel's conclusion—anticipates Scott's more extended exploration of the potential of such "global hospitality" in *Anne of Geierstein* (which I discuss in Chapter Five).

In *The Talisman,* cultural origins, precedents, and hierarchies become ever more confused. The ease with which Saladin temporarily transforms Sir Kenneth into a mute, gigantic African slave, for example, destabilizes the traditionally fixed opposition between pale European and dark-skinned heathen taken for granted by many of Scott's peers. Saladin's transformative agency even allows the bonds of European chivalry to be re-forged between England's and Scotland's royal families, since it is thanks to his African disguise that the disgraced Sir Kenneth is able to re-enter Richard's camp and save the king's life. Since Scott eschews free indirect discourse, readers cannot know how Sir Kenneth's brief stint as a subaltern may alter his previous Eurocentrism.[73] Certainly, it seems likely that Scott's original readers' perspectives would have been challenged through their engagement with a novel that consistently proposes cross-cultural exchange, not civilizational clash, as the privileged paradigm of global interaction.[74]

In his post–September 11, 2001, manifesto, *Welcome to the Desert of the Real,* Žižek argues repeatedly that "the clash of civilizations" describes nothing more than a dangerous fantasy. The real planetary dichotomy today is not the modern Judeo-Christian West versus the atavistic Islamic East, Žižek explains, not only because—as *The Talisman* amply demonstrates—neither of these entities has ever existed monolithically, but also because the forces of globalization and fundamentalism are equally enmeshed in our planet-wide capitalist world system. Hence Žižek's cutting re-deployment of Benjamin Barber's influential dichotomy: "Jihad and McWorld are the two sides of the same coin; Jihad is already McJihad."[75] For a radical Leftist like Žižek, this situation approaches travesty. But for Scott, as for the Enlightened tradition he inherited and adapted for popular consumption, there is value in the idea that our differences are not as absolute as we imagine them. To be discontented with the "clash of civilizations" paradigm is not only to reject its underlying assumptions, but also to believe—even without possessing a magic talisman—that there may be ways of thinking difference beyond seemingly intractable oppositions like East versus West and Muslim versus Christian.

Responding to a historian's complaint about *The Talisman*'s inaccuracies, Scott asserted that "romantic fiction naturally includes the power of such invention, which is indeed one of the requisites of the art."[76] If anyone was allowed such imaginative license during the Romantic era, it was undoubtedly "the Wizard of the North," as Scott was known in his day. In my final full chapter, I continue to consider Scott's influential interventions into post-

Napoleonic Romantic globalism via an examination of the geopolitics of several of his European-themed historical novels. In doing so, I intend to measure both how far Romantic globalism had come since its inception several decades earlier, and the extent to which Scott's late novels, far from being inferior productions as they were once characterized, extend in sophisticated ways his fictive explorations of the origins of modern world order.

CHAPTER FIVE

Modern Sovereignty and Global Hospitality in Scott's European Waverley Novels

IN THE final months of 1826, Walter Scott took a much-needed break from domestic concerns by traveling from his home at Abbotsford to London and Paris. The previous months had been very difficult: in January Scott was bankrupted following the collapse of the printing and publishing businesses on which he had staked his fortune, and in May his wife, Charlotte, had died suddenly. Scott was in dire need of a change of scenery, and the ensuing trip—which was not without the attendant difficulties of long-distance travel in the early nineteenth century, especially while in ill health— was a success. In London, Scott met with King George and secured a promise of royal patronage for his son's future diplomatic service, then managed to do some last-minute research for his forthcoming, monumental nine-volume *Life of Napoleon* (1827).

Paris, too, was the scene of several triumphs. Here, Scott met with his self-proclaimed American disciple, James Fennimore Cooper, dined with the *crème de le crème* of Parisian society, exchanged pleasantries with the French monarch, and even took in a performance of Gioachino Rossini's new opera *Ivanhoe* (1826)—based, of course, on Scott's novel of the same name. Later, he wrote in his journal that "[i]t was an opera and of course the story greatly mangled and the dialogue in a great part nonsense." Nevertheless, Scott was touched: "Yet it was strange to hear anything like the words which I (then in an agony of pain with spasms in my stomach) dictated . . . now recited in a foreign tongue and for the amusement of a strange people."[1] In a slightly later entry, he records his general satisfaction with his novels' French reception:

> Ere I leave *la belle France* however it is fit I should express my gratitude for the unwontedly kind reception which I met with at all hands. It would be an unworthy piece of affectation did I not allow that I have been pleased—highly pleased—to find a species of literature intended only for my own country has met with such an extensive and favourable reception in a foreign land where there was so much *a priori* to oppose its progress.[2]

The "species of literature" to which Scott refers is his own historical novels and the *a priori* impediment he imagines might have dampened their French sales is likely the still-fresh memory of the Napoleonic Wars. Scott's pleasure at finding these fears unfounded owes something, no doubt, to the fact that, as Margaret Cohen and Carolyn Dever confirm, "political hostilities diminished neither the intensity nor the cultural centrality of Anglo-French intellectual and literary exchange."[3] But it likely owes more to Scott's unprecedented popularity abroad as well as at home. Although the figures of his European sales have yet to be reconstructed fully, one quantitative indication of Scott's popularity abroad is the National Library of Scotland's *Bibliography of Scottish Literature in Translation*, which contains close to three thousand entries for Scott, mostly for European translations.[4] But sales figures do not tell the whole story of an author's success in this period, since the most common method of obtaining books during the long Romantic era was not to buy them—most Waverley Novels were initially published in expensive editions of more than twenty shillings—but to rent them from a circulating library. Factoring in lending library readerships hugely multiplies Scott's presence in the literary marketplace, such that, as William St. Clair puts it, "If there are links between texts, books, reading, cultural formation, and mentalities, then Scott is the author to whom, above all, we should look."[5]

I will return to the significance of Scott's foreign popularity at this chapter's conclusion. Primarily, however, in this chapter I explore through close reading the potential impact of Scott's later, European Waverley Novels on British readers' worldviews—a view that had become ever more confidently global since Napoleon's defeat.[6] Granted, Scott's early "Scotch novels" seem to fit traditional descriptions of him as purveying a relatively insular British nationalism: his first novel, *Waverley; or, 'Tis Sixty Years Since*, ends with a quintessential marriage of English and Scottish protagonists, and readers could finish it satisfied that Britain's future was both bright and unified. Even this inward-looking debut, however, cannot be read without reference to Europe; in addition to carefully reconstructing the novel's many allusions to Continental (especially French) politics and culture, Michael Simpson persuasively demonstrates that the post-Trafalgar composition of *Waverley*—indicated by Scott's insistence that the novel's "present" is sixty years after its 1745 setting—effectively replaces "a Britain that defensively coheres in order to avoid becoming an object of continental empire" with "a Britain that smoothly re-centres Europe on itself."[7] A European perspective, in other words, presents from the start a key horizon of the Waverley Novels. Scott's global perspective, moreover, develops significantly after *Waverley*: as Ian Duncan, Ken McNeil, and Penny Fielding have demonstrated in their interpretations of *Rob Roy*, Scott is keenly interested in how "the national" is constantly produced by the intersection of local and global forces and flows.[8] Despite the traditional critical association of Scott with Romantic nationalism, few Romantic-era authors were more prescient than Scott in recognizing that the fates of modern nations were entirely intertwined with the emerging global order.

For these reasons—and despite the traditional disparagement of Scott's decision, starting with *Ivanhoe*, to write novels on subjects beyond Scotland and before living memory—reappraising the significance of Scott's non-Scottish novels is particularly important. The previous chapter's concluding section brought forward a number of elements of Scott's Crusader novel, *The Talisman*, which complicate reading that text as straightforwardly supportive of British expansionism or exclusivity. In this chapter, I investigate what two of Scott's other late novels, *Quentin Durward* and *Anne of Geierstein*, can tell us about his—and by extension, given his unprecedented popularity, his era's—understanding of modern Europe's political and cultural formation. Paying particular attention to the themes of subjectivity, sovereignty, and hospitality as these fictions develop them, I argue, can illuminate Scott's influential vision of the path toward Western geopolitical modernity. If the vision of national sovereignty and its subjectivizing effects on individuals that Scott depicts in *Quentin Durward* seems uncomfortably totalizing, then *Anne of Geierstein* subsequently makes available a concept of global hospitality that is not only compensatory but also potentially emancipatory, inasmuch as the latter can be understood in Jacques Rancière's sense of a "process . . . consist[ing] in the polemical verification of equality."[9]

MAKING THE MODERN SUBJECT IN *QUENTIN DURWARD*

Quentin Durward is Scott's first novel set entirely outside the British Isles. As if aware of this risk, Scott prefaces it with one of his most elaborate frame narratives. Although his authorship was largely an open secret, the Author of Waverley did not publicly reveal himself until after his bankruptcy, instead inventing a host of authorial and editorial stand-ins to cover his tracks. In the introduction to *Quentin Durward,* Scott assumes the voice of an unnamed Scottish landowner who has temporarily moved to France to take advantage of the cheap living in the wake of Napoleon's defeat. The years following Waterloo were unexpectedly hard on the British economy, which experienced (in Susan Manning's words) "a period of economic depression induced by the huge cost of sustaining the Napoleonic Wars and exacerbated by a series of disastrous harvests," as well as by the influx of decommissioned soldiers who overwhelmed the employment market, causing a drastic fall in corn prices.[10] Not surprisingly, poor laborers were disproportionately affected by this constellation of events.

Yet as if anticipating Marx's famous dictum that ideology, like a *camera obscura,* projects an inverted image of the world,[11] Scott's narrator claims that rich landowners have suffered the most from the severe economic downturn:

> Having deeply considered all these things, I am no longer able to disguise from my readers, that I am neither so unpopular nor so low in fortune, as not to have my share in the distresses which at present afflict the monied and landed interest of these realms. Your authors who live upon a mutton chop may rejoice that it has fallen to threepence per pound. . . . But we who belong to the tribe which are ruined by peace and plenty—we who have land and beeves, and sell what these poor gleaners must buy—we are driven to despair by the very events which would make all Grub-street illuminate all its attics, if Grub-street could spare candle-ends for the purpose.[12]

At first glance, this passage seems of a piece with Scott's well-known general distrust of "the mob" and his post-Waterloo anxiety regarding social unrest.[13] In addition, his personal communications from this period convey growing alarm that the economic downturn was beginning to affect the landed classes. In a letter of 25 August 1822 (during the writing of *Quentin Durward*), Scott explains to "the Committee of Ladies for relief of the Irish peasantry" that he won't contribute to their cause because he resides "in a country at present suffering greatly from unpaid rents and a general depreciation of agricultural produce."[14] Writing to his son Walter a few months later, Scott explains that he likewise can't do much for the family of his brother Thomas in Canada: "What they may expect me to do I know not but I know I cannot and will not do very much for between the expence of building and the great depreciation of land-produce of every kind which makes my estate worth little income at present I have enough to do with my own exigencies" (7: 274).

In this context, the unnamed narrator in *Quentin Durward*'s introduction sounds suspiciously like Scott himself. Yet we must not miss the purposeful distance Scott creates between himself and his apparent mouthpiece. Beyond the question of whether Scott seriously expected readers to sympathize with an aristocratic narrator who places his own, relatively minor deprivations above the real distresses of the laboring orders, there are other gaps as well. The narrator's use of the overly formal noun "beeves" for "cows," for example, suggests that his worldview is as elitist as his diction. Moreover, his lack of self-awareness is highlighted by his earlier remark that "I never heard a man whose credit was *actually* verging to decay talk of the diminution of his funds" (3; my italics).

Later in the introduction, Scott's narrator meets the Marquis at whose decrepit chateau he eventually "discovers" the old manuscript that forms the text of *Quentin Durward* itself. The question of authorial identification subsequently becomes even more complicated when the Marquis, describing his aged manservant, remarks, "He sometimes reminds me of a character in the Bridle of Lammermore [sic], which you must have read, as it is the work of one of your *gens de letters, qu'on appelle, je crois, le Chevalier Scott*" (10–11). The narrator must then awkwardly correct his host on two counts: first, regarding the title of the novel in question (there being, as the narrator amusingly protests, "nothing about a bridle in the whole story" [11]); and second, regarding the supposed impossibility of Walter Scott being the author of *The Bride of Lammermoor*. As the narrator reveals in a coy aside,

> [N]o one could know so well as myself, that my distinguished literary countryman [Scott], of whom I will always speak with the respect his talents deserve, was not responsible for the slight works which the humour of the public had too generously, as well as too rashly, ascribed to him. Surprised by the impulse of the moment, I might even have gone farther, and clenched the negative by positive evidence, owning to my entertainer that no one else could possibly have written these works, since I myself was the author. . . . (11)

In this passage, Scott literally exceeds himself. When the Marquis subsequently expresses relief that "he was glad to hear these sort of trifles were not written by a person of condition," the narrator admits that he then "became so much afraid of committing myself, that I did not even venture to explain to my aristocratic friend, that the gentleman whom he had named [Scott] owed his advancement, for aught I had ever heard, to certain works of his, which may, without injury, be compared to romances in rhime" (11).

Elsewhere, I have argued that Scott's insistence on publishing his novels anonymously until his financial collapse was motivated, at least in part, by his desire to act as the British nation's mouthpiece.[15] Yet here the rules of the game seem to have changed. Since within this fictional world the Author of Waverley is expressly *not* to be identified with Walter Scott, we may deduce that *Quentin Durward*'s superficially approving attitude toward feudalism in general, and the *ancien régime* of fifteenth-century France in particular, should not be accepted uncritically. More immediately, the above passage prompts us to consider why Scott here splits his authorial identity in two: one for the author of poetical romances and one for the Waverley Novels. The usual answer might invoke the relatively low status of novel writing in the period: as the Marquis himself points out, Scott preferred to be known solely as a poet. Yet as Ina Ferris has shown, the Author of Waverley played a key role in making novel writing permanently respectable.[16] In this case, moreover, I want to argue that Scott's self-splitting into poet and novelist corresponds roughly to the division identified by Žižek between Enlightenment and post-Enlightenment forms of subjectivity. While recognizing that the historicity of Žižek's critical narrative is debatable, a brief foray into it can help illuminate both the stakes of Scott's anonymity game and also the construction of modern subjectivity on which *Quentin Durward*'s nation-building plot depends.

According to Žižek, the ideal pre-Enlightenment subject identifies itself as "a full, substantial entity, identical to a particular content."[17] As feudalism gives way to more modern forms of social relations and national identities, however, the individual is exposed to increasing pressure from outside forces, especially the pressure of the sovereign demand of absolute loyalty to the state. In exchange for renouncing his self-identical individuality in favor of identification with state interests, the subject nominally receives wealth, status, and the other benefits and trappings of modern, national citizenship. Yet this bargain is threatened by the Terror of the French Revolution, says Žižek, because with the threat of execution always (literally) hanging over the subject's head, "the appearance of an equivalent exchange collapses . . . [now] the subject gets nothing in exchange for its sacrifice" (27). On the far side of the Terror emerges the modern, post-Enlightenment subject whose sense of self depends on his identification, not with the state in its positivity, but rather with the violence of state-sanctioned power in its negative form. This transformation, says Žižek, can be understood as a historicized version of the

Lacanian narrative of the subject's symbolic castration, the price each of us must pay to enter the Symbolic Order:

> Consequently, the move from S to $ entails a radical shift in the very notion of the subject's self-identity: in it, I identify myself to that very void which a moment ago threatened to swallow the most precious kernel of my being. This is how the subject qua $ emerges from the structure of exchange: it emerges when "something is exchanged for nothing," that is to say, it is the very "nothing" I get from the symbolic structure, from the Other, in exchange for sacrificing my "pathological" particularity, the kernel of my being. (27–28)

The modern subject, in other words, gives up his or her personal subjectivity (now denominated a "'pathological' particularity" in need of cleansing) in exchange for the right, or rather the obligation, to identify with the interests of a larger entity—the State, here standing in for the Symbolic Order or the big Other of Lacanian discourse—which is effectively a subjective void.

Alongside the French Revolution, there is a second revolution that plays as important a role in Žižek's historicizing of the Lacanian narrative of subject formation: the financial revolution that saw bills of credit supplement and then replace traditional forms of specie. Žižek's insight, again following Lacan, is to align the "barred" (i.e. non-self-identical) subject of political modernity with the anonymous subject of financial modernity: hence the aptness of the symbol "$" to designate the self-divided subject. Žižek observes that bills of credit were originally made out to specific individuals, but

> [i]n order to arrive at paper money as we know it today, this deictic promise with concrete dates and names has to be depersonalized into a promise made to the anonymous "bearer" to pay the gold-equivalent of the sum written on paper money—thus, the anchoring, the link to a concrete individual was cut loose. And the subject who came to recognize itself as this anonymous "bearer" is the very subject of [modern] self-consciousness. (28–29)

The historical alignment of this double transformation is perhaps too neat: since the "paper credit" revolution took place over the course of the eighteenth century, it was arguably the conversion to a regime of financial speculation that made possible the French Revolution, not vice versa.[18] Nevertheless, Žižek's account helps conceptualize the formation of a subject who could productively inhabit the "realm of . . . homogeneity and equivalence," to recall Jameson's description of modern, global space-time.[19]

Scott did not possess our contemporary critical vocabulary, of course, but he had good reasons to be interested in thinking through the modern subject's emergence and insertion into contemporary symbolic networks. Not only was he bankrupted by an overextension of credit stemming from his publishing and printing ventures, but also late in his career he wrote a series of public letters protesting the British government's decision to bar Scottish banks from issuing small bills of credit.[20] We need not be surprised, then, to find that the doubled Scott of *Quentin Durward*'s introduction accords well with Žižek's formulae: "Walter Scott" the "person of condition" and author of traditional "romances in rhime" corresponds to the Enlightenment subject with a proper name and self-possessed identity; the unnamed narrator and supposed author of *Quentin Durward* is the post-Enlightenment, self-divided, anonymous "bearer" of modernity.[21] To be sure, this distinction between Scott-the-poet and Scott-the-novelist is also a little too neat; the Author of Waverley continued to write poetry during his novelistic career (often by inserting verses into his novels), and as we saw in Chapter Three, many of his "romances in rhime" are markedly modern in outlook. Nevertheless, applying Žižek's provocative theories to *Quentin Durward* helps clarify the novel's stakes. It helps us see, that is, that Scott's frame introduction presents in miniature the theme that will occupy the rest of the novel: how to account for the formation of a modern citizen-subject who can smoothly be fitted into the new European nation-state, which in turn becomes the fundamental building block of the emerging global order.

THE VIOLENCE OF MODERN SOVEREIGNTY

From the opening paragraph of *Quentin Durward*'s first chapter, Scott demonstrates that his interest in fifteenth-century France is not merely historical but also geared toward understanding the present: "The latter part of the fifteenth century prepared a train of future events, which ended by raising France to that state of formidable power, which has ever since been, from time to time, the principal object of jealousy to the other European nations" (23). The France of Louis XI's time was still struggling both to assert its territorial rights—rights which were "[c]rucial to the formation of the world scale taking shape"[22]—and to create and maintain some semblance of internal coherence in the face of resistance from its powerful nobility, especially the Dukes of Burgundy and Bretagne, who in Scott's words "had come to wear their feudal bonds so lightly, that they had no scruple in lifting the standard against their liege and sovereign lord" (23). A strong, centralized government was needed to unite the country by replacing feudal bonds and antagonisms with the principles of modern state sovereignty.

Louis XI, in Scott's estimation, was the right monarch for this job. According to *Quentin Durward*'s 1831 *magnum opus* introduction, Louis helped guide France toward modernity both by "disuniting and dispersing [the] grand and dangerous alliance of the great crown vassals of France against the Sovereign" and by using ever greater numbers of professional mercenaries to fight France's wars, such that "the wily monarch commenced that system which, acted upon by his successors, at length threw the whole military defence of the state into the hands of the Crown."[23] Nonetheless, Scott avoids portraying Louis as anachronistically over-aware of his historical significance. The king is more Machiavellian than purposefully modernizing, a figure "whose character, evil as it was in itself, met, combated, and in a great degree neutralized, the mischief of the time" (41). Scott's Louis is a Janus-faced composite of pre- and post-Enlightened qualities: shrewd and patient in matters of statecraft, he is also highly superstitious, putting as much faith in astrology as in *realpolitik*. Especially emblematic of Louis' split character is his penchant, shared with *The Talisman*'s Saladin, for going incognito. But Louis' disguises are not very good; his habit of roaming the countryside as "the merchant Pierre" is obvious to most readers and characters alike (although not to Quentin, as we'll see). Judith Wilt observes that this kind of open secret can be very effective, since it reinforces "a ruling Power keeping the secret of his own nature . . . infinitely malleable, deniable, expandable, pervasively invisible."[24] This paradoxical fortifying of Louis' sovereign authority reinforces the fact that, despite his fondness for disguise, the King's essential nobility is repeatedly described as shining through whatever common costume he dons. The first time Scott's titular hero meets the disguised Louis, for example, he repeatedly notices aspects of his interlocutor that betray innate superiority: a "countenance [that] was partly attractive and partly forbidding," combined with "sunken eyes . . . at once commanding and sinister" (33) and a voice whose "grave sternness . . . spite of all the youth could do, damped and overawed him" (35).

So why does Louis go to such lengths to perpetuate disguises that are, by Scott's design, so transparent? The answer lies, I think, in Louis' favorite alter ego: a silk merchant. Asked to speculate on the disguised king's simulated profession, Quentin guesses that he "may be a money-broker, or a corn-merchant," to which Louis replies with a smile, "You have hit our capacities rarely. . . . My business is indeed to deal in as much money as I can" (32).

In light of this remark, and despite more conventional critical readings of Louis as "something of a medieval Napoleon" due to his charismatic leadership,[25] the French king appears closer to Napoleon's apocryphal denigration of the British as a "nation of shopkeepers" (a phrase that in fact originated with Adam Smith, as we saw in Chapter One). In this regard, Louis' habit of shuttling between the roles of king and merchant is analogous to Scott's doubled authorial persona in *Quentin Durward*'s introduction. Whereas Scott's self-splitting between poet-gentleman and novelist-bourgeoisie maintains these identities' minimal separation, however, Louis' synthesis of monarch and merchant divulges a different (albeit related) insight: that political and economic influences are structurally homologous in the era of modern state sovereignty. The merchant who trades in goods and the politician who trades in power are both performing the same set of functions: accumulating, investing, and then returning to themselves as much capital, real or political, as possible.

The homology worked out in *Quentin Durward* between modern economic and political power supports Anne Frey's argument that Scott is one of several post-Napoleonic Romantic authors who, following the decline of Jacobinism, can best be understood as subscribing to "State Romanticism." By this, Frey means not only their commitment to a strong British state and governmental apparatus, but also their belief in the power of literature to contribute actively to the modern state's authority and legitimacy. In particular, Frey reads Scott as endorsing what Michel Foucault calls "pastoral governmentality"—a secularized version of "the Christian ideal of pastoral care as a model for the way in which a state supervises and forms its citizens."[26] This model, which Foucault argues emerges in eighteenth-century Europe, involves a corresponding shift in the understanding of political authority, away from "a king's sovereignty over a territory" and toward "the state's ability to govern a population."[27] This shift helps explain Scott's ambivalent portrayal of Louis XI in *Quentin Durward* (which becomes more decisively negative in the *magnum* revisions).[28] Notwithstanding his modernizing tendencies, Louis is an absolute monarch who does not hesitate to invoke his kingly mandate whenever the structurally generated nature of his authority threatens to be revealed too explicitly. He is thus a prime example of what Žižek calls a "vanishing mediator": in the process of helping transform feudal socio-political arrangements into modern ones, Louis actively (albeit inadvertently) helps produce the conditions of his own obsolescence.[29] The transition to modern sovereignty and governmentality that Louis' machinations facilitate in turn consolidates the model of the secular nation-state that forms the backbone of the contemporary world system.[30]

Frey's categorization of Scott as a "State Romantic" on a par with later-career establishment apologists like Wordsworth and Coleridge, however, has limitations. In particular, like many critics who focus solely on the Scottish Waverley Novels when reading Scott, Frey arguably overestimates his conservatism.[31] We can correct this imbalance by attending to how Scott—emboldened, perhaps, by his turn to European rather than British subjects—takes careful account in *Quentin Durward* of the costs of the modern state's arrogation of sovereignty to itself, including its denial of protection to those who refuse (or are unable) to become "proper" citizen-subjects.[32]

The novel opens with Louis' power sorely challenged on several fronts, most significantly by Charles of Burgundy, whose father once gave the young Louis asylum. Burgundy is now bent on independence—a move that threatens the territorial integrity of France. Unwilling to confront his rival directly (which would not only be militarily risky, but would confer legitimacy on Charles' pretensions), Louis has been deploying a network of spies and provocateurs to keep the Duchy of Burgundy in a state of unrest. In particular, he regularly employs members of the gypsy bands that traverse Western Europe to do his dirty work of surveillance and agitation. The gypsies are considered neither French nor Burgundian, however, and with no territorial home they receive no protection from any established power. In other words, in ways that are central to the novel's representation of the structural violence immanent to modern state formation, they are simultaneously inside and outside the feudal system whose transformation they are unwittingly facilitating. They too are vanishing mediators, but lack even the temporary security of Louis' kingly status.

This is not the first time Scott uses gypsy characters for political purposes. In *Guy Mannering, or The Astrologer* (1815), Meg Merrilies ensures that the novel's hero, Harry Bertram, is restored as the rightful inheritor of his family's estate, but Meg herself is killed before she can enjoy his triumph. In *Quentin Durward*, the primary gypsy character is Hayraddin Maugrabin, an enigmatic figure of unknown provenance who, in a manner reminiscent of Byron's heroes, combines characteristics of East and West:

> His dress was a red turban of small size, in which he wore a sullied plume, secured by a clasp of silver; his tunic, which was shaped like those of the Estradiots, a sort of troops whom the Venetians at that time levied in the provinces on the eastern side of their gulf, was green in colour, and tawdrily laced with gold; he wore very wide drawers or trowsers of white, though none of the cleanest, which gathered beneath the knee, and his swarthy legs were quite bare.... In a crimson sash this singular horseman

wore a dagger on the right side, and on the left a short crooked Moorish sword.... (176)

Hayraddin is a hybrid whose very dress indicates his outsider status; as Andrew Lincoln indicates, "[t]he grotesqueness of the gypsy may register the polite subject's anxiety about what has already been repudiated as part of polite identity...."[33] Although the above description appears fanciful, Scott's anthropological interest in "Bohemians" seems sincere. In a long *magnum* edition note appended to the first appearance of gypsies in *Quentin Durward*, he writes that

> it is well known that this extraordinary variety of the human race exists in nearly the same primitive state, speaking the same language, in almost all the kingdoms of Europe, and conforming in certain respects to the manners of the people around them, but yet remaining separated from them by certain material distinctions, in which they correspond with each other, and thus maintain their pretensions to be considered as a distinct race.[34]

Unlike other nations, which according to the Scottish Enlighteners progress near-inexorably through discrete stages of social development, gypsies apparently do not evolve; Scott shared this assumption with "many etymologists, antiquarians, historians, missionaries, and reformers" of his day.[35]

Accordingly, although gypsies may successfully assimilate into modern nation-states, their ability to do so is limited. Scott explains:

> Their pretensions to read fortunes, by palmistry and by astrology, acquired them sometimes respect, but oftener drew them under suspicion as sorcerers; and lastly, the universal accusation that they augmented their horde by stealing children, subjected them to doubt and execration. From this it happened, that ... they incurred almost everywhere sentences of banishment and, where suffered to remain, were rather objects of persecution than of protection from the law.[36]

Gilles Deleuze and Félix Guattari write at length on how the principle of nomadism always runs counter to the State's centralizing imperatives.[37] In this case, however, the early modern political situation of the gypsies represented by Scott more closely reflects the paradoxical logic of the ban articulated by Giorgio Agamben: "He who has been banned is not, in fact, simply set outside the law and made indifferent to it but rather *abandoned* by it, that is, exposed and threatened on the threshold in which life and law, outside and inside, become indistinguishable. It is literally not possible to say whether the one who has been banned is outside or inside the juridical order."[38] Agamben's name for the figure caught in this paradoxical position is drawn from Roman law: *homo sacer*, the individual who can be killed with impunity, but whose death holds no sacrificial value. Agamben finds the twentieth-century concentration camp inmate to be the ultimate and horrific embodiment of *homo sacer*, but his definition applies, albeit in a necessarily diminished fashion, to the gypsies of *Quentin Durward*. They too find themselves simultaneously inside and outside the political order of fifteenth-century France, permitted to live as long as they serve Louis' interests, but liable to be exterminated as soon as they do not.[39]

As if to highlight this literally exclusive status, Scott makes Hayraddin one of the most remarkable figures of any Waverley Novel. Hayraddin is a freethinker who provides a clear alternative to Quentin's unreflective belief in the King's authority and the legitimacy of his territorial sovereignty. Following the gypsy's denial of allegiance, religion, or even a fixed address, a baffled Quentin pronounces Hayraddin "destitute of all that other men are combined by": "You have no law, no leader, no settled means of subsistence, no house or home . . . no country—and, may Heaven enlighten and forgive you, you have no God!" (178). Hayraddin's response is revelatory: "I have liberty . . . I crouch to no one—obey no one—respect no one.—I go where I will—live as I can—and die when my day comes." But the price of such apparent liberty is precisely Hayraddin's status as *homo sacer*, as Quentin reminds him: "But you are subject to instant execution, at the pleasure of the Judge . . . where, then, is your boasted freedom?" (179). Hayraddin's remarkable rejoinder is worth quoting in full:

> "In my thoughts," said the Bohemian, "which no chains can bind; while yours, even when your limbs are free, remain fettered by your laws and your superstitions, your dreams of local attachment, and your fantastic visions of civil policy. Such as I are free in spirit when our limbs are chained—You are imprisoned in mind, even when your bodies are most at freedom." (179)

Like Saladin in *The Talisman* rebutting Sir Kenneth's claims to Christian superiority, Hayraddin articulates a comprehensive alternative to the dogmas of early modern Europe. In images reminiscent of William Blake's "mind-forg'd manacles,"[40] the gypsy's speech reveals the constraints of Quentin's limited, normative worldview.

To be sure, Scott does not present Hayraddin or his views in an exclusively appealing light; on the contrary, he frequently reminds us that the gypsy is grotesque, godless, and literally unattractive, especially when compared to Quentin. Yet Hayraddin's "banned" status goes beyond mere exclusion from the rapidly developing European geopolitical order, for according to Agamben, *homo sacer* is not merely a by-product or excrescence of modern sovereign power but essential to its very composition. In *Quentin Durward*, this means that Hayraddin is both necessary to the novel's plot—he first acts as Louis' agent, then disguises himself as Burgundy's herald in order to save Louis' life—and also entirely disposable. (The gypsy is ultimately hanged by Charles for his impersonation; Quentin, by contrast, is quickly forgiven when he eventually perpetrates a similar hoax.) Hayraddin's death even facilitates Quentin's triumph, since he leaves Scott's hero not only with crucial knowledge of impending military actions but also with enough money to claim the hand of the novel's aristocratic heroine.[41] In death as in life, Hayraddin occupies the place of the vanishing mediator: he is both essential to France's future, and must finally be destroyed in order for it to become part of the "formation of the world scale taking shape in the sixteenth century . . . as part of the building of national states and national capitalisms."[42]

How does Scott take us to this place where violence and sovereignty have become inextricably intertwined? When *Quentin Durward* begins, its titular hero has only recently escaped to France from a still-primitive Scotland. Hoping to make his fortune as a mercenary, Quentin proves a wayward prospective employee: when the novel opens, he has already alienated himself from Burgundy by beating one of Charles' foresters for shooting his falcon, and then proceeds unintentionally to insult the disguised King Louis at their first meeting. Moreover, when "Maitre Pierre" asks Quentin whether he will seek employment in the king's honor guard, the Scottish Archers,[43] our naïve hero responds in the negative: "Your King Louis—God bless him, I say, for he is a friend and ally of Scotland—but he lies here in his Castle, or only rides from one fortified town to another; and gains cities and provinces by politic embassies, and not in fair fighting" (47). Quentin sees Louis' intriguing and political manipulation as newfangled statecraft, unworthy of a true leader; further, Quentin believes he can remain a free and neutral agent, operating autonomously from the various forces competing to shape France's political destiny. When the disguised king tries to tempt Quentin into his service by describing the Archers' luxurious living quarters, his offer is rebuffed.

This desire to remain a self-directed, wholly rational economic actor initially aligns Quentin with the nomadic gypsies. Such an association, however, repeatedly endangers him: during the novel's opening chapters he is assumed to be a Bohemian several times by the king's provost-marshal, who first mistakes Quentin for a spy as he fords a river, then repeats this error with malicious willfulness when Quentin is caught trying to assist an actual gypsy who has just been hanged. The latter scene encapsulates the increasing tension between Quentin's desire to remain politically independent and the ever-strengthening authority of the French monarch. Arriving just after the moment of execution, Quentin asks why no one has tried to help the dying man. In return, "One of the peasants, turning on him an eye from which fear had banished all expression but its own ... pointed to a mark cut upon the bark of the tree, having the same rude resemblance to a *fleur-de-lys* which certain talismanic scratches, well known to our revenue officers, bear to a *broad arrow*" (72). This anachronistic reference is to the British government's habit of marking official property with an arrow for easy identification by customs officers. Scott's comparison reinforces the previously established isomorphism between sovereign authority and economic exchange. By ignoring the mark of Louis' sovereignty—Scott writes that his protagonist subsequently cuts down the gypsy's corpse, "[n]either understanding nor heeding the import of this symbol" (72)—Quentin unintentionally undermines Louis' symbolic authority and devalues his political capital. Subsequently threatened with execution, Quentin avoids his own hanging only by agreeing on the spot to what he had previously refused: joining the Scottish Archers.[44]

This episode displays the violence of sovereign power at its most explicit. Although Quentin nominally "chooses" to swear loyalty to Louis, the alternatives are not really "whether to take service with you or no," as Quentin hopes, but rather as his cousin (who is already an Archer) corrects him, "whether you choose to do so, or be hanged" (81). Quentin's "choice" to join the King's personal bodyguards is structurally identical to the paradox of the "forced choice" that Žižek repeatedly identifies as exemplary of the modern subject's plight: "Our freedom of choice effectively often functions as a mere formal gesture of consent to our own oppression and exploitation."[45] In other words, Quentin—insofar as he embodies, like most of Scott's Waverley Novel heroes, the ideal citizen of the modern nation-state[46]—chooses life over death only by "voluntarily" giving up his right to choose his life for himself.

What *Quentin Durward* (the novel) implicitly recognizes, then, is what Quentin Durward (the Waverley Hero) discovers: the price to be paid for the construction of the modern, sovereign nation-state—the foundational geopolitical unit of the global world-system—is the reductive transformation of all its citizens into potential *homines sacri*. This initially seems counterintuitive, since the most obvious figure of bare life is the one who is banned by the sovereign state, not protected by it. Yet Agamben argues that sovereign and outcast are constituted by the same logic of exclusion: "*The sovereign sphere is the sphere in which it is permitted to kill without committing homicide and without celebrating a sacrifice, and sacred life—that is, life that may be killed but not sacrificed—is the life that has been captured in this sphere*" (83). *Quentin Durward* may challenge the historicity of this claim, locating the birth of modern sovereign power in fifteenth-century France (between Agamben's classical jurisprudence and Foucault's eighteenth-century governmentality), but it confirms its dependence on the originary identification of citizen-subjects as inherently "bare lives."[47] From here, it is but a small step to define the modern subject as a bearer of "universal (pre-political) human rights" whose existence—especially if and when it lacks "the specific political rights of a citizen, or member of a particular political community"—is endlessly open to intervention, manipulation, and of course termination by state powers that, in the twentieth century, will declare themselves "guardians" of such rights worldwide.[48] The subject of human rights is bare life on the scale of "worldwideification."

As if to distract from the recognition that Quentin, the ideal modern citizen-subject, and Hayraddin, the ultimate outcast, are entirely fungible within the new regime of sovereignty, Scott involves Quentin in more heroic activity than most of his other, notoriously passive Waverley Heroes; after joining Louis' bodyguard, the Scotsman slays evildoers and pursues his fortune with a sense of alacrity sorely absent in Edward Waverley or Frank Osbaldistone (of *Rob Roy*). The novel's main plot is a protracted, self-consciously fantastical quest which, although designed by Louis to fail, ends up restoring Quentin's dignity—albeit in the residual sense of his chivalric honor rather than his political agency—as well as making his fortune. In the words of the novel's blustering conclusion, Quentin is ultimately rewarded with "possession of Wealth, Rank, and Beauty!" (399). This "moral of excellent tendency" (400) is almost enough to help us forget that the early chapters of *Quentin Durward* repeatedly draw attention to the enormity of the sacrifices—culminating in the biopolitical reduction of all citizens to bare life—required for the attainment of those material riches.

ALPINE ABYSSES AND SECRET SYSTEMS IN *ANNE OF GEIERSTEIN*

Almost from the moment of *Quentin Durward*'s completion, Scott felt he had not finished thinking through modern Europe's political origins. His publisher, Robert Cadell, encouraged the Author of Waverley to return to the "French ground [that] is untrodden but by yourself."⁴⁹ The new novel Scott eventually produced is indeed a sequel of sorts to *Quentin Durward*. *Anne of Geierstein* takes place some six years after the close of its predecessor, and it too depicts the profound transformations that were converting feudal principalities into sovereign nation-states—the backbone of the post-Napoleonic modern world order. Where *Quentin Durward* focuses on Louis' attempts to modernize and centralize France, however, *Anne of Geierstein* revolves around a fictionalized attempt by Lancastrian exiles, led by the Earl of Oxford, to garner Charles of Burgundy's support against the Yorkists. (In its greater license than its predecessor with the historical record, *Geierstein* arguably bears the same relation to *Quentin Durward* that *Redgauntlet* [1824]—Scott's historical fantasia of a final, fictional attempt by Bonnie Prince Charlie to reclaim the British throne in the 1760s—bears to *Waverley*.) The failure of this plot-within-a-plot allows Scott both to revisit the themes and concerns of *Quentin Durward* and to introduce into his version of European geopolitical history an ethical dynamic, which I call "global hospitality," that looks to restore the egalitarian potential of Romantic globalism.⁵⁰

Some familiarity with the details of *Geierstein*'s tortuous plot will help with the later elucidation of its themes. The above-mentioned conspiracy fails because although Charles agrees to help the Lancastrians, he is killed before he can do so, fighting at the Battle of Nancy against independent Swiss cantons previously angered by his hostile behavior. The theme of a small, independent people repelling the advances of a larger power was of great personal interest to Scott; indeed, midway through the novel Charles observes that the Swiss are to the Burgundians as the Scots are to the English.⁵¹ Regarding the Swiss as upstart peasants, Charles repeatedly denies the legitimacy of their claims to independence, and his eventual death at their hands serves as neat historical justice.

Critical discussions of *Anne of Geierstein* tend to focus on its two most distinctive features: the striking imagery of the sublimely dangerous landscape with which the novel opens, and the subterranean scene involving the medieval Germanic secret tribunal of which the Earl of Oxford runs afoul.⁵² These sensational components are in fact linked: both figure the deep senses of uncertainty and dislocation that afflict the novel's main characters, psychologically as well as politically. When Arthur Philipson, disguised like his noble father Oxford as a humble merchant (thus making good on Louis' disguises in *Quentin Durward*), swings by a tree trunk over an Alpine precipice in the novel's second chapter, Scott details the vertigo that grips him:

> The effects of his terror, indeed, were physical as well as mental, for a thousand colours played before his eyes, his stomach was suddenly and severely affected, he lost at once the obedience of those limbs which had hitherto served him so admirably; his arms and his hands, as if no longer at his own command, now clung to the branches of the tree, with a cramp-like tenacity over which he seemed to possess no power, and now trembled in a state of such complete nervous relaxation, as led him to fear that they were becoming unable to support him longer in his position. (21)

This is an unusually intense description of fear for Scott, especially with regard to an otherwise bold character who, as Alexander Welsh notes, is the only Waverley Hero who purposefully and directly kills another major character.[53] (Arthur slays his rival, Rudolph of Donnerhugel, in combat in the penultimate chapter.) Arthur's terror in this scene becomes so great that he must be rescued by the novel's eponymous heroine, who "restore[s] his confidence" by twice jumping the gap from tree to cliff, until "shame now overcame terror so much, that Arthur . . . took heart of grace, and successfully achieved the formidable step which placed him on the same cliff with his kind assistant" (26). As she will do several more times throughout the narrative, Anne uses her calm and competent influence to aid her eventual lover.[54]

Some chapters later, Arthur's father is subject to an even more disorienting experience.[55] Staying at an inn on the German side of the Rhine while en route to Charles' camp, the Earl of Oxford (disguised as Philipson senior) has the unnerving experience of feeling the floor literally drop from under him as he is lowered in his bed to a subterranean trial arranged by the Vehme Gericht. This second appearance of the threat or feeling of plunging into an abyss confirms Scott's interest, not only in the typically Romantic exploration of extreme psychological states, but also in how the early modern era itself was a dizzying time of dislocation and change. The political landscape of late fifteenth-century Europe was highly volatile, with towns, cities, and even whole principalities changing hands regularly as feudal lords jockeyed for power with ambitious monarchs against the backdrop of the increasingly ragged Holy Roman Empire.[56] Scott's repeated depictions of vertigo in *Anne of Geierstein* dramatically literalize these dislocations, while also recalling the Žižekian subject's plunge into identification with the void of modern subjectivity.

Notwithstanding the intrigue of these individual experiences, however, Scott is always more interested in depicting larger-scale socio-political transformations than personal ones. In this way, Philipson's appearance before the secret tribunal becomes an explicit confrontation between the norms of feudalism and those of a more modern, inherently more global worldview. For Scott, the Vehme Gericht represents everything that was insupportable, albeit fascinating, about governance and justice in feudal Europe. Much of his introduction to the *magnum opus* edition of *Anne of Geierstein* involves rebutting earlier criticisms of his representation of the Germanic secret society. In the novel itself, one of the Tribunal's members defends its existence by tracing its genealogy back to "the most Christian and holy Roman Emperor, Charlemagne," who supposedly created it "for the conversion of the heathen Saxons, and punishing such of them as revolted again to their Pagan practices" (226). Whatever its origin, the Vehme Gericht became a potent extra-judicial force in the territories along the Rhine, operating with relative impunity and exercising considerable influence. (One of Scott's key plot revelations is that Anne's father turns out to be the head of the tribunal that interrogates Oxford.) Its enmeshment in the feudal order is underscored by Scott's remarks that "all were conscious that the power of the Tribunal depended much more on the opinion of its being deeply and firmly rooted in *the general system,* than on any regard or esteem for an institution, of which all felt the severity" (226; my italics). Scott's use of the phrase "the general system" here seems telling. As Clifford Siskin argues, not only has "invoking The System ... become a primary modern means of totalizing and rationalizing our experience of the social," but also the very concept of "the system" as a reified, all-encompassing entity reflects our inheritance of Enlightenment models of knowledge filtered through Romanticism.[57] Our ability to "blame the system," Siskin argues, is more than just a legacy of the tangled relationship between these two worldviews: it indexes the moment when "the genre of system" became available as a way to describe the inevitable mediations in and through which knowledge is produced and disseminated.[58]

We can see some of this historical legacy being negotiated in *Anne of Geierstein*. The novel suggests that the fraying feudal system is to blame for the flourishing of the Vehme Gericht, especially as the latter has taken over judiciary functions inadequately administered by individual lords and embattled monarchs. In fact, Charles of Burgundy is deeply unhappy with the Vehme Gericht's growing influence, especially given that its relative independence mirrors that of the upstart Swiss. (His fear of the Tribunal's autonomy is realized when it orders the execution of one of his lackeys.) The elder Geierstein, in his guise as the Black Priest of St. Paul's, even tells Philipson that Charles has no authority over the Tribunal: "The Duke may execute his serfs and bondsmen at his pleasure, but there is a spell upon my life, which is proof to all his power" (200). Scott's Vehme Gericht, in contrast to Radcliffe's ultimately sympathetic depiction of the Inquisition in *The Italian*, is thus both a product of feudalism and an index of its fateful juridical and political shortcomings.

As a historical novelist, Scott relishes the opportunity to indulge in depictions of conspiratorial menace; as a modern Briton, he recognizes that the Vehme Gericht is an atavistic institution whose existence runs counter to Europe's modernization. As we saw in *Quentin Durward,* Scott was well aware of the potential downsides of the state's monopoly on legitimate violence. Publishing *Anne of Geierstein* six years later, Scott now emphasizes the advantage of that same political consolidation of authority: the modern nation-state's ability to achieve, in Jürgen Habermas' words, "the legitimate ordering of [its inhabitants'] collective existence through the means of positive law."[59] Rejecting the historian Francis Palgrave's argument that the Vehme Gericht might have influenced early English judicial practices, Scott gives Philipson a series of speeches that alternately outlines the Tribunal's flaws, sketches out the affirmative values of state-sanctioned justice, and recognizes the latter's limitations.

Responding to the accusation that while in Italy he slandered the Vehme Gericht, Philipson begins by proudly asserting his national identity: "I am an Englishman, one of a nation accustomed to yield and receive open-handed and equal justice dealt forth in the broad light of day" (226). This declaration is followed by the qualification that "I am, however, a traveler, who knows that he has no right to oppose the rules and laws of other nations, because they do not resemble those of his own." The cosmopolitan sentiment here is notable, as is Philipson's "insistence on the juridical as opposed to the merely moral dimension"[60] of the respect due to the "rules and laws of other nations." In other words, Philipson's admission of wrongdoing is not a sign of cultural relativism; rather, his enshrinement of each nation-state's right to sovereignty within its own borders embraces the core of the Kantian ideal of perpetual world peace coordinated by an international league of sovereign nations. This acknowledgment, however, is immediately qualified by yet another significant assertion, when Philipson claims that he is only obligated to recognize the Tribunal's authority within its (admittedly unofficial and ambiguous) jurisdiction:

> But this caution can only be called for in lands, where the system about which we converse is in full force and operation. If we speak of the institutions of Germany, being at the time in France or Spain, we may without offence to the country in which they are current, dispute concerning them, as students debate upon a logical thesis in a university. (226–27)

The authority of a juridico-political institution, Philipson claims, is territorially limited: if it can bind someone to abide by laws she does not necessarily agree with while within the relevant borders, it also allows her to be critical of them when outside those borders.[61] Philipson stresses that "I say also, I had a right to express these opinions, whether sound or erroneous, in a neutral country.... But I deny that I have ever spoken against the institutions of *your* Vehme, in a country where it had course as national mode of justice" (227; my italics). With the pronoun "your," Philipson reiterates that the Tribunal is literally a foreign institution to him. In sum, Scott here effectively anticipates the outlines of a global order, based not on the post-national politics of something like Hardt and Negri's radical multitude (produced by the biopolitical reduction of citizens to their lowest common denominator, bare life), but rather on what Craig Calhoun calls the "global integration" that can be realized only by "allowing people inhabiting diverse locations in the world, diverse traditions, and diverse social relationships opportunities to choose the institutions in and through which they will integrate."[62]

Philipson's position strengthens as the chapter continues. When the presiding judge demands that he relate the exact nature of his criticism of the Tribunal, the disguised Earl responds powerfully:

> My opinion was unfavourable, and I expressed myself thus:—No laws or juridical proceedings can be just or commendable, which exist and operate by means of a secret combination. I said, that justice could only live in the open air, and that when she ceased to be public, she degenerated into revenge and hatred. I said, that a system, of which your own jurists had said, *non frater a fratre, non hospes a hospite, tutus* [brother is not safe from brother, nor host from guest], was too much adverse to the laws of nature to be connected with or regulated by those of religion. (227)

Now, Philipson supplements his earlier argument regarding the Vehme's territorially limited authority with a decisive stand against its juridical practices. Invoking "the laws of nature," Scott insists that, from an Enlightened perspective of normative justice, the Vehme Gericht falls far short of modern standards of admissible evidence and fair trial. In this way, Scott turns Philipson's "admission of guilt" into an effective condemnation of the very system that has accused him. Although his acquittal is accompanied by a warning from the judge "to cross thyself when thou dost so much as think of the Holy and Invisible Tribunal" (229), Oxford emerges victorious, theoretically as well as literally, from his confrontation with the Vehme.

TOWARD GLOBAL HOSPITALITY

The themes raised by Philipson's successful defense of the advantages of limited sovereignty are carried into the rest of *Anne of Geierstein*, especially the conflict between the Swiss and Burgundy. Scott represents the former in strikingly positive terms; with their egalitarian manners, simple dress, hardy temperament, and pastoral lifestyle, the Swiss embody the virtues of honest, rural freemen. (The exception is the perpetually arrogant Rudolph.) Having won their freedom in a series of wars with Austria during the fourteenth century, the Cantons view themselves as an independent confederation—a Kantian League of Nations writ small—owing allegiance to no external power. Accordingly, they are a constant thorn in Charles' side, who repeatedly disparages their pretensions to sovereignty and equality. Angered at their perceived role in the loss of the town of La Ferette, Charles describes how the Swiss "have shaken off all reverence for authority, assume airs of independence, form leagues, make inroads, storm towns, doom and execute men of noble birth at their pleasure" (291).

In the context of Scott's fictive explorations of the originary systemic violence of modern Europe's geopolitical organization, however, the Swiss do not only stand for national sovereignty; they also represent a principle of hospitality with the potential to restore an ethical dimension to global relations, both individually and nationally. Such a dimension, observes Seyla Benhabib, is implicit in Kant's concept of "cosmopolitan right" because "the obligation to show hospitality to foreigners and strangers cannot be enforced; it remains a voluntarily incurred obligation on the part of the political sovereign."[63] As a positive rearticulation of Žižek's "forced choice," the obligation to be hospitable is less than a norm but more than a preference: it enacts the impulse to care for another, regardless of one's opinion of or relation to him.[64] For Derrida, the concept of hospitality is essential to any genuine interaction with others: "Pure and unconditional hospitality, hospitality *itself*, opens or is in advance open to someone who is neither expected nor invited, to whomever arrives as an absolutely foreign *visitor*, as a new *arrival*, nonidentifiable and unforeseeable, in short, wholly other."[65] Authentic hospitality embraces others unconditionally, allowing them to enter one's domain on their terms rather than one's own. This makes hospitality different in kind from the sympathetic cosmopolitanism of Radcliffe's romances, especially insofar as the latter tends to establish bonds with others primarily by assimilating them to the standards and norms of the self-same. The problematic elements of tolerance, as discussed at the end of Chapter Two, are productively absent in true hospitality. Derrida admits that such unconditional hospitality is "to be sure, practically impossible," yet he strongly endorses it as "the very condition of the political and the juridical."[66] Placed in its properly political context, global hospitality not only promises to make room for genuine difference in a way that sympathetic cosmopolitanism arguably does not, but also re-establishes the fundamentally ethical ground of international rights and relations. It thus provides a hopeful counterbalance to Žižek's and Agamben's concerns that modernity essentially reduces individuals to empty, anonymous subjects or *homines sacri*.

How does such global hospitality work in *Anne of Geierstein*? The novel begins with several acts of quotidian hospitality. After Arthur is rescued from his perilous situation by Anne, both he and his father are taken in by Anne's uncle, Arnold Biederman, a nobleman who works the land and embodies the spirit of Swiss egalitarianism. The Englishmen are so struck by the openness with which they are welcomed that Arthur subsequently attempts to suppress his growing affection for Anne on the grounds that

> in yielding to the feelings which impelled him to cultivate the acquaintance of this amiable young person, he would certainly incur the serious displeasure of his father, and probably also that of her uncle, by whose hospitality they had profited, and whose safe-conduct they were in the act of enjoying. (71)

Later, when Arthur comments that he sees no overt signs of privilege in Biederman's relations with his social inferiors, Rudolph replies that Arthur has been spared such treatment because he is a guest: "You are a stranger . . . and the old man has too much hospitality to lay you under the least restraint" (85–86). Arthur in turn wishes to repay such hospitality, not merely from a sense of duty or obligation, but also from a sincere desire to incur his share of the responsibilities of the polity that has so willingly embraced him.

By contrast, the Swiss envoys experience a distinct lack of hospitality on their journey to parlay with Burgundy. Most notably, the town of Bâle (Basel), where they had hoped to stop for the night, refuses them entrance under pressure from Charles. Upon being greeted by a magistrate and some citizens, the Swiss travelers "prepared themselves to hear, and make a suitable reply to, the hospitable invitation which they naturally expected to receive" (75). When they are turned away, Biederman explicitly invokes such expectations, exclaiming, "This is a singular message to the deputies of the Swiss Confederacy . . . from the citizens of Bâle. . . . The shelter of their roof, the protection of their walls, the wonted intercourse of hospitality, is what no friendly state hath a right to refuse to the inhabitants of another" (76). Nevertheless, he and his fellows are refused entrance, provoking a parting exclamation against the "brutal inhospitality" of the Bernese (78). All is not entirely lost, however, because when the Swiss arrive at the abandoned castle outside the city where they have been allowed to camp, they find it stocked with provisions; by such efforts "these poor men of Bale have saved their character for hospitality" (79).

This pattern—in which the Swiss find their hospitality less than fully reciprocated—is repeated throughout the novel. At La Farette they are harassed by Charles' men; at the Burgundian court they are mistreated and insulted until provoked to declare war. The exiled Englishmen, for their part, experience a spectrum of attitudes toward foreigners as they travel. Whereas Oxford is treated to a less than hospitable experience at the inn under which he is questioned by the Vehme Gericht, Arthur fares better when he stays the night at Arnheim castle, the ancestral home of the Geiersteins, where Anne is also in residence. When he expresses "hope that his experiencing the hospitality of the castle would occasion no trouble to the inmates" (233), Arthur is assured that it will not. Accordingly, although the unexpected presence of Geierstein's steward creates comic embarrassment for the young lovers, Arthur passes a pleasantly awkward night at Anne's estate. To their credit, moreover, the Englishmen consistently recognize the hospitality they are repeatedly shown by the Swiss themselves. When Charles asks Philipson—now openly the Earl of Oxford once more—to accompany him into battle, for example, the latter refuses, explaining that "I will not carry arms, especially against those people of Helvetia, from whom I have experienced hospitality, unless it be for my own personal defence" (313–14). The duke's unexpected acceptance of this position confirms the high esteem in which hospitality is held in *Anne of Geierstein*. His own shows of generosity toward Oxford are always self-interested, however, since Burgundy thinks he can use the earl to help stake his claim for the disputed territory of Lorraine.

Charles' battlefield death clears the way for authentic acts of hospitality to take priority once again. In the novel's final chapters, the townspeople of Nancy gratefully welcome the Swiss after their victory.[67] Despite having fought on Charles' side, Oxford and his son are "received with the utmost kindness by the Landamman [Biedermann], who assured them of his protection and friendship" (402). This reassertion of hospitality facilitates the novel's happy ending in which Anne and Arthur marry and eventually return to England, where Arthur participates in the Battle of Bosworth that puts Henry VII on the throne. In this way, Scott makes the principle of hospitality the vehicle, not just of the properly ethical dynamic that should inform global relations, but also of the path to English (and then British) modernity marked by the ascension of the Tudor line.

SCOTT'S NEW WORLD ORDER

Anne of Geierstein was not Scott's final Waverley Novel; it was, however, the last to be written before he suffered the series of strokes that led to his death in September 1832. It represents his most clear-sighted fictional investigation of the political origins of the modern global world order in at least two senses. The Europe whose contemporary origins Scott rethinks in *Quentin Durward* and *Anne of Geierstein* is the political and economic bloc that will be the center of the capitalist world-system until the middle of the twentieth century, but it is also, as Étienne Balibar observes, an entity that is internally "multiple": "always home to tensions between numerous religious, cultural, linguistic, and political affiliations, numerous readings of history, numerous modes of relations with the rest of the world. . . . "[68] Europe, in other words, is a perpetual ethico-political work-in-progress. The crux of Scott's historical vision in his European Waverley Novels lies in his recognition of the profoundly human nature and dimensions of this experiment, that is, both the constructedness of the European entity (it is man-made, and therefore both imperfect and alterable), and the subjectivizing effects of Europe's coming-into-being.

To label Scott a political thinker is arguably to misrecognize the fundamental nature of his storytelling talent. Yet Scott's gift for producing fictions is itself part of his contribution to our understanding of the modern operations of political sovereignty. When Scott became de facto stage manager of George IV's 1822 visit to Edinburgh—the first time a Hanoverian monarch had set foot in Scotland since before the 1745 Jacobite rebellion—he encouraged both the king and his Scottish subjects to engage in performances of fealty based far less on the historical record than on Scott's own previous fictions of Anglo-Scottish rapprochement. The results were, quite literally, spectacular.[69] "The King's Jaunt," as George IV's visit became known, proved what *Quentin Durward* and *Anne of Geierstein* each confirm, albeit in different registers: the principle of sovereignty—the essence of the modern nation-state, and thus of every neo-Kantian conception of globality—is strengthened, not diminished, by the exposure of its inherent fictionality. The same can be said, moreover, of the concept of global hospitality I have argued *Anne of Geierstein* puts forth as a counterbalance or supplement to the structural violence inherent to sovereign power. It too is based on the profound, and profoundly moving, fiction that each of us is capable of extending unconditional acceptance to all others.

This chapter has explored how Scott's European-themed Waverley Novels contribute to the post-Napoleonic expansion and deepening of Britons' understanding of their increasingly global world order. To conclude, I want to return to the scene of European reading with which I began, on the hunch that Scott's Continental audiences were not necessarily learning the same lessons as his Anglo-British readers. Introducing a recent collection of essays on Scott's influence in Europe, Murray Pittock writes that "[i]n societies struggling for independence against regional powers or colonial oppressors, with suppressed languages, disordered civic societies and no historiography save that of native resentment and patriotic resistance, the radical undertow in Scott's writing could seem more prominent than it did to a British audience."[70] Although Scott himself may have been pleasantly surprised by *Quentin Durward*'s warm reception in France, his widespread European popularity throughout most of the nineteenth century appears in keeping with the highly modular form of nationalism his novels promote.[71] Such national promotions, however, must be placed alongside the globalizing impulses that are an equally important component of Scott's capacious oeuvre. Certainly, the sheer scope of his popularity seems to have influenced the emergence of the "world republic of letters," which in turn both reflected and furthered the increasing systematicity of global relations.[72] That not just French but also Italian, Spanish, Hungarian, Slovenian, and a host of other national (or would-be national) writers could find inspiration and take cues from Scott's fictions confirms that the model of state sovereignty sponsored by the Waverley Novels was essentially suited to consolidating the modern world-system.[73] I have argued for a new appreciation of how Scott's fictional conceptualizations of the forms and modes of modern sovereignty and global hospitality extend well beyond the borders of Britain, and of any individual nation-state. In this precise critical sense, Scott may be the first truly global author.

CONCLUSION

Romanticism, Mediation, Globalization

JOHN LE CARRÉ's bestselling novel, *The Constant Gardener* (2001), vividly depicts the depths to which British global influence had sunk by the start of the twenty-first century. Set in Kenya, it recounts the attempts of a British bureaucrat named Justin Quayle to track down the murderers of his wife, an idealistic activist who had threatened to expose a multinational pharmaceutical corporation for using vulnerable Africans as unwitting test subjects. Aside from the sensationalistic plot and le Carré's skillful narrative manipulations, the book's main interest resides in its unsentimental assessment of Britain's greatly reduced and thoroughly compromised role in our contemporary world order.

Confronted with evidence that the Kenyan government has been colluding with the corporation in question, the head of the British embassy at the High Commission in Nairobi, Sandy Woodrow, defends his inaction by asserting that Britain needs to maintain good relations with its former colonies: "Commerce is not a sin. Trading with emerging countries is not a sin. Trade helps them to emerge, in fact. It makes reforms possible. The kind of reforms we all want. It brings them into the modern world. It enables *us* to help *them*. How can we help a poor country if we're not rich ourselves?"[1] Tessa Quayle's curt reply—"Bullshit"—exposes how Woodrow's halting speech echoes and then exposes contemporary neoliberal discourse: it begins as a paean to the mutually beneficial exchanges of contemporary globalization but devolves into a hollow justification of further enrichment of the mother country-turned-senior-trading partner. Later, at Tessa's funeral, Woodrow gazes at a stained glass window of Saint Andrew before indulging in an internal monologue that oscillates between nostalgia and self-flagellation: "What must they think of us? he marveled, transferring his misty gaze to the black faces in the congregation. What did we imagine we were doing here, back in those days, plugging our white British God and our white Scottish saint while we used the country as an adventure playground for derelict upper-class swingers?"[2]

Woodrow's evocation of "those days" draws on a host of by-now familiar, condemnatory representations of Victorian high imperialism. One of my main goals, by contrast, has been to demonstrate that such depictions do not represent the full variety of British globalism in the late-eighteenth and early-nineteenth centuries. In doing so, I have not meant to deny that some Romantic-era writers harbored straightforwardly imperial ambitions for Britain. The military officer-turned-strategist Sir Charles Pasley, for instance, authored his influential *Essay on the Military Policy and Institutions of the British Empire* (1810) specifically to urge Britain to adopt an ambitious plan not only to defeat Napoleon but also to replace his program of Continental conquests with its own. Gould Francis Leckie, the would-be colonizer of Sicily and sometime friend of Byron, had already penned a similarly titled manifesto, *An Historical Survey of the Foreign Affairs of Great Britain* (1808), which was only slightly less ambitious in its recommendation that Britain channel its imperial aspirations toward an "insular empire" made up primarily of island fortresses.[3] Outrightly imperialistic sentiments, often greatly in excess of what Britain was actually capable of realizing, can be found throughout the period's literature, lending themselves to what Makdisi has recently called "the constitution of a collective cultural and political identity, the definition of an imperial culture as against its civilizational 'others.'"[4]

Nevertheless, as I have argued throughout this book, there was simultaneously another macropolitics being developed during this period, and it deserves critical attention too. What I am calling Romantic globalism held not only that Britons needed to learn to see themselves as members of a nation whose geopolitical destiny was intimately bound up with those of the rest of the world, but also that such relations could be conceived as cooperative and egalitarian rather than competitive and hierarchical. The theoretical and conceptual foundations for this global worldview, I have argued, were laid in the Scottish Enlightenment; found fictional purchase and dissemination in the sympathetic cosmopolitanism of Radcliffe's Gothic romances; saturated the popular wartime poetry of Hemans, Barbauld, Grant, and Scott; underwrote the sophisticated dismantlings of binary thinking in Byron's and Scott's

Eastern-themed texts; and deeply informed the representations of modern sovereignty and global hospitality put forward in Scott's European Waverley Novels.

Boiling down my critical narrative to these essentials no doubt exposes some of its partialities. Put more positively, I hope it provides readers with plenty of opportunities to see where my developmental account of the British Romantics' representations of and responses to early globalization might be extended, supplemented, altered, or contested. Consider one point of alternative intervention: although the close of my fifth chapter emphasizes the significance of global hospitality in Scott's *Anne of Geierstein,* this theme could be examined in the works of many other Romantics. These might include Coleridge's 1800 "Argument" to his revised and retitled "The Ancient Mariner, A Poet's Reverie," which explains that the eponymous hero's excruciating punishments result from his "contempt of the laws of hospitality" in shooting the Albatross; Austen's celebration of the "degree of hospitality so uncommon" in the Harvilles' warm reception of Wentworth, Anne, and the other travelers to Lyme in *Persuasion;* and Percy Shelley's exalted placement of social sympathy at the core of human nature in his *Defence of Poetry* (1821/1840).[5] The incorporation of any (or all) of these alternative texts would alter the contours of my critical narrative, and similar substitutions or additions could no doubt be made at earlier points in my argument as well. I not only anticipate, but positively look forward to such developments.

At the same time, however, I believe the overall arc of my account of Romantic globalism's evolution—from the Scottish Enlightenment, through Romantic poetry, and into Romantic fiction, with Scott looming increasingly large after the turn of the nineteenth century—possesses a number of solid merits. First, Byron's popularity and celebrity notwithstanding, it accords with the current scholarly consensus that by the Romantic era's end, the novel had mostly overtaken poetry as the most important as well as the most popular medium of cultural transmission in the English-speaking world. The explanations for this generic shift are wide-ranging and overdetermined, from changes in copyright laws and publishing and distribution methods, to the rise of journalistic reviewing and anthologizing, to the internal fitness of the novel form itself. Among recent accounts that pursue the last of these arguments, Nancy Armstrong's observation that the Romantic-era novel helped model forms of subjectivity that mediated (however ambivalently) between individual and collective modes of identification is especially apt: "Between 1789 and 1819, the novel accordingly shifts its moral investment to the supplementary qualities associated with citizenship and yet remains aesthetically bound and committed to those qualities associated with an earlier individualism it must now renounce."[6] My argument in *Romantic Globalism*—that Radcliffe and Scott were also interested (albeit in significantly different ways) in encouraging modes of *global* citizenship—can thus be added, I think, to Armstrong's story of the novel's ideological work in the nineteenth century. In Scott's case, he did not merely write novels, but also reviewed and reissued them throughout his career; as Armstrong reminds us, Scott edited Defoe's novels in 1809, and wrote introductions for the canon-forming *Ballantyne's Novelist's Library* between 1821 and 1824. Add to this the thematization of mediation in Scott's poetry and prose, and one quickly apprehends his particular gift for forecasting and trend setting the shifting dynamics of cultural transmission.[7] I hope the critical narrative I have told does some justice both to the evolving literary landscape of the long Romantic era, and to Scott's central position within it.

The version of Romantic globalism I have put forward also concurs, I think, with recent scholarship on the historical development of cultural information's means of dissemination, as well as changes in our modes of thinking information itself. In the introduction to *This Is Enlightenment,* Siskin and Warner claim that the Enlightenment is best understood today as "an event in the history of mediation"—a provocative assertion that draws attention away from the content of Enlightenment texts (the study of which nevertheless continues to yield insights with respect to the durability and influence of Enlightenment motifs like Smith's "invisible hand"[8]) and toward their imbrication in "the mechanics of mediation, the role of technologies, the influence of genres, the dynamic of association, and the aggregate effect of elementary protocols."[9] Although questions of mediation have been raised in this book primarily in generic terms, I hope it will serve to stimulate further work by others, especially insofar as a "truly global sociology of modernities"[10] will inevitably need to recognize globalization itself to be at least one, and possibly several, "event[s] in the history of mediation."

My argument in *Romantic Globalism* accords particularly well with Siskin's thesis that the central concept of "system" undergoes a significant transformation over the course of the long eighteenth century. According to Siskin, Scottish Enlighteners like Smith were particularly dedicated to "writing systems . . . of a very particular kind: master systems that would simplify and popularize by arranging and methodizing *all* earlier systems."[11] Whereas Siskin posits that the literati became victims of their own success due to their overproduction of (meta)systems, I have argued that their systematizing and theorizing of the basic principles of the disciplines we now call economics and anthropology succeeding in setting the "floor plan" (to re-invoke

Jameson's term) for modern globalism. Yet my account agrees with Siskin's systemic description of the cognitive structure of the Scottish Enlighteners' projects, as well as with his thesis that, in the Romantic era, the earlier systematizing impulse is fractured and fragmented into first poetic and then novelistic forms of increasingly professional specialization. "System" does not disappear, although it becomes nearly unmentionable; rather, it becomes embedded into the literary and other media forms with which we are now more familiar. Siskin's turn to the Author of Waverley as his primary example of this trend—"Scott put systems into history as the new touchstone of novelistic narrative"[12]—substantiates my assertion that Scott's contributions to the development of modern globalism must not be underestimated.

In the rest of this conclusion, I want finally to sketch some preliminary answers to two broad but interrelated questions that have implicitly animated the preceding chapters. First, what might be gained when we begin to rethink our contemporary experiences of globalization in literary historical, and specifically Romantic, terms? Second, what difference does it make when we begin to rethink the history of Romanticism in global terms?

Today, the most vocal and visible proponents of globalism tend to be united by their strong belief in the total efficacy of free market capitalism, at least in theory. (In practice, as Wallerstein points out, they almost always support protectionist state policies for their own interests.[13]) Its critics, by contrast, are extremely wary of the oft-heard claim that, as Harish Trivedi skeptically puts it, "globalization benefits everyone, that is, both the globalizer and the globalized."[14] The proponents of Romantic globalism I have discussed would not have recognized the terms of Trivedi's dichotomy, a not-so-subtle echo of the colonizer–colonized dyad that continues to form the conceptual backbone of most postcolonial criticism. Yet I suspect they would have embraced unironically the underlying sentiment, since for the Scottish Enlighteners, as for their Romantic successors, globalization appeared to offer not just greater opportunities for the egalitarian distribution of wealth, but also greater opportunities for Britons to reach out imaginatively to the rest of the world. Sympathetic cosmopolitanism had limitations, and global hospitality may still be largely an unrealized ideal, but recovering the history of Romantic globalism may yet help us find ways to (re)incorporate an ethical imperative and an egalitarian dynamic into our thinking about globalization today, especially given the general failure (even after 2008's "Great Recession") to dislodge neoliberalism from its ideological hegemony.[15]

"[S]uch a possibility," as Jean-Luc Nancy states with regard to the work of imagining "the sense of a world that would become rich from itself without any reason either sacred or cumulative," must by definition never become "the object of a programmatic and certain calculation."[16] Yet some versions of this work are already being accomplished by the various activists, scholars, associations, and networks gathered loosely under the alter-globalization movement. Seeking alternatives to neoliberalism's hegemony, but without opposing globalization altogether, alter-globalist movements are, in the words of political scientist John Keane, "marked by a cross-border mentality": "Their participants . . . do not see their concerns as confined within a strictly bounded community or locality. They are convinced that toxic chemicals and human rights and debt relief and compassion for those whose dignity has been violated know no borders. For them the world is one world."[17] The specific items in this list of global concerns—environmental, economic, and socio-political problems too large and metastasizing too quickly to be dealt with effectively by any one entity or nation—might not be entirely recognizable from a Romantic-era standpoint (although issues like the growing national debt were certainly of concern to many Britons of the period). Nevertheless, the varieties of Romantic globalism I have traced clearly share with contemporary alter-globalists the sense that the planet, its peoples, and its problems must be understood and treated horizontally, not vertically.

This basic structural orientation is arguably the starting point for any ethical attitude to the world. In the preface to *The Worlding Project: Doing Cultural Studies in the Era of Globalization,* David Watson describes how that volume's contributors collectively seek to present "a whole new way to globalize. . . . For this is a globalization filled with human potential: respecting differences and exchanging ideas, synthesizing rather than stratifying, opening the marketplace rather than seeking out new markets, and acknowledging the possibilities of change rather than accepting the model of capitalism's last man standing."[18] Watson's diction reflects our twenty-first-century moment, but his sentiments were largely shared, I think, by those Romantics who understood, implicitly or explicitly, the ethical obligations that increasing global interconnectedness both facilitates and necessitates. Moreover, the Scottish Enlighteners' theorizations, and their Romantic successors' literary deployments of the enhanced mobility of affect and intellect adequate to their globalizing era, are still being more fully developed. We live at a time, as Pheng Cheah describes, in which "the various material networks of globalization have formed a world that is interconnected enough to generate political institutions and nongovernmental organizations (NGOs) that have a global reach in their regulatory functions as well as global forms of mass-based political consciousness or popular feelings of belonging to a shared world."[19]

Cheah is somewhat skeptical of these claims, and rightly so; nevertheless, he ultimately endorses a position that sees emancipatory possibilities in the conceptual developments of contemporary globalization[20]—developments that the Scottish Enlighteners and Romantics discussed in this book surely helped pioneer.

This brings me to consider briefly the second question posed above: how might Romanticism begin to look different when it is brought into focus, both as a movement (as problematic as that designation remains) and as an era, through the lens of long-durational globalization? To choose one possible avenue: a fuller appreciation of the global dynamics informing and permeating the work of many Romantics—especially those, like Radcliffe, Hemans, Byron, and Scott, who purposefully and successfully engaged a large reading public—provides a counterweight to the arguments of critics, like Michael Löwy and Robert Sayre, who see Romanticism as fundamentally backward-looking and anti-modern.[21] Certainly, some authors and strains of British Romanticism are driven by nostalgia and melancholy, and I do not want to be misunderstood as claiming that the Romantics—even the popular and well-compensated ones—were free from anxiety regarding the present and future state of things.[22] But the iterations of Romantic globalism I have sought to recover and unpack in this book do present a fundamentally more optimistic side of British Romanticism, one that also moves away from (for example) Baucom's largely condemnatory account of its dehumanizing, "speculative" tendencies and returns to greater visibility its idealistic, egalitarian, and progressive dynamics.[23]

Now more than ever, these may be precisely the Romantic elements we most need to recall. In *Not for Profit: Why Democracy Needs the Humanities*, Martha Nussbaum argues forcefully for the value of humanistic teaching and learning in our globalized age. Although she runs the risk of reducing the humanities to a set of narrowly utilitarian functions, Nussbaum's position is not the Arnoldian construction of literature as a secular religion whose lessons must be learned by heart; rather, it is closer to the Shelleyan vision of literature as a vehicle for enhancing one's abilities to feel, authentically and deeply, connections to and with others. In a passage that explicitly recalls the cosmopolitanism of the eighteenth century, Nussbaum asserts that the study of history, literature, and the other arts can help students become "citizens of the world, meaning people who see their own nation as part of a complex interlocking world, in economic, political, and cultural relationships with other nations and peoples."[24] It is difficult to imagine language and sentiments that would echo more precisely those of the late-eighteenth- and early-nineteenth-century Britons whose writings I have examined here. If *Romantic Globalism* has succeeded in opening up new, globally aware avenues of inquiry for future studies to explore, extend, and revise, then so much the better—both for our understanding of Romanticism, and for our understanding of our own global moment.

NOTES

INTRODUCTION

1. Samuel Taylor Coleridge, "Fears in Solitude," in William Wordsworth and Samuel Taylor Coleridge, *Lyrical Ballads and Related Writings*, eds. William Richey and Daniel Robinson (Boston: Houghton Mifflin, 2002), 11. 173-78. Subsequent citations appear parenthetically.

2. The word "globalization" first appears in the Webster dictionary in 1961, and the Supplement to the *Oxford English Dictionary* in 1972; see Suman Gupta, *Globalization and Literature* (Malden, MA: Polity, 2009), 6.

3. I borrow the phrase "global imaginary" from Manfred Steger, *The Rise of the Global Imaginary: Political Ideologies from the French Revolution to the Global War on Terror* (Oxford: Oxford University Press, 2008).

4. Zygmunt Bauman, *Globalization: The Human Consequences* (New York: Columbia University Press, 1998), 2.

5. Manfred Steger, *Globalization: A Very Short Introduction* (New York: Oxford University Press, 2003), 13.

6. Bill Ashcroft, *Post-Colonial Transformation* (New York: Routledge, 2001), 213.

7. See Arjun Appadurai, *Modernity at Large: Cultural Dimensions of Globalization* (Minneapolis: University of Minnesota Press, 1996); Carlo Galli, *Political Spaces and Global War*, ed. Adam Sitze, trans. Elisabeth Fay (Minneapolis: University of Minnesota Press, 2010); Michael Hardt and Antonio Negri, *Empire* (Cambridge, MA: Harvard University Press, 2000); Fredric Jameson, "Notes on Globalization as a Philosophical Issue," in *The Cultures of Globalization*, eds. Jameson and Masao Miyoshi (Durham, NC: Duke University Press, 1998), 54-77.

8. Appadurai, *Modernity at Large*, 27.

9. See Steger, *Globalization: A Very Short Introduction*, 2nd ed. (New York: Oxford University Press, 2009), 20.

10. See, for example, Liah Greenfeld, *Nationalism: Five Roads to Modernity* (Cambridge, MA: Harvard University Press, 1993).

11. See Benedict Anderson, *Imagined Communities: Reflections on the Origin and Spread of Nationalism*, revised ed. (London: Verso, 1991); Ernest Gellner, *Nations and Nationalism*, 2nd ed. (Ithaca, NY: Cornell University Press, 2006).

12. Robertson's five phases are "germinal" (1400–1750); "incipient" (1750–1875); "take-off" (1875–1925); "struggle for hegemony" (1925–69); and "uncertainty" (1969-present). See Roland Robertson, *Globalization* (New York: Sage, 1992), 25–31; quoted in Paul Jay, *Global Matters: The Transnational Turn in Literary Studies* (Ithaca, NY: Cornell University Press, 2010), 36.

13. See, e.g., Jay, *Global Matters*, 37.

14. See Immanuel Wallerstein, *The Modern World System I: Capitalist Agriculture and the Origins of the European World-Economy in the Sixteenth Century* (New York: Academic Press, 1974). Wallerstein's oeuvre is impressively large and varied; for a helpful outline of his methods and main theses, see his *World-Systems Analysis: An Introduction* (Durham, NC: Duke University Press, 2004).

15. Hardt and Negri, *Empire*, 9–10.

16. Saskia Sassen, "Spatialities and Temporalities of the Global: Elements for a Theorization," *Public Culture* 12.1 (2000): 218. Significantly, Hardt and Negri have begun to subscribe to this view as well, endorsing Sassen's work in their *Commonwealth* (Cambridge, MA: Belknap Press, 2009), 223–24.

17. See, for example, James Annesley, *Fictions of Globalization: Consumption, the Market, and the Contemporary American Novel* (London: Continuum, 2009); Vilashini Cooppan, *Worlds Within: National Narratives and Global Connections in Postcolonial Writing* (Stanford, CA: Stanford University Press, 2009); Gupta, *Globalization and Literature*; Jay, *Global Matters*. Special journal issues of note include "Globalizing Literary Studies," ed. Giles Gunn, *PMLA* 116.1 (January 2001): 16–188; "Anglophone Literatures and Global Cultures," eds. Susie O'Brien and Imre Szeman, *South Atlantic Quarterly* 100.3 (Summer 2001): 603–852.

18. C. A. Bayly, *The Birth of the Modern World, 1780–1914: Global Connections and Comparisons* (Malden, MA: Blackwell, 2004), 41.

19. Bayly, *Birth of the Modern World*, 45.

20. James Belich, *Replenishing the Earth: The Settler Revolution and the Rise of the Anglo-World, 1783–1939* (Oxford: Oxford University Press: 2009), 21.

21. Belich, *Replenishing the Earth*, 23.

22. A related intellectual trend has been the recent rise of "personal" or "domestic" histories of empire; see, for example, Linda Colley, *The Ordeal of Elizabeth Marsh: A Woman in World History* (New York: Pantheon, 2007); Emma Rothschild, *The Inner Life of Empires: An Eighteenth-Century History* (Princeton, NJ: Princeton University Press, 2011).

23. John Darwin, *The Empire Project: The Rise and Fall of the British World-System, 1830–1970* (Cambridge: Cambridge University Press, 2009), xi. Darwin both draws on and revises the path-breaking work of John Gallagher and Ronald Robinson; see esp. their formative article, "The Imperialism of Free Trade," *Economic History Review* 6.1 (1953): 1–15.

24. See Bernard Porter, *The Absent-Minded Imperialists: Empire, Society, and Culture in Britain* (Oxford: Oxford University Press, 2005).

25. Richard Price, "One Big Thing: Britain, Its Empire, and Their Imperial Culture," *Journal of British Studies* 45.3 (July 2006): 608.

26. Jonathan Arac and Harriet Ritvo, eds., *Macropolitics of Nineteenth-Century Literature: Nationalism, Exoticism, Imperialism* (Durham, NC: Duke University Press, 1995).

27. See Edward Said, *Orientalism* (New York: Vintage, 1978).

28. Edward Said, *Culture and Imperialism* (New York: Vintage, 1993), 90. Although Said's perceived besmirching of Austen's wholesomeness set off a firestorm of condemnation in the popular press, it has also been criticized on more substantive interpretive grounds; for an excellent recent overview of Said's interpretation and subsequent critical developments, see Elizabeth A. Bohls, *Romantic Literature and Postcolonial Studies* (Edinburgh: Edinburgh University Press, 2013), 40–47.

29. See, e.g., Gayatri Chakravorty Spivak, *An Aesthetic Education in the Era of Globalization* (Cambridge, MA: Harvard University Press, 2012); Vivek Chibber, *Postcolonial Theory and the Specter of Capital* (London: Verso, 2013). Whereas Spivak, one of the originators of postcolonial theory, has begun to find its key terms in need of revision but still productive, Chibber questions the very assumptions on which postcolonialism, especially in its Subaltern Studies form, founds its analytical approach.

30. Saree Makdisi, *Romantic Imperialism: Universal Empire and the Culture of Modernity* (Cambridge: Cambridge University Press, 1998), 16–17.

31. Cf. Makdisi's interpretation of Blake as a critic of both imperialism and early globalization in *William Blake and the Impossible History of the 1790s* (Chicago: University of Chicago Press, 2003), as well as his synoptic accounts of a variety of Romantics' positions on empire in recent pieces on "Romantic Cultural Imperialism," in *The Cambridge History of English Romantic Literature*, ed. James Chandler (Cambridge: Cambridge University Press, 2009), 601–20, and "Worldly Romanticism," introduction, special issue of *Nineteenth-Century Literature* 65.4 (March 2011): 429–32. Published too recently to be integrated sufficiently into this introduction, another recent study that appears cut from the same cloth as Makdisi's early work, inasmuch as its ingenious readings of Romantic texts seem to assume their production in an always already essentially imperial atmosphere, is Dermot Ryan's *Technologies of Empire: Writing, Imagination, and the Making of Imperial Networks, 1750–1820* (Newark, NJ: University of Delaware Press, 2013).

32. Katie Trumpener, *Bardic Nationalism: The Romantic Novel and the British Empire* (Princeton, NJ: Princeton University Press, 1997); Nigel Leask, *British Romantic Writers and the East: Anxieties of Empire* (Cambridge: Cambridge University Press, 1993); Nigel Leask, *Curiosity and the Aesthetics of Travel Writing, 1770–1840: 'From an Antique Land'* (Cambridge: Cambridge University Press, 2002); Alan Bewell, *Romanticism and Colonial Disease* (Baltimore: Johns Hopkins University Press, 1999); Rajani Sudan, *Fair Exotics: Xenophobic Subjects in English Literature, 1720–1850* (Philadelphia: University of Pennsylvania Press, 2002); Elizabeth Chang, *Britain's Chinese Eye: Literature, Empire, and Aesthetics in Nineteenth-Century Britain* (Stanford, CA: Stanford University Press, 2010); Tara Ghoshal Wallace, *Imperial Characters: Home and Periphery in Eighteenth-Century Literature* (Lewisburg, PA: Bucknell University Press, 2010); Laura Doyle, *Freedom's Empire: Race and the Rise of the Novel in Atlantic Modernity, 1640–1940* (Durham, NC: Duke University Press, 2008). As well, John Barrell's *The Infection of Thomas de Quincey: A Psychopathology of Imperialism* (New Haven, CT: Yale University Press, 1991) deserves mention as an important precursor to many of these more recent texts. Two additional studies published too recently to be adequately accounted for in my text, but which look to offer greater nuance for thinking the intertwined development of imperial and global dynamics, are James Mulholland, *Sounding Imperial: Poetic Voice and the Politics of Empire* (Baltimore: The Johns Hopkins University Press, 2013) and Eugenia Zuroski Jenkins, *A Taste for China: English Subjectivity and the Prehistory of Orientalism* (Oxford: Oxford University Press, 2013). Jenkins, for example, argues that the East/West binarism described so influentially

by Said was not natural but instead arose in mid-eighteenth century Britain as a "counterintuitive rejection of a deeply rooted aristocratic paradigm, namely the fluidity of cultural identities in a cosmopolitan world" (188).

33. Ian Baucom, *Specters of the Atlantic: Finance Capital, Slavery, and the Philosophy of History* (Durham, NC: Duke University Press, 2005), 106. Baucom's book likewise participates in ongoing debates about the production of modern disciplinary knowledges, and the intersection of literary and other genres of facticity, being carried out most thoroughly by Mary Poovey in her *A History of the Modern Fact: Problems of Knowledge in the Sciences of Wealth and Society* (Chicago: University of Chicago Press, 1998) and *Genres of the Credit Economy: Mediating Value in Eighteenth- and Nineteenth-Century Britain* (Chicago: University of Chicago Press, 2008).

34. See Samuel Baker, *Written on the Water: British Romanticism and the Maritime Empire of Culture* (Charlottesville: University of Virginia Press, 2010).

35. Mary Favret, *War at a Distance: Romanticism and the Making of Modern Wartime* (Princeton, NJ: Princeton University Press, 2010), 12.

36. Kevis Goodman, *Georgic Modernity and British Romanticism: Poetry and the Mediation of History* (Cambridge: Cambridge University Press, 2004), 67–105.

37. See Penny Fielding, *Scotland and the Fictions of Geography: North Britain, 1760–1830* (Cambridge: Cambridge University Press, 2008); Richard Maxwell, *The Historical Novel in Europe, 1650–1950* (Cambridge: Cambridge University Press, 2009); Michael Wiley, *Romantic Migrations: Local, National, and Transnational Dispositions* (Houndmills, Basingstoke: Palgrave Macmillan, 2008); Esther Wohlgemut, *Romantic Cosmopolitanism* (Houndmills, Basingstoke: Palgrave Macmillan, 2009).

38. Jay, *Global Matters*, 41.

39. Jürgen Osterhammel and Niels P. Petersson, *Globalization: A Short History*, trans. Dona Geyer (Princeton, NJ: Princeton University Press, 2005), 17–18.

40. A very short list might include Richmond Barbour, *Before Orientalism: London's Theatre of the East, 1576–1626* (Cambridge: Cambridge University Press, 2003); Jonathan Burton, *Traffic and Turning: Islam and English Drama, 1579–1624* (Newark, NJ: University of Delaware Press, 2005); Robert Markley, *The Far East and the English Imagination, 1600–1730* (Cambridge: Cambridge University Press, 2006). See also the recent collection *A Companion to the Global Renaissance*, ed. Jyotsna G. Singh (Malden, MA: Wiley-Blackwell, 2009).

41. Recent examples of important studies in the long eighteenth century that move well beyond Britain's canonical and national borders include Srinivas Aravamudan, *Enlightenment Orientalism: Resisting the Rise of the Novel* (Chicago: University of Chicago Press, 2012); Tim Fulford, Debbie Lee, and Peter J. Kitson, *Literature, Science and Exploration in the Romantic Era: Bodies of Knowledge* (Cambridge: Cambridge University Press, 2004); Simon Gikandi, *Slavery and the Culture of Taste* (Princeton, NJ: Princeton University Press, 2011); *The Global Eighteenth Century*, ed. Felicity Nussbaum (Baltimore: The Johns Hopkins University Press, 2003).

42. Kapil Raj, *Relocating Modern Science: Circulation and the Construction of Knowledge in South Asia and Europe, 1650–1900* (Houndmills, Basingstoke: Palgrave Macmillan, 2007), 10. In order better to fit the somewhat different interests of my project, I have elided the word "scientific" from Raj's quotation.

43. This argument (as well as a mostly different set of spotlighted texts and authors) sets the present study apart from Elizabeth Bohls' recent *Romantic Literature and Postcolonial Studies*, which was published as *Romantic Globalism* was going to press. As part of a series aimed at "introducing the diverse body of postcolonial criticism, theory and scholarship in

literary studies" through historically specific studies (vii), Bohls' text forthrightly assumes "the fact of empire" (2) and the existence of "the imperial state" (6) in the Romantic era—two long-standing assumptions of literary historical postcolonial scholarship that my study seeks to complicate. In fact, however, many of Bohls' specific interpretations go well beyond these reifications, taking close account of what she elsewhere calls "the intimate interpenetration between metropole and colonies, the British Isles and the rest of the world" (11).

44. Jacques Derrida, "Globalization, Peace, and Cosmopolitanism," in *Negotiations: Interventions and Interviews, 1971–2001*, ed. and trans. Elizabeth Rottenberg (Stanford, CA: Stanford University Press, 2002), 374–75. The term "mondialisation" appears in Derrida's oeuvre at least as early as *Specters of Marx: The State of the Debt, the Work of Mourning, and the New International* (trans. Peggy Kamuf [New York and London: Routledge, 1994]), which many consider the text that inaugurated a new, more explicitly political phase of Derrida's career.

45. Jean-Luc Nancy, *The Creation of the World or Globalization*, trans. François Raffoul and David Pettigrew (Albany, NY: State University of New York Press, 2007), 28.

46. Robert Mitchell, "Global Flows: Romantic-era Terraforming," unpublished manuscript.

47. Here I draw on the terms of Seyla Benhabib's reading of Kant in *The Rights of Others: Aliens, Residents and Citizens* (Cambridge: Cambridge University Press, 2004), 25–48.

48. Franco Moretti, *Graphs, Maps, Trees* (London: Verso, 2005), 18–19.

49. See William St. Clair, *The Reading Nation in the Romantic Period* (Cambridge: Cambridge University Press, 2004).

50. Robert Crawford, "Walter Scott and European Union," *Studies in Romanticism* 40.1 (Spring 2001): 140.

51. See, for example, Miranda Burgess' recent reconsideration of the period's treatment of feeling in the context of "the global circumstances of British Romanticism" (245), in "Transport: Mobility, Anxiety, and the Romantic Poetics of Feeling," *Studies in Romanticism* 49.2 (Summer 2010): 229–60; and Adriana Craciun's rereading of Shelley's most famous novel in the context of the era's polar expeditions, in "Writing the Disaster: Franklin and Frankenstein," *Nineteenth-Century Literature* 65.4 (March 2011): 433–80.

52. David Simpson's *Romanticism, Nationalism, and the Revolt against Theory* (Chicago: University of Chicago Press, 1993) remains one of the most fruitful studies of the context and legacy of Burkean conservatism.

53. See Manuel Castells, *The Information Age*, 3 vols. (Malden, MA: Blackwell, 1996, 1998, 2000), esp. vol. 1, *Economy, Society, and Culture—The Rise of the Network Society*.

54. See, e.g., Paul Virilio, *Speed and Politics*, trans. Mark Polizzotti (Los Angeles: Semiotext[e], 1986), and more recently *The Great Accelerator*, trans. Julie Rose (Malden, MA: Polity, 2012).

55. Cf. Peter Sloterdijk's observation, vis-à-vis the obstacles to global democracy today, that "money and images are the two great, vital systems that can be deployed for the steering of mass needs. Language, on the other hand, is increasingly marginalized": "The Space of Global Capitalism and Its Imaginary Imperialism: An Interview with Peter Sloteridjk," in *Peter Sloterdijk's Spherological Poetics of Being*, eds. Willem Schinkel and Liesbeth Noordegraaf-Eelens (Amsterdam: University of Amsterdam Press, 2011), 187. On the role of media in shaping knowledge production and transmission in the long-eighteenth-century and Romantic eras, see, e.g., *This Is Enlightenment*, eds. Clifford Siskin and William Warner (Chicago: University of Chicago Press, 2010); Maureen N. McLane, *Balladeering, Minstrelsy, and the Making of British Romantic Poetry* (Cambridge: Cambridge University Press, 2008).

56. Cf. Bruno Latour, *Irreductions*, in *The Pasteurization of France*, trans. Alan Sheridan and John Law (Cambridge, MA: Harvard University Press, 1988), esp. 201–3 for his parable-like account of how Portuguese colonizers succeeded, not because they were stronger or more modern that the natives they eventually overwhelmed, but because "they came *together*, each one *separated* and *isolated* in his virtue, but *all supported* by the whole" (italics in original). Latour expands this networked account of imperial activity in *On the Modern Cult of the Factish Gods*, trans. Catherine Porter and Heather Maclean (Durham, NC: Duke University Press, 2010), esp. 1–66.

57. Immanuel Wallerstein, *Utopistics, or, Historical Choices of the Twenty-First Century* (New York: New Press, 1998), 1.

CHAPTER ONE

1. The phrase's first recorded usage is by W. R. Scott in 1900; see John Robertson, *The Case for the Enlightenment: Scotland and Naples, 1680–1760* (Cambridge: Cambridge University Press, 2005), 25.

2. David Hume, *The Letters of David Hume*, ed. J. Y. T. Grieg, 2 vols. (Oxford: Oxford University Press, 1932), 1: 255.

3. Richard B. Sher, *The Enlightenment and the Book: Scottish Authors and Their Publishers in Eighteenth-Century Britain, Ireland, and America* (Chicago: University of Chicago Press, 2006), 44.

4. See Alexander Broadie, *The Scottish Enlightenment: The Historical Age of the Historical Nation* (Edinburgh: Birlinn, 2007), 7–13, for a helpful overview of the ways in which, despite appearances to the contrary, seventeenth-century Scotland laid the foundations for its eighteenth-century intellectual flowering. See also David Allan, *Virtue, Learning, and the Scottish Enlightenment* (Edinburgh: Edinburgh University Press, 1993), 29–146.

5. David Hume, *A Treatise of Human Nature*, 2nd ed., eds. L. A. Selby-Bigge and P. H. Nidditch (Oxford: Oxford University Press, 1978), xvi.

6. Contributions were also made in the maths and sciences, but these have generally received less attention; see Broadie, *Scottish Enlightenment*, 186–218.

7. See my *Feeling British: Sympathy and National Identity in Scottish and English Writing, 1707–1832* (Lewisburg, PA: Bucknell University Press, 2007), esp. 26–60. Cf. Juliet Shields, *Sentimental Literature and Anglo-Scottish Identity, 1745–1820* (Cambridge: Cambridge University Press, 2010), esp. 7–12.

8. See Jürgen Habermas, *The Philosophical Discourse of Modernity: Twelve Lectures*, trans. Frederick Lawrence (Cambridge, MA: The MIT Press, 1987), esp. lectures five and six.

9. Jonathan Israel, *Enlightenment Contested: Philosophy, Modernity, and the Emancipation of Man, 1670–1752* (Oxford: Oxford University Press, 2006), 52.

10. Roland Robertson, *Globalization*, 8; qtd. in Gupta, *Globalization and Literature*, 4.

11. Fredric Jameson, "The Realist Floor-Plan," in *On Signs*, ed. Marshall Blonsky (Baltimore and London: The Johns Hopkins University Press, 1985), 373. In fact, Scottish Enlightenment mathematicians were integral to the development and popularization of the calculus which enabled formulae like Jameson's.

12. A few years later, Jameson would develop his concept of "cognitive mapping" as a way to describe how ideologies manifest themselves as sets of internalized conceptual frameworks. With regard to the cognitive maps made available by British imperialism at its height, for example, Jameson recognized that "the truth of [any individual] experience

no longer coincides with the place in which it takes place. . . . [I]t is bound up with the whole colonial system of the British Empire" ("Cognitive Mapping," in *Marxism and the Interpretation of Culture*, eds. Cary Nelson and Lawrence Grossberg [Urbana: University of Illinois Press, 1988], 349–50). See also Goodman's redeployment of this passage in *Georgic Modernity and British Romanticism*, 6.

13. Matthew Wickman, "Alba Newton and Alasdair Gray," in *Scotland as Science Fiction*, ed. Caroline McCracken-Flesher (Lewisburg, PA: Bucknell University Press, 2012), 176–77.

14. On the Scottish Enlightenment's contributions to global geography, see the work of Charles W. J. Withers, e.g. "Geography, Natural History and the Eighteenth-Century Enlightenment: Putting the World in Place," *History Workshop Journal* 39 (1995): 137–63.

15. Uday Singh Mehta, *Liberalism and Empire: A Study in Nineteenth-Century British Liberal Thought* (Chicago and London: University of Chicago Press, 1999), 40. See also Dipesh Chakrabarty's observation that Enlightenment thinkers like Hume and Smith "often offered as universally applicable hypotheses that were clearly derived from very particular and specific cultural practices of the societies they themselves knew" (*Provincializing Europe: Postcolonial Thought and Historical Difference*, 2nd ed. [Princeton, NJ: Princeton University Press, 2007], 127).

16. The formulation "Scottish past/British present," it should be noted, may be literally true on the political level, but nevertheless oversimplifies the continuation of strong feelings of Scottish nationalism in at least some sectors, even within the parameters of the 1707 Union. See, for example, Graeme Morton, *Unionist Nationalism: Governing Urban Scotland, 1830–1860* (Edinburgh: Tuckwell Press, 1999).

17. This argument recurs at the end of the later essay "Of Commerce," where Hume states that "the fewer goods or possessions . . . any people enjoy, the fewer quarrels are likely to arise amongst them, and the less necessity will there be for a settled police or regular authority to protect and defend them from foreign enemies, or from each other" (*Essays: Moral, Political, and Literary*, ed. Eugene F. Miller [Indianapolis: Liberty Fund, 1985], 267).

18. For a discussion of this concept, which was explicitly developed in Foucault's lectures rather than his published books, see Michel Foucault, *Security, Territory, Population: Lectures at the Collège de France, 1977–78*, ed. Michel Senellart, trans. Graham Burchell (New York: Picador, 2007), 108–9.

19. Hume more or less repeats this argument in his later essay "Of the Origin of Government." There, however, he simplifies his position by omitting to mention that commerce, like war, can be the cause of governmental formations. Whether this represents a change in Hume's thinking or simply an omission for the sake of abridgement is a matter of speculation. In his *Enquiry Concerning the Principles of Morals* (1st ed. 1751), he likewise states that "nations can subsist without intercourse" (*Enquiries Concerning Human Understanding and Concerning the Principles of Morals*, 3rd ed., eds. L. A. Selby-Bigge and P. H. Nidditch [Oxford: Clarendon Press, 1975], 206). This remark's context, however, is important: Hume is distinguishing between promises made by individuals, which are binding because humans cannot survive without each other, and treaties made by nations, which are not. Russell Hardin notes that "[p]erhaps in the increasingly globalized world in which at least economic interactions are thick and manifold, states will begin to seem like persons in the extent to which they do and must rely upon each other": *David Hume: Moral and Political Theorist* (New York: Oxford University Press, 2007), 131.

20. In preparation for writing these pieces, Hume read closely a variety of earlier French and British writers on economic themes; see John Robertson, *Case for the Enlightenment*, 363.

21. Joseph Addison, *The Spectator* 69 (May 19, 1711), in *The Commerce of Everyday Life: Selections from* The Tatler *and* The Spectator, ed. Erin Mackie (Houndmills, Basingstoke: Palgrave Macmillan, 1998), 204, 206.

22. David Hume, "Of Commerce," in *Essays: Moral, Political, and Literary*, ed. Eugene F. Miller (Indianapolis: Liberty Fund, 1985), 253–67. Subsequent citations to this and other essays drawn from this collection ("Of the Balance of Trade," "Of the Jealousy of Trade," "Of the Balance of Power," "Of the Study of History") will appear parenthetically.

23. Saskia Sassen, *A Sociology of Globalization* (New York: W. W. Norton, 2007), 3.

24. Galli, *Political Spaces and Global War*, 57 (emphasis in original).

25. Eugene F. Miller, note 3 to Hume's "Of the Balance of Trade," in *Essays*, 309.

26. Claudia M. Schmidt, *David Hume: Reason in History* (University Park, PA: Penn State University Press, 2003), 307.

27. For an in-depth discussion and analysis of the price-specie-flow mechanism and its place in Hume's economic theory, see John Berdell, *International Trade and Economic Growth in Open Economies: The Classical Dynamics of Hume, Smith, Ricardo and Malthus* (Cheltenham, UK: Edward Elgar, 2002), 17–21. Berdell argues that, while Hume does not entirely renounce mercantilism, he unequivocally promotes "the desirability of freer trade" among nations (20).

28. As Wallerstein shrewdly observes, however, while contemporary capitalists pay lip service to free trade, in practice they rely heavily on protectionist and domestic-business-friendly governmental policies; see *World-Systems Analysis: An Introduction*, 25–26.

29. Robertson, *Case for the Enlightenment*, 370.

30. Karen O'Brien, "Poetry, Knowledge, and Imperial Globalization," in *The Postcolonial Enlightenment: Eighteenth-Century Colonialism and Postcolonial Theory*, eds. Daniel Carey and Lynn Festa (Cambridge: Cambridge University Press, 2009), 286. I particularly disagree with Israel's reductive portrayal of Hume as a tacit supporter of empire; see Israel, *Enlightenment Contested*, 593. Cf. Sankar Muthu, *Enlightenment against Empire* (Princeton, NJ: Princeton University Press, 2003), for a spirited defense of many Enlighteners' grave reservations concerning imperialism.

31. Mehta, *Liberalism and Empire*, 38.

32. For more on the influence of Turgot, Quesnay, Condorcet, and the other physiocrats on Smith, see Andrew S. Skinner, *A System of Social Science: Papers Relating to Adam Smith*, 2nd ed. (Oxford: Oxford University Press, 1996), 114–16, 192–93; Emma Rothschild, *Economic Sentiments: Adam Smith, Condorcet, and the Enlightenment* (Cambridge, MA: Harvard University Press, 2001), 81–82; Donald Winch, *Riches and Poverty: An Intellectual History of Political Economy in Britain, 1750–1834* (Cambridge: Cambridge University Press, 1996), 91. Smith himself critiques what he calls the "agricultural systems of political oeconomy" in Book 4, Chapter 9 of *Wealth of Nations*. (He also repeatedly, and somewhat confusingly, refers to mercantilism as "the commercial system.") For recent accounts of Steuart's work, see Poovey, *Genres of the Credit Economy*, 127–43; Ikuo Omori, "The 'Scottish Triangle' in the Shaping of Political Economy: David Hume, Sir James Steuart, and Adam Smith," in *The Rise of Political Economy in the Scottish Enlightenment*, eds. Tatsuya Sakamoto and Hideo Tanaka (London: Routledge, 2003), 103–18.

33. Winch, *Riches and Poverty*, 19.

34. Cf. Siskin's observation that, throughout his career, Smith (and, to a lesser extent, many of the other literati) was devoted to creating "systems of a very particular kind: master systems that would simplify and popularize by arranging and methodizing *all* earlier sys-

tems": "Mediated Enlightenment: The System of the World," in *This Is Enlightenment*, eds. Siskin and William Warner (Chicago: University of Chicago Press, 2010), 168.

35. For brief, recent summaries of Smith's basic economic theories as laid out in Books I–III of *Wealth of Nations*, see Skinner, "Economic Theory," in *The Cambridge Companion to the Scottish Enlightenment*, ed. Alexander Broadie (Cambridge: Cambridge University Press, 2003), 194–200; Geoffrey Ingham, *Capitalism* (Malden, MA: Polity, 2008), 7–13.

36. Immanuel Wallerstein, *The Capitalist World-Economy* (Cambridge: Cambridge University Press, 1979), 66.

37. Adam Smith, *The Correspondence of Adam Smith*, eds. Ernest Campbell Mossner and Ian Simpson Ross (Oxford: Clarendon, 1977), 251; quoted in Rothschild, *Economic Sentiments*, 7.

38. Adam Smith, *An Inquiry into the Nature and Causes of the Wealth of Nations*, 2 vols., ed. R. H. Campbell and A. S. Skinner (Indianapolis: Liberty Fund, 1981), I.429, I.451. Subsequent citations will appear parenthetically by volume and (continuous) page numbers. On the seventeenth- and eighteenth-century preoccupation with the "general domain" of wealth, see Michel Foucault, *The Order of Things: An Archaeology of the Human Sciences* (New York: Vintage, 1970), 166.

39. See, for example, Rothschild, *Economic Sentiments*, Chapter Two.

40. See, e.g. Ingham's remark that "[p]ro-globalization arguments for the extension of market capitalism are fundamentally Smithian" (*Capitalism* 14).

41. See Rothschild, *Economic Sentiments*, 52–71, for the arc of Smith's posthumous reputation from subversive to conservative. Cf. Bernard Semmel, *The Rise of Free-Trade Imperialism: Classical Political Economy, the Empire of Free Trade and Imperialism, 1750–1850* (Cambridge: Cambridge University Press, 1970).

42. Quoted in Rothschild, *Economic Sentiments*, 56.

43. Richard F. Teichgraeber III, *"Free Trade" and Moral Philosophy: Rethinking the Sources of Adam Smith's* Wealth of Nations (Durham, NC: Duke University Press, 1986), 166. One could argue that Smith's vision was only realized—and then only imperfectly—with the late-twentieth century establishment of the single-market European Union.

44. See Skinner, *System of Social Science*, 186–87, for a summary of these and other features of the economic relations between Britain and North America at the time of Smith's writing.

45. Deidre Shauna Lynch, *The Economy of Character: Novels, Market Culture, and the Business of Inner Meaning* (Chicago: University of Chicago Press, 1998), 25.

46. Thus Smith, despite his clear affiliation with what Israel sees as the essentially conservative "moderate Enlightenment," takes up a position—albeit from an economic rather than a moral or ontological standpoint—essentially similar to that of Israel's radical, anti-imperial Enlightenment. For a reading of Smith that cuts against this grain, however, see Dermot Ryan, *Technologies of Empire*, 17–39. Ryan's argument—that Smith's theory of the imagination facilitates systematic empire-building—is innovative but declines to engage fully with Smith's economic arguments against imperialism.

47. Ingham, *Capitalism*, 205.

48. Slavoj Žižek, *Tarrying with the Negative: Kant, Hegel, and the Critique of Ideology* (Durham, NC: Duke University Press, 1993), 209.

49. Wallerstein, *Capitalist World-Economy*, 162.

50. As Giovanni Arrighi notes with some bemusement, "Smith thought that the widening and deepening of exchanges in the world market economy would act as an unstoppable

equalizer of relations between the West and the non-West": *The Long Twentieth Century: Money, Power, and the Origins of Our Times* (London: Verso, 1994).

51. David Harvey, *Justice, Nature and the Geography of Difference* (Malden, MA: Blackwell, 1996), 295. The term was first popularized by Neil Smith in his *Uneven Development: Nature, Capital, and the Production of Space* (New York: Blackwell), 1984.

52. Cf. Jacques Derrida, "Plato's Pharmacy," in *Dissemination*, trans. Barbara Johnson (Chicago: University of Chicago Press, 1981), 63–171.

53. Cf. Samuel Baker's observation regarding James Mill's writings: "Drawing on Scottish Enlightenment stadial theory, Mill would subsequently do much to translate conjectural history into a prototypical theory of uneven development that accounted for global cultural difference as a function of differently paced economic life" (*Written on the Water*, 10).

54. Michel Foucault, *Discipline and Punish: The Birth of the Prison*, trans. Alan Sheridan (New York: Vintage, 1979), 31.

55. See James Chandler, *England in 1819: The Politics of Literary Culture and the Case of Romantic Historicism* (Chicago: University of Chicago Press, 1998).

56. For reasons that will become clear, I distinguish between conjectural history (as practical methodology) and stadial theory (as theoretical framework), rather than consolidate them into "stadial history," as is often done.

57. Broadie, *Scottish Enlightenment*, 47.

58. Hume, "Of the Study of History," in *Essays*, 566–67.

59. Quoted in Broadie, *Scottish Enlightenment*, 66.

60. Not all the literati approved of this method; Adam Ferguson, for example, disliked that "[o]ur method . . . too frequently, is to rest the whole on conjecture," and claimed to eschew such historiographical speculation in favor of analyzing "the character of man, as he now exists. . . .": *An Essay on the History of Civil Society* (New Brunswick, NJ: Transaction, 1980), 75, 3. Similarly, William Robertson "prided himself on his exact documentation" in such volumes as his *History of Scotland* (1759) and *History of the Reign of Emperor Charles V* (1769): see John Kenyon, *The History Men* (London: Weidenfeld and Nicolson, 1983), 64. In fact, both Ferguson and Robertson make ample use of conjecture at various points in their writings; nevertheless, Ferguson in particular differs from the other literati both in his scruples regarding the validity of conjectural history and in his strong pessimism regarding the tendency of civilized nations to fall into decay due to a weakening of social bonds and military vigor over time. He also subscribes to a stadial theory of history that involves only three stages (primitive, barbaric, commercial) rather than four. See, e.g., Gottlieb, *Feeling British*, 54–60.

61. Adam Smith, *Lectures on Jurisprudence*, ed. R. L. Meek, D. D. Raphael, and P. G. Stein (Indianapolis: Liberty Fund, 1982), 14.

62. Maureen Harkin, "Adam Smith's Missing History: Primitives, Progress, and Problems of Genre," *ELH* 72.2 (Summer 2005): 434.

63. See Murray G. H. Pittock, "Historiography," in *The Cambridge Companion to the Scottish Enlightenment*, ed. Alexander Broadie (Cambridge: Cambridge University Press, 2003), 259–62. David Spadafora names William Worthington's *Essay on the Scheme and Conduct, Procedure and Extent of Man's Redemption* (1750) as "probably the first piece of published writing in Britain to enunciate fully a doctrine of general progress" (*The Idea of Progress in Eighteenth-Century Britain* [New Haven, CT: Yale University Press, 1990], 228). For a wider-ranging study of earlier theories of progress, see Ronald L. Meek, *Social Science and the Ignoble Savage* (Cambridge: Cambridge University Press, 1976), 5–36.

64. Although it does not focus on the Scottish Enlightenment and was published too late for me to engage with in depth in this book, Tony Brown's *The Primitive, the Aesthetic, and the Savage: An Enlightenment Problematic* (Minneapolis: University of Minnesota Press, 2012) offers a number of insights on the three elements of his title as they proliferate and intersect in Enlightened discourse.

65. Quoted in Chandler, *England in 1819*, 108. As Chandler observes, Hartley's statement "make[s] it possible to conceptualize culture as a shared object of study for the fields of history and ethnography"—fields that the literati certainly did not see as mutually exclusive.

66. Chandler, *England in 1819*, 107.

67. The combination of conjectural history and stadial theory is deployed on several occasions by Smith in *Wealth of Nations*; the most extensive comes at the end of Book V, where Smith analyzes the changing costs of maintaining a national fighting force. See *Wealth of Nations* II.689–98.

68. Roxann Wheeler, *The Complexion of Race: Categories of Difference in Eighteenth-Century British Culture* (Philadelphia: University of Pennsylvania Press, 2000), 182. See also Meek, *Social Science and the Ignoble Savage*, 176.

69. Henry Home, Lord Kames, *Sketches of the History of Man*, 3 vols., ed. James A. Harris (Indianapolis, IN: Liberty Fund, 2007). Subsequent citations will appear parenthetically.

70. Mark Salber Phillips, *Society and Sentiment: Genres of Historical Writing in Britain, 1740–1820* (Princeton, NJ: Princeton University Press, 2000), 179.

71. Meek, *Social Science and the Ignoble Savage*, 160.

72. Timothy Fulford, *Romantic Indians: Native Americans, British Literature, and Transatlantic Culture, 1756–1830* (Cambridge: Cambridge University Press, 2006), 42.

73. Wheeler, *Complexion of Race*, 187.

74. For the book's full publishing history, see Sher, *Enlightenment and the Book*, 383, 642–43; for Millar's influence in Germany specifically, see Fania Oz-Salzburger, *Translating the Enlightenment: Scottish Civic Discourse in Eighteenth-Century Germany* (Oxford: Oxford University Press, 1995), 57, 65, 72. The citation regarding James Madison's ownership of a copy of *Origins* is on the back cover of the paperback Liberty Fund edition of John Millar, *The Origin of the Distinction of Ranks*, ed. Aaron Garrett (Indianapolis, IN: Liberty Fund, 2006). Subsequent references will appear parenthetically.

75. As Knud Haakonssen indicates, in Millar "the economic elements dominate and are necessary for any social change, but they are hardly ever alone or sufficient": *Natural Law and Moral Philosophy: From Grotius to the Scottish Enlightenment* (Cambridge: Cambridge University Press, 1996), 178.

76. These include "the fertility or barrenness of the soil, the nature of its productions, the species of labour requisite for procuring subsistence, the number of individuals collected together in one community, their proficiency in arts, the advantages which they enjoy for entering into mutual transactions and for maintaining an intimate correspondence" (Millar, *Origin of the Distinction*, 83–84).

77. Chandler, *England in 1819*, 129.

78. Nancy, *Creation of the World*, 28.

79. For a more detailed survey of Enlightened theories of climate's influence on civilizational development, see Jan Golinski, *British Weather and the Climate of Enlightenment* (Chicago: University of Chicago Press, 2007), esp. 170–202.

80. Rey Chow, *The Age of the World Target: Self-Referentiality in War, Theory, and Comparative Work* (Durham, NC: Duke University Press, 2006), 71.

81. See, for example, Millar's statement that men "[l]iving at ease, and in a state of tranquility, and engaged in the exercise of peaceable professions . . . become averse from every enterprise that may expose them to danger, or subject them to pain and uneasiness" (*An Historical View of the English Government*, eds. Mark Salber Phillips and Dale R. Smith [Indianapolis, IN: Liberty Fund, 2006], 751).

82. Reinhart Koselleck, "The Eighteenth Century as the Beginning of Modernity," in *The Practice of Conceptual History: Timing History, Spacing Concepts*, trans. Todd Samuel Presner and others (Stanford, CA: Stanford University Press, 2004), 166.

83. As many critics have observed, it seems likely that the Scottish literati were prompted to this recognition by the observation of uneven development in their own backyards, as it were, which is to say, in the highly obvious differences of wealth and situation between the underdeveloped Scottish Highlands, and the rapidly commercializing Lowlands.

84. See, e.g. Alain Badiou's comprehensive denunciation of globalization as merely the latest iteration of "imperial capitalism," in *The Rebirth of History: Times of Riots and Uprisings*, trans. Gregory Elliot (London: Verso, 2012), 9–12.

85. Hume's and Smith's positions on the slave trade are somewhat less clear. The latter opposed it (at least in writing) primarily on the grounds of its perceived economic inefficiency; Hume, based on the evidence of a notorious footnote in his essay "Of National Characters," seems to have believed in the natural inferiority of Africans, and therefore may have supported it. For a powerful examination of the Enlightenment's generally willful ignorance of actually existing slavery, and the consequences of that omission, see Susan Buck-Morss, *Hegel, Haiti, and Universal History* (Pittsburgh: University of Pittsburgh Press, 2009).

86. Michael Malherbe, "The Impact on Europe," in *The Cambridge Companion to the Scottish Enlightenment*, ed. Alexander Broadie (Cambridge: Cambridge University Press, 2003), 311; see 307–11 for a brief discussion of Hume's broad reception in eighteenth-century Germany before Kant. For a more thorough (and technical) account of Kant's answer to Hume, see Arthur Melnick, "Kant's Proofs of Substance and Causation," in *The Cambridge Companion to Kant and Modern Philosophy*, ed. Paul Guyer (Cambridge: Cambridge University Press, 2006), 215–17. For a contrasting view, i.e. one that questions the efficacy of Kant's response to Hume, see Cairns Craig, *Associationism and the Literary Imagination: From the Phantasmal Chaos* (Edinburgh: Edinburgh University Press, 2007), 48–51. A provocative contemporary rebuttal of Kant's transcendental analytic can be found in Quentin Meillassoux, *After Finitude: An Essay on the Necessity of Contingency*, trans. Ray Brassier (London: Continuum, 2008).

87. Oz-Salzburger, *Translating the Enlightenment*, 23.

88. Immanuel Kant, "Toward Perpetual Peace: A Philosophical Project," in *Practical Philosophy*, trans. and ed. Mary J. Gregor (Cambridge: Cambridge University Press, 1996), 320. Subsequent citations to this and *The Metaphysics of Morals* in the same volume will appear parenthetically. See also Pauline Kleingeld, "Kant's Theory of Peace," in *The Cambridge Companion to Kant and Modern Philosophy*, ed. Paul Guyer (Cambridge: Cambridge University Press, 2006), 481.

89. Elisabeth Ellis, *Kant's Politics: Provisional Theory for an Uncertain World* (New Haven, CT: Yale University Press, 2005), 75.

90. As Kant optimistically opines in his first definitive article, republics are naturally unlikely to seek war, since such an action requires the consent of citizens who are unlikely to give it.

91. Benhabib, *The Rights of Others*, 40–41.
92. See Kleingeld, "Kant's Theory of Peace," 480.
93. Kleingeld, "Kant's Theory of Peace," 477.
94. Ellis, *Kant's Politics*, 70.
95. Peter Fenves, *Late Kant: Towards Another Law of the Earth* (New York: Routledge, 2003), 92–113.
96. In Katerina Deligiorgi's helpful words, "the idea of perpetual peace retains a role in our practical deliberations, guiding our practices and aspirations within history," even as its prospect always recedes before us: *Kant and the Culture of Enlightenment* (Albany, NY: State University of New York Press, 2005), 127. For a much more skeptical treatment of Kant's ideas on the subject of world governance—one that finds him instituting a state of affairs that essentially clears the way for perpetual war against any enemy deemed "unjust"—see Daniel Heller-Roazen, *The Enemy of All: Piracy and the Law of Nations* (New York: Zone Books, 2009), 184–189. But Muthu defends Kant vigorously in *Enlightenment against Empire*, 196–99.
97. Cf. Oz-Salzburger, "The Political Theory of the Scottish Enlightenment," in *The Cambridge Companion to the Scottish Enlightenment*, ed. Alexander Broadie (Cambridge: Cambridge University Press, 2003), 157–77.
98. Robert J. Holton, *Cosmopolitanisms: New Thinking and New Directions* (Houndmills, Basingstoke: Palgrave Macmillan, 2009), 4.

CHAPTER TWO

1. The rapid dissemination of Enlightened ideas through the British public sphere's various outlets (including journals, newspapers, lending libraries, learned societies, public lecture series, and coffeehouses) likely contributed to its rapid modernization throughout the Romantic and Victorian eras. Cf. David Allan, *Making British Culture: English Readers and the Scottish Enlightenment, 1740–1830* (London: Routledge, 2008).
2. Max Horkheimer and Theodor Adorno, *Dialectic of Enlightenment*, ed. Gunzelin Schmid Noerr, trans. Edmund Jephcott (Stanford, CA: Stanford University Press, 2002), 1.
3. Horace Walpole, *The Castle of Otranto*, ed. W. S. Lewis, introduction and notes E. J. Clery (Oxford: Oxford University Press, 1996), 5.
4. Deidre Shauna Lynch, "Gothic Fiction," in *The Cambridge Companion to Fiction in the Romantic Era*, eds. Richard Maxwell and Katie Trumpener (Cambridge: Cambridge University Press, 2008), 47.
5. The ability of the Gothic novel's habitual reader to predict what will happen in any given Gothic text is precisely what leads Catherine Morland, the heroine of Austen's *Northanger Abbey* (1818), to expect to find villains and murderers even in her own rather mundane sphere of existence.
6. For some important representative examples, see Alan Bewell, *Wordsworth and the Enlightenment: Nature, Man, and Science in the Experimental Poetry* (New Haven, CT: Yale University Press, 1998); Miranda J. Burgess, *British Fiction and the Production of Social Order, 1740–1830* (Cambridge: Cambridge University Press, 2000); Peter Knox-Shaw, *Jane Austen and the Enlightenment* (Cambridge: Cambridge University Press, 2004); and the essays in *Enlightening Romanticism, Romancing the Enlightenment: British Novels from 1750 to 1832*, ed. Miriam L. Wallace (Aldershot, UK: Ashgate, 2009).

7. This link was first definitively made by Duncan Forbes, "The Rationalism of Sir Walter Scott," *The Cambridge Journal* 7 (1953): 20–35; see also Peter Garside, "Scott and the 'Philosophical Historians,'" *Journal for the History of Ideas* 36 (1975): 497–512; Graham McMaster, *Scott and Society* (Cambridge: Cambridge University Press, 1981); Ian Duncan, *Scott's Shadow: The Novel in Romantic Edinburgh* (Princeton, NJ: Princeton University Press, 2007), esp. 101–15.

8. See Stefan Andriopoulos, "The Invisible Hand: Supernatural Agency in Political Economy and the Gothic Novel," *ELH* 66.3 (Summer 1999): 739–58. On the Gothic's representations of progress, see esp. Mary Poovey, "Ideology in *The Mysteries of Udolpho*," *Criticism* 21 (1979): 307–30.

9. See my *Feeling British*, passim. This theme has been taken up even more recently in Shields, *Sentimental Literature and Anglo-Scottish Identity*.

10. On the conjunction of sympathy and abolitionism, see e.g. Brycchan Carey, *British Abolitionism and the Rhetoric of Sensibility: Writing, Sentiment, and Slavery, 1760–1807* (Houndmills, Basingstoke: Palgrave Macmillan, 2005); Christine Levecq, *Slavery and Sentiment: The Politics of Feeling in Black Atlantic Antislavery Writing, 1770–1860* (Durham, NH: University of New Hampshire Press, 2008).

11. I discuss the two "minor" novels published in Radcliffe's lifetime (*The Castles of Athlin and Dunbayne* [1789] and *A Sicilian Romance* [1790]), as well as locate the Radcliffean Gothic in a more complete generic context, in a quasi-companion piece to this chapter, "No Place Like Home: From Local to Global (and Back Again) in the Gothic Novel," in *Representing Place in British Literature and Culture, 1660–1830: From Local to Global*, eds. Gottlieb and Juliet Shields (Aldershot, UK: Ashgate, 2013), 85–101.

12. Markman Ellis, "Enlightenment or Illumination: The Spectre of Conspiracy in Gothic Fictions of the 1790s," in *Recognizing the Romantic Novel: New Histories of British Fiction, 1780–1830*, eds. Jillian Heydt-Stevenson and Charlotte Sussman (Liverpool: Liverpool University Press, 2008), 86. Although I take issue with several aspects of Ellis' argument—later in his chapter, he makes a (to my mind) dubious distinction between "British empiricism" and "Continental enlightenment," and his reading of Lewis' *The Monk* differs greatly from my own—I share his desire to demonstrate the deep connections between the Gothic and the Enlightenment. For one of the few readings of the Gothic to make these connections explicit, see James P. Carson, "Enlightenment, Popular Culture, and the Gothic," in *The Cambridge Companion to the Eighteenth-Century Novel*, ed. John Richetti (New York: Cambridge University Press, 1996), 255–76.

13. On Radcliffe's well-established use of the terms of Burkean aesthetics, see, for example, Angela Wright, *Gothic Fiction: A Reader's Guide to Essential Criticism* (Houndmills, Basingstoke: Palgrave Macmillan, 2007), 38–41. For intellectual points of contact between Radcliffe and the Scottish Enlightenment, see Knox-Shaw, *Jane Austen and the Enlightenment*, 111–14; and JoEllen DeLucia, "From the Female Gothic to a Feminist Theory of History: Ann Radcliffe and the Scottish Enlightenment," *The Eighteenth Century: Theory and Interpretation* 50.1 (2010): 101–15. DeLucia's main argument—that parallels can be drawn between the ways literati like Millar "used women's social status to gauge historical progress," and Radcliffe's own interests in these and related phenomena—complements my own sense that, regardless of whether Radcliffe actually read the Scottish Enlighteners, she was in tune with their primary theories. By contrast, although Stephen Ahern has also recently connected Radcliffe to the Enlightenment, he finds her depictions of character to be fundamentally antithetical to Enlightened understandings of psychology and moral volition; see his *Affected Sensibilities: Romantic Excess and the Genealogy of the Novel, 1680–1810* (New York: AMS Press, 2007), 151–72.

14. E. J. Clery, *The Rise of Supernatural Fiction, 1762–1800* (Cambridge: Cambridge University Press, 1995), 114.

15. The connection between these two phenomena is implicit in the fact that Smith famously preceded *Wealth of Nations* with *Theory of Moral Sentiments*. Moreover, the much-remarked apparent incongruity between these seminal treatises is resolved by the recognition that, in both, Smith not only posits circulation (of sentiments, of money) as the basis of social cohesion, but also confirms the centrality of the sympathetic imagination to sociability, since in each type of exchange individuals must imaginatively project themselves into others' positions in order to achieve mutually satisfactory outcomes.

16. On the conjunction of sympathetic and economic theories more generally in the period, see Robert Mitchell, *Sympathy and the State in the Romantic Era: Systems, State Finance, and the Shadows of Futurity* (New York: Routledge, 2007).

17. Quoted in Richter Norton, *Mistress of Udolpho: The Life of Ann Radcliffe* (Liverpool: Liverpool University Press, 1999), 1.

18. This tradition of snubbing by male critics has been carried on, as recently as 2004, by Terry Eagleton, whose *The English Novel: An Introduction* (Oxford: Blackwell, 2004) omits even a single mention of Radcliffe.

19. Ellen Moers, *Literary Women* (Garden City, NY: Doubleday, 1976), 126.

20. See Poovey, "Ideology in *The Mysteries of Udolpho*"; Burgess, *British Fiction and the Production of Social Order*, 169. For a more extended account of the reputational ups and downs of the Gothic genre, see Terry Castle, "The Gothic Novel," in *Boss Ladies, Watch Out! Essays on Women, Sex, and Writing* (New York: Routledge, 2002), 73–107.

21. Cannon Schmitt, "Techniques of Terror, Technologies of Nationality: Ann Radcliffe's *The Italian*," *ELH* 61.4 (Winter 1994): 855.

22. Cf. Peter Walmsley, "The Melancholy Briton: Enlightenment Sources of the Gothic," in *Enlightening Romanticism, Romancing the Enlightenment*, ed. Miriam L. Wallace (Aldershot, UK: Ashgate, 2009), 39–53.

23. Toni Wein, *British Identities, Heroic Nationalisms, and the Gothic Novel, 1764–1824* (Houndmills, Basingstoke: Palgrave Macmillan, 2002), 96, 150.

24. The contemporary historical study that established this perspective is Linda Colley's *Britons: Forging the Nation, 1707–1832* (New Haven, CT: Yale University Press, 1992). In his introduction to the book that subsequently incorporated his original *ELH* article on Radcliffe, Schmitt defends his position by claiming that Colley's argument ceases to apply to the Victorian era (on which the rest of Schmitt's study focuses)—an argument that, whatever its merits, in any case fails to explain why Schmitt nevertheless insists that it is Englishness, not Britishness, which is at stake even for a Romantic-era novelist like Radcliffe. See Schmitt, *Alien Nation: Nineteenth-Century Gothic Fictions and English Nationality* (Philadelphia: University of Pennsylvania Press, 1997), 14–16.

25. Robert Miles, *Ann Radcliffe: The Great Enchantress* (Manchester: Manchester University Press, 1995), 3.

26. Norton, *Mistress of Udolpho*, x, xi.

27. See Norton, *Mistress of Udolpho*, 14–40, for more on Radcliffe's probable relationships with these men, and more generally for the progressive politics of the Unitarians of her day.

28. Cf. Ingrid Horrocks, "More Than a Gravestone: *Caleb Williams*, *Udolpho*, and the Politics of the Gothic," *Studies in the Novel* 39.1 (Spring 2007), where she notes that Godwin's journal from 1794 "makes a number of references to 'call[ing] on Radcliffe'" (34).

29. Norton, *Mistress of Udolpho*, 60–61.

30. William Wordsworth, *The Prelude, or Growth of a Poet's Mind*, ed. Ernest de Selin-

court (Oxford: Oxford University Press, 1960), X. 693–94. Subsequent citations appear parenthetically.

31. I follow here George Soule's reading in "*The Prelude* and the French Revolution," *Charles Lamb Bulletin* 129 (2005): 9–19.

32. Miles parses what Radcliffe keeps for her later romances, and what she throws away, from *Athlin and Dunbayne* in *Ann Radcliffe: The Great Enchantress*, 73–85.

33. See, e.g., John Brewer, *The Pleasures of the Imagination: English Culture in the Eighteenth Century* (New York: Farrar, Strauss, and Giroux, 1997), 655.

34. George Dekker, *The Fictions of Romantic Tourism: Radcliffe, Scott, and Mary Shelley* (Stanford, CA: Stanford University Press, 2005), 93.

35. Cf. Blakey Vermeule, *Why Do We Care about Literary Characters?* (Baltimore: The Johns Hopkins University Press, 2010), 35–41.

36. Quoted in Deborah D. Rogers, ed., *The Critical Response to Ann Radcliffe* (Westport, CT: Greenwood Press, 1994), 5, 7.

37. Ann Radcliffe, *The Romance of the Forest*, ed. Chloe Chard (Oxford: Oxford University Press, 1986), 5. Subsequent citations appear parenthetically.

38. Edmund Burke, *A Philosophical Inquiry into the Origin of our Ideas of the Sublime and the Beautiful*, ed. James T. Boulton (Notre Dame, IN: University of Notre Dame Press, 1968), 110.

39. For more on the conjuncture between sympathy, observation, and sexual provocation, see Laura Hinton, *The Perverse Gaze of Sympathy: Sadomasochistic Sentiments from* Clarissa *to* Rescue 911 (Albany, NY: State University of New York Press, 1999).

40. See, e.g., Derrida's analysis of Kierkegaard's insight that "the instant of decision is madness," in *The Gift of Death*, trans. David Wills (Chicago: University of Chicago Press, 1995), 65–66.

41. To recap: the Marquis had promised to forgive La Motte's debts and have him reinstated in Parisian society in return for getting rid of Adeline and thus securing the Marquis' inheritance of the estates of his late half-brother (whom he has previously had murdered).

42. Schmitt, "Techniques of Terror," 856–57.

43. William Wordsworth, "LINES Written a few miles about TINTERN ABBEY, on revisiting the banks of the WYE during a Tour, July 13, 1798," in *Lyrical Ballads: 1798 and 1800*, by Wordsworth and Samuel Taylor Coleridge, eds. Michael Gamer and Dahlia Porter (Peterborough, Ontario: Broadview Press, 2008), 11. 3, 5. The category of the "greater Romantic lyric" is developed by M. H. Abrams in his classic article "Structure and Style in the Greater Romantic Lyric," in *From Sensibility to Romanticism: Essays Presented to Frederick A. Pottle*, eds. Frederick Hilles and Harold Bloom (New York: Oxford University Press, 1965), 527–60.

44. The phrase "green and pleasant land," used to describe England, is from William Blake's prefatory poem to his 1804 epic *Milton* (line 16). The rise of domestic tourism in Romantic-era Britain has been well documented; see, for a seminal example, Carole Fabricant, "The Literature of Domestic Tourism and the Public Consumption of Private Property," in *The New Eighteenth Century: Theory, Politics, English Literature*, eds. Felicity Nussbaum and Laura Brown (New York: Methuen, 1987), 254–75, 310–13.

45. See, e.g., Anne Chandler, "Ann Radcliffe and Natural Theology," *Studies in the Novel* 38.2 (Summer 2006): 133–53.

46. Buck-Morss, *Hegel, Haiti, and Universal History*, x.

47. Kwame Anthony Appiah, *Cosmopolitanism: Ethics in a World of Strangers* (New York: Norton, 2006), xv.

48. William Enfield, Review of *The Mysteries of Udolpho*, *The Monthly Review* 15 (Nov. 1794): 278–83, in Rogers, ed. *Critical Response to Radcliffe*, 25.

49. Elihu Hubbard Smith, quoted in Rogers, *Critical Response*, 26. The allusion here is to a line from Horace's *Ars poetica*, "parturient montes, nascetur ridiculus mus," i.e., the mountains will give birth; a ridiculous mouse will be born.

50. See Terry Castle, "The Spectralization of the Other in *The Mysteries of Udolpho*" in *The Female Thermometer: Eighteenth-Century Culture and the Invention of the Uncanny* (New York: Oxford University Press, 1995), 120–39; and Margaret Russett, "Narrative as Enchantment in *The Mysteries of Udolpho*," *ELH* 65.1 (1998): 159–86.

51. Samuel Baker, "The Transmission of Gothic: Feeling, Philosophy, and the Media of *Udolpho*," in *Public Emotions*, eds. Janet Staiger, Ann Cvetkovich, and Ann Reynolds (London: Routledge, 2010), 91.

52. Only once does Montoni find himself even slightly moved by "the divinity of pity, beaming in Emily's eyes": when she pleads for her aunt's dignified death. See Ann Radcliffe, *The Mysteries of Udolpho*, ed. Bonamy Dobrée, intro. and notes Terry Castle (Oxford: Oxford University Press, 1998), 305, 366. Further citations appear parenthetically.

53. See Ingrid Horrocks, "'Her ideas arranged themselves': Re-membering Poetry in Radcliffe," *Studies in Romanticism* 47.4 (Winter 2008): 507–27.

54. Cf. Deidre Lynch, "Gothic Libraries and National Subjects," *Studies in Romanticism* 40.1 (Spring 2001): 29–48. Lynch's full argument—which ranges well beyond Radcliffe—is that the Romantic-era Gothic novel is at least as invested in complicating the notion of a national community as in policing it.

55. April Alliston, "Transnational Sympathies, Imaginary Communities," in *The Literary Channel: The Inter-National Invention of the Novel*, eds. Margaret Cohen and Carolyn Dever (Princeton, NJ: Princeton University Press, 2002), 140.

56. Quoted in Rogers, *Critical Response*, 25.

57. Emma McEvoy, introduction to Matthew Lewis, *The Monk*, ed. Howard Anderson (New York: Oxford University Press, 1995), xii–xiii. Further citations appear parenthetically.

58. See, for example, Slavoj Žižek, *Welcome to the Desert of the Real!: Five Essays on September 11 and Related Dates* (New York: Verso, 2002): "Here I cannot resist the temptation to recall the Freudian opposition of the public Law and its obscene superego double . . ." (38).

59. For a more redemptive reading of *The Monk*—one that finds Lewis to be in fact more searching and honest than Radcliffe in his explorations of the darker sides of the human drives and desires—see Ahern, *Affected Sensibilities*, 173–202.

60. See Fredric Jameson, *The Political Unconscious: Narrative as a Socially Symbolic Act* (Ithaca, NY: Cornell University Press, 1982). See also Ronald Paulson, "Gothic Fiction and the French Revolution," *ELH* 48.3 (Fall 1981): 532–54. Published too recently for me to consult, Angela Wright's *Britain, France, and the Gothic: The Import of Terror, 1764–1820* (Cambridge: Cambridge University Press, 2013), promises a decisive intervention into the politics of the Gothic novel controversy.

61. James Watt, *Contesting the Gothic: Fiction, Genre, and Cultural Conflict, 1764–1832* (Cambridge: Cambridge University Press, 1999), 42–69.

62. Peter Mortensen, "The Englishness of the English Gothic Novel: Romance Writing in an Age of Europhobia," in *"Better in France?": The Circulation of Ideas across the Channel in the Eighteenth Century*, ed. Frédéric Ogée (Lewisburg, PA: Bucknell University Press, 2005), 272.

63. The phrase "delicate Gothic" is from Yael Shapira, "Where the Bodies Are Hidden: Ann Radcliffe's 'Delicate' Gothic," *Eighteenth-Century Fiction* 18.4 (Summer 2006): 1–24.

64. Ann Radcliffe, *The Italian, or The Confessional of the Black Penitents*, ed. Frederick Garber, intro. and notes E. J. Clery (Oxford: Oxford University Press, 1998), 1. Subsequent citations appear parenthetically.

65. See Schmitt, "Techniques of Terror": 853; Diego Saglia, "Looking at the Other: Cultural Difference and the Traveler's Gaze in *The Italian*," *Studies in the Novel* 28.1 (Spring 1996): 14. Saglia subsequently notes that when the assassin catches the Englishman's eye, "[t]he Other's looking back represents an act of resistance to being regimented and inscribed in the subject's categories, so that the relationship between what is Italian and the foreign point of view is crossed by menacing uncertainties"; nevertheless, Saglia still concludes his reading of this opening tableau by characterizing it as "a constant negotiation between opposite forces and impulses" (15).

66. Quoted in an anonymous review of Lowth's *A Letter to the Right Reverend Author of The Divine Legation of Moses*, *The Critical Review* 20 (1765): 413.

67. A conjunction of vices that Jane Austen very well may have noted here first.

68. See Schmitt, "Techniques of Terror": 859–60.

69. Ann Radcliffe, *A Journey made in the Summer of 1794, through Holland and the Western Frontier of Germany, with a Return down the Rhine: to which are added, Observations during a tour to the Lakes of Lancashire, Westmoreland, and Cumberland* (London: G. G. and J. Robinson, 1795), v–vi.

70. A similar argument, albeit made in much more detail, can be found in Angela Wright's "Inspiration, Toleration and Relocation in Ann Radcliffe's *A Journey Made in the Summer of 1794, through Holland and the Western Frontier of Germany* (1795)," in *Romantic Localities: Europe Writes Place*, eds. Christoph Bode and Jacqueline Labbe (London: Pickering and Chatto, 2010), 131–43.

71. Katarina Gephardt, "Hybrid Gardens: Travel and the Nationalization of Taste in Ann Radcliffe's Continental Landscapes," *European Romantic Review* 21.1 (February 2010): 3–28. Despite her title, Gephardt ultimately shares my view that Radcliffe's cosmopolitanism has been underrated. Radcliffe's landscape descriptions are the subject of much criticism; see, for example, the content and especially the Works Cited list of Benjamin Brabon's "Surveying Ann Radcliffe's Gothic Landscapes," *Literature Compass* 3/4 (2006): 840–45. On Radcliffe's Gothic representations of Italy in particular, see Pam Perkins, "John Moore, Ann Radcliffe and the Gothic Vision of Italy," *Gothic Studies* 8.1 (May 2006): 35–51.

72. See esp. the much-remarked scene in Volume 2, Chapter 2, 158–59.

73. Mark Canuel, *Religion, Toleration, and British Writing, 1790–1830* (Cambridge: Cambridge University Press, 2002), 79.

74. Again, Paulson led the way in interpreting Ambrosio's career as an effective critique of the excesses of the French Revolution; see his "Gothic Fiction and the French Revolution."

75. Quoted in Rogers, *Critical Response*, 96.

76. Jane Austen, *Northanger Abbey*, 2nd ed., ed. Claire Grogan (Peterborough, ON: Broadview Press, 2002), 195.

77. See, for example, the arguments of Claudia Johnson, *Jane Austen: Women, Politics, and the Novel* (Chicago: University of Chicago Press, 1988), 34; and Knox-Shaw, *Austen and Enlightenment*, 114.

78. See, for example, Slavoj Žižek, "Multiculturalism, the Reality of an Illusion," http://www.lacan.com/essays/?page_id=454, accessed 24 February 2010; "Tolerance as an Ideological Category," *Critical Inquiry* 34.4 (Summer 2008): 660–82.

79. Wendy Brown, *Regulating Aversion: Tolerance in the Age of Identity and Empire* (Princeton, NJ: Princeton University Press, 2006), 85–86.

80. Although she does not cite Brennan, this seems to be the same logic employed by Wohlgemut in *Romantic Cosmopolitanism*.

81. Timothy Brennan, "Cosmo-Theory," in *Wars of Position: The Cultural Politics of Left and Right* (New York: Columbia University Press, 2006), 205–6.
82. Slavoj Žižek, *First as Tragedy, Then as Farce* (London: Verso, 2009), 119.
83. Edmund Burke, *Reflections on the Revolution in France*, ed. L. G. Mitchell (New York: Oxford University Press, 1993), 58.
84. Cf. Slavoj Žižek, "Against Human Rights," *New Left Review* 34 (July–August 2005): 115–31.
85. For studies of the literary culture of British conservatism in the 1790s, see e.g. Kevin Gilmartin, *Writing against Revolution: Literary Conservatism in Britain, 1790–1830* (Cambridge: Cambridge University Press, 2007); M. O. Grenby, *The Anti-Jacobin Novel: British Conservatism and the French Revolution* (Cambridge: Cambridge University Press, 2005).

CHAPTER THREE

1. Jane Austen, *Persuasion*, ed. James Kinsley, intro. and notes Deidre Shauna Lynch (New York: Oxford University Press, 2008), 59–60.
2. For more on Wentworth's characterization—especially Austen's simultaneous synthesis and critique of Nelson and the rakish anti-heroes of Byron's Turkish Tales—see Jocelyn Harris, "'Domestic Virtues and National Importance': Lord Nelson, Captain Wentworth, and the English Napoleonic War Hero," *Eighteenth-Century Fiction* 19.1–2 (Fall/Winter 2006–07): 181–205.
3. Anne K. Mellor, *Mothers of the Nation: Women's Political Writing in England, 1780–1830* (Bloomington: Indiana University Press, 2000), 7.
4. Stephen C. Behrendt, "'A few harmless Numbers': British Women Poets and the Climate of War, 1793–1815," in *Romantic Wars: Studies in Culture and Conflict, 1789–1822*, ed. Philip Shaw (Aldershot, UK: Ashgate, 2000), 14.
5. George Gordon, Lord Byron, *Childe Harold's Pilgrimage* Canto 1, in *Selected Poems*, eds. Susan J. Wolfson and Peter Manning (New York: Penguin, 2005), 900.
6. Favret, *War at a Distance*, 9.
7. See David A. Bell, *The First Total War: Napoleon's Europe and the Birth of Warfare as We Know It* (Boston: Houghton Mifflin, 2007).
8. Quoted in Stephen C. Behrendt, "'Certainly not a Female Pen': Felicia Hemans's Early Public Reception," in *Felicia Hemans: Reimagining Poetry in the Nineteenth Century*, eds. Nanora Sweet and Julie Melnyk (Houndmills, Basingstoke: Palgrave Macmillan, 2001), 98.
9. Marlon B. Ross, foreword to *Felicia Hemans: Reimagining Poetry*, eds. Sweet and Melnyk, xii. For a recent excavation of an even-more overlooked female Romantic-era poet, whose post-Napoleonic reminiscences provide a useful counterbalance to Hemans' and others' charged nationalism, see Timothy Ruppert, "Waterloo, Napoleon, and the Vision of Peace in Louisa Stuart Costello's *The Maid of the Cyprus Isle*," *Studies in Romanticism* 51.4 (Winter 2012): 555–78.
10. Quoted in Nanora Sweet, "History, Imperialism, and the Aesthetics of the Beautiful: Hemans and the Post-Napoleonic Moment," in *At the Limits of Romanticism: Essays in Cultural, Feminist, and Materialist Criticism*, eds. Mary A. Favret and Nicola Watson (Bloomington: Indiana University Press, 1994), 172.
11. Cf. Diego Saglia's comments on *England and Spain*'s neoclassicism, in *Poetic Castles in Spain: British Romanticism and Figurations of Iberia* (Amsterdam: Rodopi, 2000), 115.
12. Behrendt, "'Certainly not a Female Pen': Felicia Hemans's Early Public Reception," 95.

For more on Hemans' reception, as well as her desire to be considered a properly feminine poet, see Marlon B. Ross, *The Contours of Masculine Desire: Romanticism and the Rise of Women's Poetry* (Oxford and New York: Oxford University Press, 1989), esp. 232–66.

13. Alexander Pope, "Windsor Forest," in *Selected Poetry and Prose*, ed. William K. Wimsat (New York: Holt, Rinehart and Winston, n.d.), 1–2; Felicia Dorothea Browne (Hemans), *England and Spain: Or, Valour and Patriotism* (London: Cadell, 1808), 1–3. Subsequent citations appear parenthetically by line number.

14. On the global concerns of *Windsor Forest*, see Suvir Kaul, *Poems of Nation, Anthems of Empire: English Verse in the Long Eighteenth Century* (Charlottesville, VA: University of Virginia Press, 2000), 26; Laura Brown, *Fables of Modernity: Literature and Culture in the English Eighteenth Century* (Ithaca, NY: Cornell University Press, 2001), 74–77. My argument is thus not that Pope's poem is not imperialistic, but rather that its global concerns are not foregrounded to the extent that they are in Hemans' poem.

15. Sweet, "History, Imperialism, and the Aesthetics of the Beautiful," 172.

16. Diego Saglia, "'A deeper and richer music': The Poetics of Sound and Voice in Felicia Hemans's 1820s Poetry," *ELH* 74.2 (Summer 2007): 353.

17. As I'll discuss below, Scott would write his own epic meditation on the Peninsular War, *The Vision of Don Roderick*, which sees the British liberation of Spain ending a series of occupations stretching back to "the fall of Spain from Gothic to Moorish rule" (Susan Oliver, *Scott, Byron, and the Poetics of Cultural Encounter* [Houndmills, Basingstoke: Palgrave Macmillan, 2005], 125).

18. Saglia notes that this is one of several occasions where Hemans imagines Napoleon as a Faust-like figure, defeated by his unholy ambitions (*Poetic Castles*, 120).

19. Here and throughout the poem, the trope of "Albion" refers to the entire island, not just the English portion of it; likewise, in the poem's title and elsewhere, Hemans means "England" to effectually denote "Britain." These slippages are less in the service of what Robert J. C. Young somewhat hyperbolically calls "the metonymic extension of English dominance over the other kingdoms with which England has constructed illicit acts of union," than in the patriotic unification of the nation against the French threat (*Colonial Desire: Hybridity in Theory, Culture and Race* [London: Routledge, 1995], 3).

20. Sweet, "History, Imperialism, and the Aesthetics of the Beautiful," 171.

21. On eighteenth-century Britain's sense of itself as a second Rome—and especially its desire to avoid Rome's fate—see Howard Weinbrot, *Britannia's Issue: The Rise of British Literature from Dryden to Ossian* (Cambridge: Cambridge University Press, 1993), 33–36.

22. The French invasion of Egypt (1798–1801) also forms the backdrop of Hemans' most famous poem, "Casabianca" (1826), which memorializes the crucial Battle of the Nile (lost by the French).

23. Rebecca Cole Heinowitz, *Spanish America and British Romanticism, 1777–1826: Rewriting Conquest* (Edinburgh: Edinburgh University Press, 2010), 132.

24. See, for example, Richard Fletcher, *The Cross and the Crescent: The Dramatic Story of the Earliest Encounters between Christians and Muslims* (New York: Penguin, 2003), who avers that "[t]owards the end of the tenth century one ruler of al-Andalus was credited with fifty-seven campaigns against the Christians in twenty-one years" (43).

25. Favret, *War at a Distance*, 32.

26. For more on the concept of "aftermath," especially as it relates to the end of the Napoleonic Wars, see Jerome Christensen, *Romanticism at the End of History* (Baltimore: Johns Hopkins University Press, 2000), 7–8.

27. John Barrell and Harriet Guest, "On the Uses of Contradiction: Economics and Morality in the Eighteenth-Century Long Poem," in *The New Eighteenth Century: Theory, Politics, English Literature*, eds. Felicity Nussbaum and Laura Brown (New York: Methuen, 1987), 123.

28. For an astute reading of Wordsworth's oft-overlooked pamphlet expressing his outrage at the deal that allowed the defeated French their free retreat, see Baker, *Written on the Water*, 153–58.

29. For the revisionist argument that the Spanish guerillas were neither as spontaneously generated nor as patriotic as myth-making accounts like Hemans' suggest, see Charles J. Esdaile, *Fighting Napoleon: Guerillas, Bandits, and Adventurers in Spain, 1808–1814* (New Haven, CT: Yale University Press, 2004).

30. See Behrendt, "'Certainly not a Female Pen,'" 93–99.

31. John Wilson Croker, "Mrs. Barbauld's *Eighteen Hundred and Eleven*," *Quarterly Review* 7.14 (June 1812): 309–313, reprinted in *The Longman Anthology of British Literature*, 3rd. ed., Vol. 2A, ed. Susan Wolfson and Peter Manning (New York: Pearson Education, 2006), 78.

32. William Keach, "A Regency Prophecy and the End of Anna Barbauld's Career," *Studies in Romanticism* 33.4 (Winter 1994): 577. For more on Barbauld's Dissenting circle, see Daniel E. White, *Early Romanticism and Religious Dissent* (Cambridge: Cambridge University Press, 2006), 66–86. Marlon B. Ross gives a brief reading of Barbauld's poem as a dissenting occasional piece in "Configurations of Feminine Reform: The Woman Writer and the Tradition of Dissent," in *Re-Visioning Romanticism: British Women Writers, 1776–1837*, ed. Carol Shiner Wilson and Joel Haefner (Philadelphia: University of Pennsylvania Press, 1994), 101–7.

33. Chandler, *England in 1819*, 114.

34. Nicholas Birns, "'Thy World, Columbus!': Barbauld and Global Space, 1803, '1811,' 1812, 2003," *European Romantic Review* 16.5 (December 2005): 548.

35. For the additional argument that Barbauld's poem angered critics because it refused to distinguish between the fates of England and Napoleonic Europe, see Heinowitz, *Spanish America and British Romanticism*, 143–44.

36. Anna Laetitia Barbauld, *Eighteen Hundred and Eleven: A Poem* (London: J. Johnson and Co., 1812), 1–2. Subsequent citations appear parenthetically by line number.

37. Ross, "Configurations," 105.

38. Croker, "Barbauld's *Eighteen Hundred and Eleven*," in Wolfson and Manning, *Longman Anthology of British Literature*, Vol. 2A, 78.

39. Mary A. Favret, "Everyday War," *ELH* 72.3 (2005): 608. Cf. Simon Bainbridge's observation, made with reference specifically to Hemans' early war poetry, that "Fancy breaks down the sense of distance between the home and the scene of war, undermining any simple construction of the private and the public space": *British Poetry and the Revolutionary and Napoleonic Wars: Visions of Conflict* (Oxford: Oxford University Press, 2003), 151. Kevis Goodman's account of the "rhizomatic underpresence" of the georgic mode on eighteenth-century and Romantic poetry's ability to "negotiate[e] temporal flux [and] spatial extension" is also apposite here and throughout this chapter (*Georgic Modernity and British Romanticism*, 1, 10).

40. Cf. Anderson, *Imagined Communities*.

41. Barbauld's apocalyptic vision was likely inspired by her reading of the Comte de Volney's *The Ruins; or Meditations on the Revolutions of Empires* (1791); see Mellor, *Mothers of the Nation*, 78.

42. Here, Barbauld echoes the conclusion of the previous generation's most famous prophesy of Britain's downfall, Oliver Goldsmith's *The Deserted Village* (1770), which imagines the forced migration of a host of traditional "rural virtues" (1.398).

43. Emily Rohrbach, "Anna Barbauld's History of the Future: A Deviant Way to Poetic Agency," *European Romantic Review* 17.2 (2006): 182.

44. Jacques Derrida, "Autoimmunity: Real and Symbolic Suicides," *Philosophy in a Time of Terror: Dialogues with Jürgen Habermas and Jacques Derrida*, ed. Giovanni Borradori (Chicago: University of Chicago Press, 2003), 94.

45. The significance of this phrase, which combines recognition of Spain's proprietary claim to New World territory with an assertion of Spanish America's right to self-determination, is further explored by Heinowitz, *Spanish America and British Romanticism*, 142–44.

46. Peter Womack, *Improvement and Romance: Constructing the Myth of the Highlands* (London: Macmillan, 1989), 186 n37.

47. Anne Grant, *Eighteen Hundred and Thirteen* (Edinburgh: James Ballantyne and Co., 1814), I.35–36. Subsequent citations appear parenthetically by canto and line number.

48. Favret, *War at a Distance*, 134.

49. Fielding, *Scotland and the Fictions of Geography*, 32–39.

50. Alok Yadav, *Before the Empire of English: Literature, Provinciality, and Nationalism in Eighteenth-Century Britain* (Houndmills, Basingstoke: Palgrave Macmillan, 2004), 175.

51. Makdisi, *Romantic Imperialism*, 134.

52. Paula R. Feldman, introduction to Felicia Hemans, *Records of Women with Other Poems*, ed. Feldman (Lexington: University Press of Kentucky, 1999), xi. On Scott's popularity, see St. Clair, *Reading Nation in the Romantic Period*.

53. Betty T. Bennett's collection *British War Poetry in the Age of Romanticism, 1793–1815* (New York: Garland, 1976) is available online, newly re-edited by Orianne Smith; see www.rc.umd.edu/editions/warpoetry, accessed 7 March 2011.

54. Simon Dentith, *Epic and Empire in Nineteenth-Century Britain* (Cambridge: Cambridge University Press, 2006), 42.

55. An excellent recent analysis of *Marmion*'s introductory epistles can be found in Alison Lumsden and Ainsley McIntosh, "The Narrative Poems," in *The Edinburgh Companion to Walter Scott*, ed. Fiona Robertson (Edinburgh: Edinburgh University Press, 2012), 42–44.

56. See Diego Saglia, "War Romances, Historical Analogies and Coleridge's *Letters on the Spaniards*," in *Romantic Wars: Studies in Culture and Conflict, 1789–1822*, ed. Philip Shaw (Aldershot, UK: Ashgate, 2000), 142.

57. Walter Scott, *The Vision of Don Roderick*. In *The Works of Sir Walter Scott* (Ware, Hertfordshire: Wordsworth Editions, 1995), I.8.7. Subsequent citations appear parenthetically.

58. Philip Shaw, *Waterloo and the Romantic Imagination* (Houndmills, Basingstoke: Palgrave Macmillan, 2002), 51.

59. John Sutherland, *The Life of Walter Scott* (Oxford: Blackwell, 1995), 158.

60. As Bell notes in *The First Total War*, such rhetoric was of course available before the Romantic era; during the Seven Years' War, for example, both English and French propagandists "highlighted atrocities committed by enemy soldiers, in order to demonstrate the perfidious qualities of the enemy nation" (80). Bell's argument, however, is that the specific intellectual circumstances of the later eighteenth century contributed to the totalization of such rhetoric during the Napoleonic Wars.

61. Scott, *The Field of Waterloo: A Poem*, in *The Poetical Works of Sir Walter Scott*, ed. J.

Robertson (London: Oxford University Press, 1940), 619. Subsequent citations appear parenthetically by line number.

62. As Carl Woodring notes, even actual eyewitnesses to Waterloo could not see more than a portion of it at any one time, such that "[a]ll contemporary representations of the battle . . . were simultaneously and interchangeably news and entertainment": "Three Poets of Waterloo," *The Wordsworth Circle* 18.2 (1987): 54.

63. The casualty count and subsequent quotation are from Ian Haywood, *Bloody Romanticism: Spectacular Violence and the Politics of Representation, 1776–1832* (Houndmills, Basingstoke: Palgrave Macmillan, 2006), 100.

64. Bainbridge, *British Poetry*, 120, 128.

65. See Bainbridge, *British Poetry*, 168–69.

66. See the Walter Scott Digital Archive, www.walterscott.lib.ed.ac.uk/works/poetry/waterloo.html#reception, accessed 18 January 2011. One anonymous squib quickly became almost as well known as the poem itself: "On Waterloo's ensanguined plain / Full many a gallant man was slain, / But none, by sabre or by shot, / Fell half so flat as Walter Scott."

CHAPTER FOUR

1. Francis Jeffrey, unsigned review of *The Bride of Abydos* and *The Corsair*, in *The Edinburgh Review* 23 (April 1814): 198–229; reprinted in *Byron: The Critical Heritage*, ed. Andrew Rutherford (New York: Barnes & Noble, 1970), 53. Subsequent citations appear parenthetically.

2. Marilyn Butler, "Byron and the Empire in the East," in *Byron: Augustan and Romantic*, ed. Andrew Rutherford (New York: St. Martin's, 1990), 67.

3. Roderick Cavaliero, *Ottomania: The Romantics and the Myth of the Islamic Orient* (London: I. B. Tauris, 2010), 92.

4. For a recent, nuanced reading of the political valences of the first "set" of Byron's Eastern Tales, see Ghislaine McDayter, *Byromania and the Birth of Celebrity Culture* (Albany, NY: State University of New York Press, 2009), 71–102.

5. Srinivas Aravamudan, *Tropicopolitans: Colonialism and Agency, 1688–1804* (Durham and London: Duke University Press, 1999), 19.

6. See Bernard Lewis, "The Roots of Muslim Rage," *The Atlantic Monthly* 266.3 (September 1990): 47–58; Samuel Huntington, "The Clash of Civilizations?," *Foreign Affairs* 72.3 (Summer 1993): 22–49; Huntington, *The Clash of Civilizations and the Remaking of World Order* (New York: Simon & Schuster, 1996). Further citations of Huntington's book appear parenthetically.

7. The most immediate motive for Huntington seems to have been to counter the more optimistic, even utopian strain of thought evident in other Western-centric, post–Cold War international analyses, most prominently Francis Fukuyama's *The End of History and the Last Man* (New York: Free Press, 1992).

8. Edward Said, "The Clash of Ignorance," October 4, 2001, www.thenation.comdoc/20011022/said, accessed 14 July 2008. Said's article was subsequently published in the October 22, 2001, print edition of *The Nation*.

9. Amartya Sen, "Civilizational Imprisonments," *The New Republic* 226.22 (June 10, 2002): 28, 32.

10. Susan Buck-Morss, "Sovereign Right and the Global Left," *Cultural Critique* 69 (Spring 2008): 155.

11. For a more general study of the distinctive features of post-Napoleonic, Romantic literary culture, see Richard Cronin, *Paper Pellets: British Literary Culture after Waterloo* (Oxford: Oxford University Press, 2010). Not coincidentally, Byron and Scott are the most cited authors in Cronin's index (only William Hazlitt rivals them).

12. *The Works of Lord Byron: Poetry*, ed. E. H. Coleridge (7 vols., rev. ed.; London and New York, 1903–05), III, 323n. Qtd. in Robert F. Gleckner, *Byron and the Ruins of Paradise* (Baltimore: The Johns Hopkins University Press, 1967), 154.

13. *The Works of Lord Byron: Letters and Journals*, ed. R. E. Prothero (6 vols., rev. ed., London and New York, 1902–04), III, 131. Quoted in Gleckner, *Ruins of Paradise*, 153.

14. Byron, *Lara: A Tale*, in *Selected Poems*, 11.1–2 and note 1. Subsequent citations appear parenthetically by line number.

15. Jerome Christensen, *Lord Byron's Strength: Romantic Writing and Commercial Society* (Baltimore: The Johns Hopkins University Press, 1993), 125.

16. Cf. Nigel Leask's note that "it is easy to slip into the critical vocabulary of psychoanalysis in describing *Lara*": *British Romantic Writers and the East*, 56.

17. Peter J. Manning, *Byron and His Fictions* (Detroit: Wayne State University Press, 1978), 52.

18. Leask, *British Romantic Writers and the East*, 55.

19. Judith Butler, *The Psychic Life of Power: Theories in Subjection* (Stanford, CA: Stanford University Press, 1997), 184.

20. See, e.g., Judith Butler, *Precarious Life: The Powers of Mourning and Violence* (London: Verso, 2004).

21. This is true even if one traces the origin of the Byronic hero back to the initial descriptions of Harold in Canto 1 of *Childe Harold's Pilgrimage*, where we are told Harold first feels the urge to travel when "[h]e felt the fullness of satiety: / Then loathed he in his native land to dwell" (in *Selected Poems*, I.4.34–35).

22. Emily A. Bernhard Jackson, "*Manfred*'s Mental Theater and the Construction of Knowledge," *SEL* 47.4 (Autumn 2007): 806.

23. Tom Mole, *Byron's Romantic Celebrity: Industrial Culture and the Hermeneutic of Intimacy* (Houndmills, Basingstoke: Palgrave Macmillan, 2007), 118.

24. My thanks to Matt Wickman for reminding me of this example. Cf. my earlier analysis of Wordsworth's strategic use of incomprehensibility in "The Solitary Reaper" in Gottlieb, *Feeling British*, 150–51.

25. I refer here to Jürgen Habermas' theory of communicative action, especially as he initially develops its eighteenth-century construction in *The Structural Transformation of the Public Sphere: An Inquiry into a Category of Bourgeois Society*, trans. Thomas Burger with Frederick Lawrence (Cambridge, MA: The MIT Press, 1989).

26. Manning, *Byron and His Fictions*, 54.

27. Makdisi, *Romantic Imperialism*, 137.

28. My thanks to Tom Mole for prompting me to take Lara's marked body into account.

29. See Leask, *British Romantic Writers and the East*, 62.

30. For the critics' generally negative response, see Byron, *Selected Poems*, 798.

31. St. Clair, *Reading Nation in the Romantic Period*, 219.

32. Caroline Franklin has argued that Byron drew on Mme. De Stael and Goethe, among other sources: "The Influence of Madame de Staël's Account of *Goethe's Die Braut von Korinth* in *De l'Allemagne* on the Heroine of Byron's *Siege of Corinth*," *Notes and Queries* 35.3 (Sept. 1988): 307–10.

33. George Gordon, Lord Byron, *The Siege of Corinth*, in *Selected Poems*, 11.44–45. Subsequent citations appear parenthetically by line number. "Acro-Corinth" refers to the monumental rock overlooking the city.

34. Maxwell, *Historical Novel in Europe*, 172.

35. Alain Badiou, *Saint Paul: The Foundation of Universalism*, trans. Ray Brassier (Stanford, CA: Stanford University Press, 2003), 99.

36. For the argument that Byron was much better informed about Islam than is often assumed, see Peter Cochran, "Byron and Islamic Culture," in *Byron's Religions*, ed. Cochran (Newcastle-Upon-Tyne: Cambridge Scholars Press, 2011), 198–212.

37. Oliver, *Scott, Byron and the Poetics of Cultural Encounter*, 168.

38. Caroline Franklin, *Byron's Heroines* (Oxford: Clarendon Press, 1992), 70. Franklin further argues that Francesca represents the logical culmination of a pattern in Byron's Eastern Tales whereby "virtuous domestic heroine[s]" are increasingly associated with "the trap of social conformity" (68).

39. Franklin, *Byron's Heroines*, 70.

40. Butler explains that "Freud identifies heightened conscience and self-beratement as one sign of melancholia, the condition of uncompleted grief" (*Psychic Life of Power*, 23). My reading thus dovetails with Cochran's identification of Francesca as a precursor to Astarte in *Manfred*: see Peter Cochran, "Introduction: Byron's Orientalism," in *Byron's Orientalism*, ed. Cochran (Newcastle-Upon-Tyne: Cambridge Scholars Press, 2008), 56.

41. Butler, *Psychic Life of Power*, 28.

42. The depiction of the siege of Ismail in the seventh and eighth cantos of *Don Juan* is a notable exception.

43. George Gordon, Lord Byron, *The Island; or, Christian and His Comrades*, in *The Works of Lord Byron* (Ware, Hertfordshire: Wordsworth Editions, 1994), II.11.1–4. Further citations appear parenthetically.

44. Jonathan Lamb, *Preserving the Self in the South Seas, 1680–1840* (Chicago: University of Chicago Press, 2001), 252.

45. Oliver, *Scott, Byron, and the Poetics of Cultural Encounter*, 196.

46. Barbara Judson, "Tragicomedy, Bisexuality, and Byronism; or, Jokes and Their Relation to Sardanapalus," *Texas Studies in Language and Literature* 45.3 (Fall 2003): 246.

47. Andrew Elfenbein, "Byron: Gender and Sexuality," in *The Cambridge Companion to Byron*, ed. Drummond Bone (Cambridge: Cambridge University Press, 2005), 63.

48. George Gordon, Lord Byron, *Sardanapalus*, in *Selected Poems*, I.2.421–36. Further citations appear parenthetically.

49. Compare Jerome Christensen's observation that "Myrrha's Greek heritage stamps her with liberalism's pedigree," in "Byron's Sardanapalus and the Triumph of Liberalism," *Studies in Romanticism* 31.3 (Fall 1992): 346.

50. Daniela Garofalo, "Political Seductions: The Show of War in Byron's *Sardanapalus*," *Criticism* 44.1 (Winter 2002): 44.

51. Jerome J. McGann, "Hero With a Thousand Faces: The Rhetoric of Byronism," *Studies in Romanticism* 31.3 (Fall 1992): 309.

52. Oliver, *Scott, Byron, and the Poetics of Cultural Encounter*, 111.

53. Bewell, *Romanticism and Colonial Disease*, 129.

54. This is the argument I pursue in my earlier treatment of Scott's novels; see Gottlieb, *Feeling British*, 170–207. See also, e.g., Duncan, *Scott's Shadow*, esp. 96–115; Caroline McCracken-Flesher, *Possible Scotlands: Walter Scott and the Story of Tomorrow* (Oxford:

Oxford University Press, 2005); Kenneth McNeil, *Scotland, Britain, Empire: Writing the Highlands, 1760–1860* (Columbus: The Ohio State University Press, 2007), 51–116.

55. In fact, Scott's interest in meditating upon international conflicts manifests itself first in *Ivanhoe*, the novel critics have traditionally faulted for leading Scott away from the Scottish materials and histories that he knew best.

56. Walter Scott, *The Talisman*, ed. J. B. Ellis with J. H. Alexander, P. D. Garside, and David Hewitt (Edinburgh: Edinburgh University Press, 2009), 6. Subsequent citations from this edition appear parenthetically. Since "the Saracen" is eventually revealed to be Saladin, who was Kurdish by birth, Scott's likening of him to an "Arab horseman" is technically erroneous, at least from a contemporary ethnic standpoint.

57. Clifford Geertz, "A Strange Romance: Anthropology and Literature," *Profession* (2003): 33. Said is equally dismissive of Scott's depictions of the East; see *Orientalism*, 101–2. For a corrective to Said's misidentification of Sir Kenneth's voice with Scott's own, see Tara Ghoshal Wallace, "Thinking Globally: *The Talisman* and *The Surgeon's Daughter*," in *Approaches to Teaching Scott's Waverley Novels*, eds. Evan Gottlieb and Ian Duncan (New York: MLA, 2009), 170–71.

58. Moreover, Scott was almost certainly familiar with these clichés from other historical and fictional sources, there being something of a vogue for Crusader tales at the time; see Andrew Lincoln, *Walter Scott and Modernity* (Edinburgh: Edinburgh University Press, 2007), 106–8. Thanks to Tony Jarrells for reminding me that Lincoln notes in passing that *The Talisman* does not conform to "Samuel P. Huntingdon's [sic] notorious phrase, a 'Clash of Civilizations'" (*Scott and Modernity*, 106).

59. Scott's last completed novel, *Count Robert of Paris* (1831), is in fact set in the time preceding the First Crusade; as in *The Talisman*, the heterogeneity of the Christian forces is of great interest to Scott here.

60. Scott, introduction to the *magnum opus* edition, *The Talisman* (London: J. M. Dent & Sons, 1977), 2.

61. Scott's decision was very likely influenced by the overwhelmingly critical assessment of the Crusades put forward by Scottish Enlightenment historians like Hume and Robertson; see Sylvia Mergenthal, "'An Imaginary Line Drawn Through Waste and Wilderness': Scott's *The Talisman*," in *Romantic Localities: Europe Writes Place*, eds. Christoph Bode and Jacqueline Labbe (London: Pickering and Chatto, 2010), esp. 212–214.

62. Scott, introduction to the *magnum opus* edition of *The Talisman* (1977), 2.

63. "To remain content with reversal is of course to operate within the immanence of the system to be destroyed": Derrida, *Dissemination*, 6.

64. David Simpson, "'Which is the merchant here? and which the Jew?': Friends and Enemies in Walter Scott's Crusader Novels," *Studies in Romanticism* 47.4 (Winter 2008): 437–38.

65. I analyze Scott's portrayal of Jews in *Ivanhoe*, with specific reference to Žižek's theory of "the Jew" as the ultimate ideological signifier, in my *Walter Scott and Contemporary Theory* (London: Bloomsbury Academic, 2013), 23–31.

66. Here Scott seems to have in mind the common eighteenth-century caricature of "the Saracen's Head" on inn and pub signs; he had previously used such signs as the basis for a quasi-comic discussion of mimesis and artistic license in the opening chapter of *The Bride of Lammermoor*.

67. For historical evidence of this phenomenon, see James Reston Jr., *Warriors of God: Richard the Lionheart and Saladin in the Third Crusade* (New York: Doubleday, 2001), 13–14.

68. Margaret Bruzelius, *Romancing the Novel: Adventure from Scott to Sebald* (Lewisburg, PA: Bucknell University Press, 2007), 97.

69. On the significance of Scott's linkage in the *magnum opus* edition of the talisman's powers to opium, see David Simpson, "Friends and Enemies," 443–44.

70. For a helpful review of recent interpretations of Saladin, see Wallace, "Thinking Globally," 172–73. See also Sylvia Mergenthal, "Scott's *The Talisman*," in *Romantic Localities*, eds. Bode and Labbe, 209–19, which additionally takes up human-animal transgressions in the novel's rhetoric and imagery.

71. See Reston, *Warriors of God*, xiv.

72. Cf. Ian Duncan, "Scott's Romance of Empire: The *Tales of the Crusaders*," in *Scott in Carnival: Selected Papers from the Fourth International Scott Conference*, eds. J. H. Alexander and David Hewitt (Aberdeen: Association for Scottish Literary Studies, 1993), 377.

73. I take up this question, as well as the novel's representation of female characters, at more length in a complementary reading of *The Talisman* in my *Walter Scott and Contemporary Theory*, 69–74.

74. James Watt observes that not just *The Talisman* but all of Scott's so-called Orientalist productions "eschew the increasingly influential language of racial essentialism . . . while at the same time focusing on the ramifications of cultural contact and exchange": "Scott, the Scottish Enlightenment, and Romantic Orientalism," in *Scotland and the Borders of Romanticism*, eds. Leith Davis, Ian Duncan, and Janet Sorensen (Cambridge: Cambridge University Press, 2004), 94.

75. Žižek, *Welcome to the Desert of the Real*, 146. See also Žižek's observation, vis-à-vis Huntington's paradigm, that "[p]seudo-naturalized ethnico-religious conflicts are the form of struggle which fits global capitalism; in our age of 'post-politics,' when politics proper is replaced by expert social administration, the only remaining legitimate source of conflicts is cultural (ethnic, religious) tension" (132).

76. Scott, introduction to the *magnum* opus edition of *The Talisman (1977)*, 2. Cf. Christensen's two postulates of the "policy of cryptoliberalism" that he labels Romantic: "that Romanticism is an ethics of imaginative, collaborative work and that any Romantic ethics is also a poetics, which provides the model for how work ought to be organized in human terms" (*Romanticism at the End of History*, 8).

CHAPTER FIVE

1. *The Journal of Sir Walter Scott*, ed. W. E. K. Anderson (Edinburgh: Canongate, 1998), 258. See also Robert Giddings, "Scott and Opera," in *Sir Walter Scott: The Long-Forgotten Melody*, ed. Alan Bold (London: Barnes and Noble, 1983), 194–218.

2. Scott, *Journal*, 267.

3. Margaret Cohen and Carolyn Dever, introduction to *The Inter-National Invention of the Novel*, eds. Cohen and Dever (Princeton, NJ: Princeton University Press, 2002), 12. Pascale Casanova notes that A. J. B. Defauconpret's contemporaneous French translations of the Waverley Novels were probably more widely read, globally speaking, than the English originals, and certainly formed the basis of many other translations of Scott: *The World Republic of Letters*, trans. M. B. Debevoise (Cambridge, MA: Harvard University Press, 2004), 146.

4. See http://boslit.nls.uk (accessed 20 September 2008).

5. St. Clair, *Reading Nation in the Romantic Period*, 420.

6. In the bitter words of the Prussian field marshal August Niedhardt von Gneisenau, the Allied victory at Waterloo left Britain "mistress of the sea and neither in this dominion nor in world trade has she now a single rival to fear." Quoted in Michael Duffy, "Contested Empires, 1756–1815," in *The Eighteenth Century, 1688–1815*, ed. Paul Langford (Oxford: Oxford University Press, 2002), 242.

7. Michael Simpson, "Wavering on Europe: Walter Scott and the Equilibrium of Empires," *Romanticism* 11.2 (2005): 133.

8. Ian Duncan, "Primitive Inventions: *Rob Roy*, Nation, and World System," *Eighteenth-Century Fiction* 15.1 (2002): 81–102; McNeil, *Scotland, Britain, Empire*, 51–82; Fielding, *Scotland and the Fictions of Geography*, 96–100. For more on how local, national, and global frames mutually produce and inflect each other, see, e.g., the essays collected in *Representing Place in British Literature and Culture, 1660–1830*, eds. Evan Gottlieb and Juliet Shields (Aldershot, UK: Ashgate, 2013).

9. Gabriel Rockhill, "Glossary of Technical Terms," in Jacques Rancière, *The Politics of Aesthetics*, trans. Gabriel Rockhill (London: Continuum, 2004), 86. Although Rancière seems unlikely to sympathize with the notably state-centered version of equality that, I argue, Scott holds out as a potential outcome of global hospitality, I think his ideas are nevertheless more compatible with Scott's historical novels that they initially seem, especially given Rancière's dictum that "[t]he real must be fictionalized in order to be thought" (38).

10. Walter Scott, *Quentin Durward*, ed. Susan Manning (Oxford: Oxford University Press, 1992), 530.

11. "If in all ideology men and their circumstances appear upside-down as in a camera obscura, this phenomenon arises just as much from their historical life-process as the inversion of objects on the retina does from their physical life-process": Karl Marx and Frederick Engels, *The German Ideology*, in *The Marx-Engels Reader*, 2nd ed., ed. Robert C. Tucker (New York: Norton, 1978), 154.

12. Walter Scott, *Quentin Durward*, eds. J. H. Alexander and G. A. M. Wood (Edinburgh: Edinburgh University Press, 2001), 4. Subsequent citations of this edition appear parenthetically.

13. See Douglas Mack and Suzanne Gilbert, "Scottish History in the Waverley Novels," in Gottlieb and Duncan, *Approaches to Teaching Scott's Waverley Novels*, 3.

14. Scott, *Letters of Sir Walter Scott*, ed. H. J. C. Grierson (London: Constable, 1933), 7: 224.

15. See Gottlieb, *Feeling British*, 172–77.

16. Ina Ferris, *The Achievement of Literary Authority: Gender, History, and the Waverley Novels* (Ithaca, NY: Cornell University Press, 1991).

17. Žižek, *Tarrying with the Negative*, 27. Subsequent citations appear parenthetically.

18. See Baucom, *Specters of the Atlantic*, 55–57. For more on Britain's financial revolution and its particular relevance to our understanding of the Romantic era, see Alexander Dick, *Romanticism and the Gold Standard: Money, Literature, and the Economic Debate in Britain, 1790–1830* (Houndmills, Basingstoke: Palgrave Macmillan, 2013).

19. Jameson, "Realist Floor-Plan," 373.

20. See, e.g., Gottlieb, *Feeling British*, 204–7; McCracken-Flesher, *Possible Scotlands*, 143–53; Dick, *Romanticism and the Gold Standard*, Chapter 5.

21. Granted, Scott's ability to lay claim simultaneously to both of these subject-positions again complicates the historicity of Žižek's scheme insofar as it suggests that, at least when the French Revolution was still recent history, self-aware authors (like Scott) were able to straddle the divide between pre- and post-Enlightenment subjectivities.

22. Saskia Sassen, *Territory, Authority, Rights: From Medieval to Global Assemblages* (Princeton, NJ: Princeton University Press, 2006), 76. Sassen describes European territorial authority as finally coalescing only in the sixteenth century.

23. Scott, introduction to *Quentin Durward*, ed. Manning, 5–6.

24. Judith Wilt, "Transmutations: From Alchemy to History in *Quentin Durward* and *Anne of Geierstein*," *European Romantic Review* 13.3 (2002): 252. Cf. Anne-Lise François, *Open Secrets: The Literature of Uncounted Experience* (Stanford, CA: Stanford University Press, 2008).

25. Crawford, "Scott and European Union": 146.

26. Anne Frey, *British State Romanticism: Authorship, Agency, and Bureaucratic Nationalism* (Stanford, CA: Stanford University Press, 2010), 89. See also Foucault, *Security, Territory, Population*; Sassen, *Territory, Authority, Rights*, Chapters 1–2.

27. Frey, *British State Romanticism*, 58.

28. Manning, introduction to *Quentin Durward*, ed. Manning, xxxii.

29. For an extended discussion of the vanishing mediator's role in the historical dialectical, see Slavoj Žižek, *For They Know Not What They Do: Enjoyment as a Political Factor*, 2nd ed. (London: Verso, 2002), 182–93.

30. See, for example, Craig Calhoun's assertion that "[n]ationalism matters not least because it has offered such a deep and compelling account of large-scale identities and structures in the world—helping people to imagine the world as composed of sovereign nation-states": *Nations Matter: Culture, History, and the Cosmopolitan Dream* (London: Routledge, 2007), 8.

31. Christensen's characterization of Scott as little more than "a conscientious official" doing the bidding of the Hanoverian regime (in *Romanticism at the End of History*) is an extreme example of the misprisions that can occur when critics do not extend their reading of Scott beyond *Waverley*.

32. I provide a complementary reading of *Quentin Durward* as an extended meditation on governmentality in *Walter Scott and Contemporary Theory*, 85–96.

33. Lincoln, *Scott and Modernity*, 23.

34. Scott, note to *Quentin Durward*, ed. Manning, 504–5.

35. Deborah Epstein Nord, *Gypsies and the British Imagination, 1807–1930* (New York: Columbia University Press, 2006), 21.

36. Scott, note to *Quentin Durward*, ed. Manning, 505–6.

37. See Gilles Deleuze and Félix Guattari, "Treatise on Nomadology—The War Machine," in *A Thousand Plateaus: Capitalism and Schizophrenia Volume II*, trans. Brian Massumi (Minneapolis: University of Minnesota Press, 1987), 351–423.

38. Giorgio Agamben, *Homo Sacer: Sovereign Power and Bare Life*, trans. Daniel Heller-Roazen (Stanford, CA: Stanford University Press, 1998), 28. Further citations appear parenthetically.

39. It bears grim mention that gypsies (Roma)—along with Jews, homosexuals, and people with various perceived mental and physical abnormalities—were among the main targets of persecution and genocide in Nazi Germany.

40. William Blake, "London," Plate 18 of *Songs of Experience* (New York: Dover, 1984), line 8.

41. For a more traditional reading of Hayraddin's role as a "pivot character" necessary to the plot, see Lionel Lackey, "Plausibility and the Romantic Plot Construction of *Quentin Durward*," *Studies in Philology* 90.1 (Winter 1993): 106–8.

42. Sassen, *Territory, Authority, Rights*, 76. Cf. Erik Simpson's interpretation of the incorporation of the gypsy's fortune into Durward's estate as "a Cinderella fantasy of wealth sniff-

ing out true nobility": "'A Good One Though Rather for the Foreign Market': Mercenary Writing and Scott's *Quentin Durward*," *Studies in Romanticism* 48.4 (Winter 2009): 681–82.

43. Scott essentially invented the Scottish Royal Company of Archers for the book's purposes; see Manning's introduction to *Quentin Durward*, ed. Manning, viii.

44. Lackey points out that this episode brings an added benefit, since the hanged man whom Quentin attempts to assist turns out to be the brother of Hayraddin, who is thus predisposed to behave kindly to Quentin later in the novel ("Plausibility and the Romantic Plot": 105).

45. Slavoj Žižek, *Violence: Six Sideways Reflections* (New York: Picador, 2008), 173, 147.

46. On the exemplary status of Scott's heroes, see Alexander Welsh, *The Hero of the Waverley Novels: With New Essays on Scott* (Princeton, NJ: Princeton University Press, 1992). Although we pursue divergent arguments, my reading of Quentin as condemned to make a "false choice" to submit to the King is complemented by Erik Simpson's insight that Scott takes pains to downplay the mercenary nature of Quentin's forced employment by Louis ("Mercenary Writing and *Quentin Durward*": esp. 672–85).

47. See, e.g., Agamben's bleak view that "[i]f today there is no longer any one clear figure of the sacred man, it is perhaps because we are all virtually *homines sacri*" (*Homo Sacer*, 115).

48. Žižek, "Against Human Rights": 126. For a more conventional story of the development of human rights, albeit one that similarly identifies the French Revolution as a watershed moment, see Lynn Hunt, *Inventing Human Rights: A History* (New York: Norton, 2007).

49. Quoted in J. H. Alexander, "Essay on the Text," in Walter Scott, *Anne of Geierstein*, ed. Alexander (Edinburgh: Edinburgh University Press, 2000), 406.

50. On the widespread deployment of conventional and historical norms of hospitality in Scott's oeuvre, see Stanley Sulkes, "The Code of Hospitality in the Waverley Novels: A Study of Sir Walter Scott's Fiction," PhD dissertation, 1976. Thanks to Kang-yen Chiu for bringing this text to my attention.

51. Walter Scott, *Anne of Geierstein*, ed. J.H. Alexander (Edinburgh: University of Edinburgh Press, 2000), 291. Subsequent citations will appear parenthetically. See also Nanora Sweet's observation that "*Anne* pits Burgundy and England against the contested (Scotland-like) Border and Highlands region of central Europe, the Rhine Valley and Switzerland": "Felicia Hemans' 'A Tale of the Secret Tribunal': Gothic Empire in the Age of Jeremy Bentham and Walter Scott," *European Journal of English Studies* 6.2 (2002): 166.

52. Like Radcliffe in her European romances, Scott in *Anne of Geierstein* had to rely on others' descriptions and illustrations for his own depictions of a landscape he had never seen in person; see Richard J. Hill, *Picturing Scotland through the Waverley Novels: Walter Scott and the Origins of the Victorian Illustrated Novel* (Aldershot, UK: Ashgate, 2010), 27–28.

53. Welsh, *Hero of the Waverley Novels*, 150.

54. Cf. Ian Duncan's observation that Anne is one of Scott's "guardian fairy-figures": *Modern Romance and Transformations of the Novel: The Gothic, Scott, Dickens* (Cambridge: Cambridge University Press, 1992), 219.

55. See Fiona Robertson, *Legitimate Histories: Scott, Gothic, and the Authorities of Fiction* (Oxford: Clarendon Press, 1994), 242.

56. For more on the specific historical details of *Anne of Geierstein*'s setting, see the very helpful historical note (with chronology) by Alexander in the Edinburgh edition, 502–519.

57. Clifford Siskin, "Novels and Systems," *Novel: A Forum on Fiction* 34.2 (Spring 2001): 202.

58. Siskin, "Mediated Enlightenment: The System of the World," 172.

59. Jürgen Habermas, "The Postnational Constellation and the Future of Democracy," in *The Postnational Constellation: Political Essays*, ed. and trans. Max Pensky (Cambridge, MA: The MIT Press, 2001), 63.

60. Seyla Benhabib, *Another Cosmopolitanism* (New York: Oxford University Press, 2006), 15. Benhabib is describing Hannah Arendt's attitude to the trial of Adolf Eichmann; my recontextualization is warranted, I think, by Benhabib's subsequent (albeit qualified) observation that Arendt is "deeply indebted to the cosmopolitan legacy of Kantian thought" (15).

61. For a trenchant analysis of the development of modern sovereignty's territorial dynamics, see Stuart Elden, *Terror and Territory: The Spatial Extent of Sovereignty* (Minneapolis: University of Minnesota Press, 2009), esp. his "Introduction: Terror and the State of Territory" (xi–xxxii).

62. Calhoun, "Is It Time to be Postnational?," in *Nations Matter*, 25.

63. Benhabib, *Another Cosmopolitanism*, 23.

64. In trying accurately to articulate this thought, I was aided by Suh-Reen Han's observation, with regard to the Kantian distinction between "philanthropy" and "right," that "[l]ove for fellow humans should come *after* hospitality, not before": "When Theory Meets the World: Kant's Post-Revolutionary Renegotiation of the Cosmopolitan Ideal," *European Romantic Review* 21.6 (December 2010): 688.

65. Derrida, "Autoimmunity," 128–29.

66. Derrida, "Autoimmunity," 129. See also Derrida's extended meditation on the concept in *Of Hospitality*, trans. Rachel Bowlby (Stanford, CA: Stanford University Press, 2000).

67. J. H. Alexander notes that the battle of Nancy is one of several historical events Scott gets wrong in *Anne of Geierstein*: the battle actually took place on January 5, 1477, not New Year's Day as Scott has it (probably from an inaccurate source.) Yet as Alexander observes, whether purposeful or not, Scott uses the error to his advantage, remarking that Arthur "almost forgave that new-year's morning all its complicated distresses" when he is subsequently granted the right to woo Anne: "The 'Amanuensis of History' in the Franco-Burgundian Novels," *European Romantic Review* 13.3 (2002): 242.

68. Étienne Balibar, "At the Borders of Europe," in *We, the People of Europe?: Reflections on Transnational Citizenship*, trans. James Swenson (Princeton, NJ: Princeton University Press, 2004), 5.

69. I am indebted in particular to Ian Duncan's interpretation of these events in *Scott's Shadow*, 3–8. Duncan's interpretation of Scott's "authenticity effects" as purposefully, patently fictional is related to Christensen's portrait of Scott as a "world pictorialist, whose aim is to engineer the viewer's full persuasion not in any particular fiction but in the good faith of the system by which effective fictions are generated" (*Romanticism at the End of History*, 164), but with this important difference: Duncan's position, which I share, allows for the possibility that Scott's uncovering of the fictionality of social constructs like sovereignty is potentially emancipatory, whereas Christensen's leads him to conclude that Scott's fictions merely "regulate accommodation" to the existing order of things (175).

70. Murray Pittock, introduction to *The Reception of Sir Walter Scott in Europe*, ed. Pittock (London: Continuum, 2006), 5.

71. For more on the "modularity" of modern Western nationalism, see Partha Chatterjee, *The Nation and Its Fragments: Colonial and Postcolonial Histories* (Princeton, NJ: Princeton University Press, 1993), 5–6. Trumpener's *Bardic Nationalism* continues to be the defining study of the interplay of central and peripheral discourses of identity in Britain and its

colonies in the Romantic era, although a number of more recent studies have productively complicated her model.

72. Cf. Casanova, *World Republic of Letters*, 35–37, for an account of the processes of linguistic and literary differentiation that took place congruently with Europe's formation into discrete nation-states. My suggestion is that "beneath" the linguistic, stylistic, and generic differences highlighted by Casanova, the formal homologies of the conceptualization of national sovereignty are just as significant.

73. See also Simon Edwards' exuberant account of the multiple European directions in which Scott's influence can be followed over the nineteenth century and beyond, in "Home and Away with Walter Scott," in Gottlieb and Duncan, *Approaches to Teaching Scott's Waverley Novels*, 77–87.

CONCLUSION

1. John le Carré, *The Constant Gardener: A Novel* (New York: Scribner, 2001), 43.
2. le Carré, *Constant Gardener*, 113.
3. Pasley's treatise was apparently popular with Jane Austen, among many others; see Vivien Jones, "Reading for England: Austen, Taste, and Female Patriotism," *European Romantic Review* 16.2 (April 2005): 221–30. Leckie's remarkable life and writings were brought to my attention by Samuel Baker; see his *Written on the Water*, esp. 193–98, 207–9.
4. Makdisi, "Romantic Cultural Imperialism," 603.
5. "Argument" to "The Ancient Mariner, A Poet's Reverie," in Wordsworth and Coleridge, *Lyrical Ballads*, 260; Percy Shelley, *A Defence of Poetry*, ed. Mary Shelley (New York: Bobbs-Merrill, 1904); Austen, *Persuasion*, 82.
6. Nancy Armstrong, *How Novels Think: The Limits of Individualism from 1719–1900* (New York: Columbia University Press, 2005), 58.
7. See Celeste Langan, "Understanding Media in 1805: Audiovisual Hallucination in *The Lay of the Last Minstrel*," *Studies in Romanticism* 40.1 (Spring 2001): 49–70; Chandler, *England in 1819*, esp. 203–349; McLane, *Balladeering*; Andrew Piper, *Dreaming in Books: The Making of the Bibliographic Imagination in the Romantic Age* (Chicago: University of Chicago Press, 2009), esp. 101–120. For more general historico-theoretical investigations of cultural transmission, see e.g. Régis Debray, *Transmitting Culture*, trans. Eric Rauth (New York: Columbia University Press, 2000); Friedrich Kittler, *Discourse Networks 1800/1900*, trans. Michael Metteer with Chris Cullens (Stanford, CA: Stanford University Press, 1990).
8. See, e.g., Eleanor Courtemanche, *The "Invisible Hand" and British Fiction, 1818–1860: Adam Smith, Political Economy, and the Genre of Realism* (Houndmills, Basingstoke: Palgrave Macmillan, 2011).
9. Siskin and Warner, "This Is Enlightenment," 23.
10. Peter Wagner, *Modernity: Understanding the Present* (Cambridge: Polity, 2012), 118.
11. Siskin, "Mediated Enlightenment," 168. For the full, earlier version of Siskin's argument regarding the special status of the Scottish Enlightenment, see his *The Work of Writing: Literature and Social Change in Britain, 1700–1830* (Baltimore: Johns Hopkins University Press, 1998), 79–102.
12. Siskin, "Mediated Enlightenment," 171.
13. Wallerstein, *World Systems Analysis*, 25–26.
14. Harish Trivedi, "From Bollywood to Hollywood: The Globalization of Hindi Cinema," in *The Postcolonial and the Global*, eds. Revathi Krishaswamy and John C. Hawley (Minneapolis: University of Minnesota Press, 2008), 206.

15. See, e.g., Jamie Peck, Nik Theodore, and Neil Brenner, "Neoliberalism Resurgent? Market Rule after the Great Recession," *South Atlantic Quarterly* 111.2 (Spring 2012): 265–88.

16. Nancy, *Creation of the World*, 49.

17. John Keane, *Global Civil Society?* (Cambridge: Cambridge University Press, 2003), 61–62. Keane lists a variety of non-governmental organizations whose activities fall under the general heading of alter-globalism, including the Global Action Project, the Earthwatch Institute, and the Association for the Taxation of Financial Transactions for the Aid of Citizens (ATTAC).

18. David Watson, preface in *The Worlding Project: Doing Cultural Studies in the Era of Globalization,* eds. Rob Wilson and Christopher Leigh Connery (Santa Cruz, CA: New Pacific Press and North Atlantic Books, 2007), 5.

19. Pheng Cheah, *Inhuman Conditions: On Cosmopolitanism and Human Rights* (Cambridge, MA: Harvard University Press, 2007), 19.

20. For a mostly positive account of the transformative role of technological globalization in recent socio-political movements, including the Arab Spring and Occupy Wall Street, see Manuel Castells, *Networks of Outrage and Hope: Social Movements in the Internet Age* (Cambridge: Polity, 2012).

21. Michael Löwy and Robert Sayre, *Romanticism against the Tide of Modernity*, trans. Catherine Porter (Durham, NC: Duke University Press, 2001).

22. See, for example, the articles in the recent special issue, "Nostalgia, Melancholy, Anxiety: Discursive Mobility and the Circulation of Bodies," ed. Peter J. Manning, *Studies in Romanticism* 49.2 (Summer 2010): 195–336.

23. Cf. Baucom, *Specters of the Atlantic*, passim.

24. Martha C. Nussbaum, *Not for Profit: Why Democracy Needs the Humanities* (Princeton, NJ: Princeton University Press, 2010), 91. Nussbaum does not claim she is the first to think along such lines, naming predecessors like Bronson Alcott, John Dewey, and Rabindranath Tagore. Although she does not discuss the Enlighteners or the Romantics beyond a brief mention of Rousseau's pedagogical ideas, she spends a great deal of time on the importance of the cultivation of sympathy, which of course was central to their thinking on the subject. Surprisingly similar conclusions are reached regarding the ongoing merits of humanistic study, albeit understood more critically via the shorthand of "sabotaging Schiller" by Gayatri Chakravorty Spivak in her newest collection, *An Aesthetic Education in the Era of Globalization* (Cambridge, MA: Harvard University Press, 2012).

BIBLIOGRAPHY

Abrams, M. H. "Structure and Style in the Greater Romantic Lyric." In *From Sensibility to Romanticism: Essays Presented to Frederick A. Pottle*, edited by Frederick Hilles and Harold Bloom. New York: Oxford University Press, 1965.
Addison, Joseph. *The Spectator* no. 69 (May 19, 1711). In *The Commerce of Everyday Life: Selections from* The Tatler *and* The Spectator, edited by Erin Mackie. Houndmills, Basingstoke: Palgrave Macmillan, 1998.
Agamben, Giorgio. *Homo Sacer: Sovereign Power and Bare Life*, translated by Daniel Heller-Roazen. Stanford, CA: Stanford University Press, 1998.
Ahern, Stephen. *Affected Sensibilities: Romantic Excess and the Genealogy of the Novel, 1680–1810*. New York: AMS Press, 2007.
Alexander, J. H. "The 'Amanuensis of History' in the Franco-Burgundian Novels." *European Romantic Review* 13, no. 3 (2002): 239–47.
Allan, David. *Making British Culture: English Readers and the Scottish Enlightenment, 1740–1830*. London: Routledge, 2008.
———. *Virtue, Learning, and the Scottish Enlightenment*. Edinburgh: Edinburgh University Press, 1993.
Alliston, April. "Transnational Sympathies, Imaginary Communities." In *The Literary Channel: The Inter-National Invention of the Novel*, edited by Margaret Cohen and Carolyn Dever. Princeton, NJ: Princeton University Press, 2002.
Anderson, Benedict. *Imagined Communities: Reflections on the Origin and Spread of Nationalism*. Revised edition. London: Verso, 1991.
Andriopoulos, Stefan. "The Invisible Hand: Supernatural Agency in Political Economy and the Gothic Novel." *ELH* 66, no. 3 (Summer 1999): 739–58.
Annesley, James. *Fictions of Globalization: Consumption, the Market, and the Contemporary American Novel*. London: Continuum, 2009.
Anonymous. Review of Robert Lowth's *A Letter to the Right Reverend Author of* The Divine Legation of Moses. *The Critical Review* 20 (London: 1765): 410–15.
Appadurai, Arjun. *Modernity at Large: Cultural Dimensions of Globalization*. Minneapolis: University of Minnesota Press, 1996.
Appiah, Kwame Anthony. *Cosmopolitanism: Ethics in a World of Strangers*. New York: Norton, 2006.

Arac, Jonathan, and Harriet Ritvo, eds. *Macropolitics of Nineteenth-Century Literature: Nationalism, Exoticism, Imperialism.* Durham, NC: Duke University Press, 1995.
Aravamudan, Srinivas. *Enlightenment Orientalism: Resisting the Rise of the Novel.* Chicago: University of Chicago Press, 2012.
———. *Tropicopolitans: Colonialism and Agency, 1688–1804.* Durham, NC: Duke University Press, 1999.
Armstrong, Nancy. *How Novels Think: The Limits of Individualism from 1719–1900.* New York: Columbia University Press, 2005.
Arrighi, Giovanni. *The Long Twentieth Century: Money, Power, and the Origins of Our Times.* London: Verso, 1994.
Ashcroft, Bill. *Post-Colonial Transformation.* New York: Routledge, 2001.
Austen, Jane. *Northanger Abbey.* 2nd edition, edited by Claire Grogan. Peterborough, ON: Broadview Press, 2002.
———. *Persuasion,* edited by James Kinsley, introduction and notes by Deidre Shauna Lynch. New York: Oxford University Press, 2008.
Badiou, Alain. *The Rebirth of History: Times of Riots and Uprisings,* translated by Gregory Elliot. London: Verso, 2012.
———. *Saint Paul: The Foundation of Universalism,* translated by Ray Brassier. Stanford, CA: Stanford University Press, 2003.
Bainbridge, Simon. *British Poetry and the Revolutionary and Napoleonic Wars: Visions of Conflict.* Oxford: Oxford University Press, 2003.
Baker, Samuel. "The Transmission of Gothic: Feeling, Philosophy, and the Media of *Udolpho.*" In *Public Emotions,* edited by Janet Staiger, Ann Cvetkovich, and Ann Reynolds. London: Routledge, 2010.
———. *Written on the Water: British Romanticism and the Maritime Empire of Culture.* Charlottesville: University of Virginia Press, 2010.
Balibar, Étienne. *We, the People of Europe? Reflections on Transnational Citizenship,* translated by James Swenson. Princeton, NJ: Princeton University Press, 2004.
Barbauld, Anna Laetitia. *Eighteen Hundred and Eleven: A Poem.* London: J. Johnson and Co., 1812.
Barbour, Richmond. *Before Orientalism: London's Theatre of the East, 1576–1626.* Cambridge: Cambridge University Press, 2003.
Barrell, John. *The Infection of Thomas de Quincey: A Psychopathology of Imperialism.* New Haven, CT: Yale University Press, 1991.
Barrell, John, and Harriet Guest. "On the Uses of Contradiction: Economics and Morality in the Eighteenth-Century Long Poem." In *The New Eighteenth Century: Theory, Politics, English Literature,* edited by Felicity Nussbaum and Laura Brown. New York: Methuen, 1987.
Baucom, Ian. *Specters of the Atlantic: Finance Capital, Slavery, and the Philosophy of History.* Durham, NC: Duke University Press, 2005.
Bauman, Zygmunt. *Globalization: The Human Consequences.* New York: Columbia University Press, 1998.
Bayly, C. A. *The Birth of the Modern World, 1780–1914: Global Connections and Comparisons.* Malden, MA: Blackwell, 2004.
Behrendt, Stephen. "'Certainly not a Female Pen': Felicia Hemans's Early Public Reception." In *Felicia Hemans: Reimagining Poetry in the Nineteenth Century,* edited by Nanora Sweet and Julie Melnyk. Houndmills, Basingstoke: Palgrave Macmillan, 2001.
———. "'A few harmless Numbers': British women poets and the climate of war, 1793–1815."

In *Romantic Wars: Studies in Culture and Conflict, 1789-1822*, edited by Philip Shaw. Aldershot, UK: Ashgate, 2000.

Belich, James. *Replenishing the Earth: The Settler Revolution and the Rise of the Anglo-World, 1783-1939*. Oxford: Oxford University Press: 2009.

Bell, David. A. *The First Total War: Napoleon's Europe and the Birth of Warfare as We Know It*. Boston: Houghton Mifflin, 2007.

Benhabib, Seyla. *Another Cosmopolitanism*. New York: Oxford University Press, 2006.

———. *The Rights of Others: Aliens, Residents and Citizens*. Cambridge: Cambridge University Press, 2004.

Bennett, Betty, ed. *British War Poetry in the Age of Romanticism, 1793-1815*. New York: Garland, 1976.

Berdell, John. *International Trade and Economic Growth in Open Economies: The Classical Dynamics of Hume, Smith, Ricardo and Malthus*. Cheltenham, UK: Edward Elgar, 2002.

Bewell, Alan. *Romanticism and Colonial Disease*. Baltimore: The Johns Hopkins University Press, 1999.

———. *Wordsworth and the Enlightenment: Nature, Man, and Science in the Experimental Poetry*. New Haven, CT: Yale University Press, 1998.

Birns, Nicholas. "'Thy World, Columbus!': Barbauld and Global Space, 1803, '1811,' 1812, 2003." *European Romantic Review* 16, no. 5 (December 2005): 545-62.

Blake, William. *Songs of Experience*. New York: Dover, 1984.

Bohls, Elizabeth A. *Romantic Literature and Postcolonial Studies*. Edinburgh: Edinburgh University Press, 2013.

Brabon, Benjamin. "Surveying Ann Radcliffe's Gothic Landscapes." *Literature Compass* 3/4 (2006): 840-45.

Brennan, Timothy. *Wars of Position: The Cultural Politics of Left and Right*. New York: Columbia University Press, 2006.

Brewer, John. *The Pleasures of the Imagination: English Culture in the Eighteenth Century*. New York: Farrar, Strauss, and Giroux, 1997.

Broadie, Alexander. *The Scottish Enlightenment: The Historical Age of the Historical Nation*. Edinburgh: Birlinn, 2007.

Brown, Laura. *Fables of Modernity: Literature and Culture in the English Eighteenth Century*. Ithaca, NY: Cornell University Press, 2001.

Brown, Tony. *The Primitive, the Aesthetic, and the Savage: An Enlightenment Problematic*. Minneapolis: University of Minnesota Press, 2012.

Brown, Wendy. *Regulating Aversion: Tolerance in the Age of Identity and Empire*. Princeton, NJ: Princeton University Press, 2006.

Bruzelius, Margaret. *Romancing the Novel: Adventure from Scott to Sebald*. Lewisburg, PA: Bucknell University Press, 2007.

Buck-Morss, Susan. *Hegel, Haiti, and Universal History*. Pittsburgh: University of Pittsburgh Press, 2009.

———. "Sovereign Right and the Global Left." *Cultural Critique* 69 (Spring 2008): 145-71.

Burgess, Miranda. *British Fiction and the Production of Social Order, 1740-1830*. Cambridge: Cambridge University Press, 2000.

———. "Transport: Mobility, Anxiety, and the Romantic Poetics of Feeling." *Studies in Romanticism* 49, no. 2 (Summer 2010): 229-60.

Burke, Edmund. *Reflections on the Revolution in France*, edited by L. G. Mitchell. New York: Oxford University Press, 1993.

———. *A Philosophical Inquiry into the Origin of our Ideas of the Sublime and the Beautiful*, edited by James T. Boulton. Notre Dame: University of Notre Dame Press, 1968.
Burton, Jonathan. *Traffic and Turning: Islam and English Drama, 1579–1624*. Newark, NJ: University of Delaware Press, 2005.
Butler, Judith. *Precarious Life: The Powers of Mourning and Violence*. London: Verso, 2004.
———. *The Psychic Life of Power: Theories in Subjection*. Stanford, CA: Stanford University Press, 1997.
Butler, Marilyn. "Byron and the Empire in the East." In *Byron: Augustan and Romantic*, edited by Andrew Rutherford. New York: St. Martin's, 1990.
Byron, Lord, George Gordon. *Selected Poems*, edited by Susan J. Wolfson and Peter Manning. New York: Penguin, 2005.
———. *The Works of Lord Byron*. Ware, Hertfordshire: Wordsworth Editions, 1994.
———. *The Works of Lord Byron: Poetry*, edited by E. H. Coleridge. 7 volumes, revised edition. London and New York: 1903–1905.
———. *The Works of Lord Byron: Letters and Journals*, edited by R. E. Prothero. 6 volumes. Revised edition. London and New York: 1902–1904.
Calhoun, Craig. *Nations Matter: Culture, History, and the Cosmopolitan Dream*. London: Routledge, 2007.
Canuel, Mark. *Religion, Toleration, and British Writing, 1790–1830*. Cambridge: Cambridge University Press, 2002.
Carey, Brycchan. *British Abolitionism and the Rhetoric of Sensibility: Writing, Sentiment, and Slavery, 1760–1807*. Houndmills, Basingstoke: Palgrave Macmillan, 2005.
Carson, James P. "Enlightenment, Popular Culture, and the Gothic." In *The Cambridge Companion to the Eighteenth-Century Novel*, edited by John Richetti. New York: Cambridge University Press, 1996.
Casanova, Pascale. *The World Republic of Letters*, translated by M. B. Debevoise. Cambridge, MA: Harvard University Press, 2004.
Castells, Manuel. *The Information Age Volume 1: Economy, Society, and Culture—The Rise of the Network Society*. Oxford: Blackwell, 1996.
———. *Networks of Outrage and Hope: Social Movements in the Internet Age*. Cambridge: Polity, 2012.
Castle, Terry. *Boss Ladies, Watch Out! Essays on Women, Sex, and Writing*. New York: Routledge, 2002.
———. *The Female Thermometer: Eighteenth-Century Culture and the Invention of the Uncanny*. New York: Oxford University Press, 1995.
Cavaliero, Roderick. *Ottomania: The Romantics and the Myth of the Islamic Orient*. London: I. B. Tauris, 2010.
Chaktrabarty, Dipesh. *Provincializing Europe: Postcolonial Thought and Historical Difference*. 2nd edition. Princeton, NJ: Princeton University Press, 2007.
Chandler, Anne. "Ann Radcliffe and Natural Theology." *Studies in the Novel* 38, no. 2 (Summer 2006): 133–53.
Chandler, James. *England in 1819: The Politics of Literary Culture and the Case of Romantic Historicism*. Chicago: University of Chicago Press, 1998.
Chang, Elizabeth. *Britain's Chinese Eye: Literature, Empire, and Aesthetics in Nineteenth-Century Britain*. Stanford, CA: Stanford University Press, 2010.
Chatterjee, Partha. *The Nation and Its Fragments: Colonial and Postcolonial Histories*. Princeton, NJ: Princeton University Press, 1993.

Cheah, Pheng. *Inhuman Conditions: On Cosmopolitanism and Human Rights.* Cambridge, MA: Harvard University Press, 2006.

Chibber, Vivek. *Postcolonial Theory and the Specter of Capital.* London: Verso, 2013.

Chow, Rey. *The Age of the World Target: Self-Referentiality in War, Theory, and Comparative Work.* Durham, NC: Duke University Press, 2006.

Christensen, Jerome. "Byron's *Sardanapalus* and the Triumph of Liberalism." *Studies in Romanticism* 31, no. 3 (Fall 1992): 333–60.

———. *Lord Byron's Strength: Romantic Writing and Commercial Society.* Baltimore: The Johns Hopkins University Press, 1993.

———. *Romanticism at the End of History.* Baltimore: The Johns Hopkins University Press, 2000.

Clery, E. J. *The Rise of Supernatural Fiction, 1762–1800.* Cambridge: Cambridge University Press, 1995.

Cochran, Peter. "Byron and Islamic Culture." In *Byron's Religions*, edited by Peter Cochran. Newcastle-Upon-Tyne: Cambridge Scholars Press, 2011.

———. "Introduction: Byron's Orientalism." In *Byron's Orientalism*, edited by Peter Cochran. Newcastle-Upon-Tyne: Cambridge Scholars Press, 2008.

Cohen, Margaret, and Carolyn Dever. Introduction to *The Inter-National Invention of the Novel*, eds. Cohen and Dever. Princeton, NJ: Princeton University Press, 2002.

Colley, Linda. *Britons: Forging the Nation, 1707–1832.* New Haven, CT: Yale University Press, 1992.

———. *The Ordeal of Elizabeth Marsh: A Woman in World History.* New York: Pantheon, 2007.

Cooppan, Vilashini. *Worlds Within: National Narratives and Global Connections in Postcolonial Writing.* Stanford, CA: Stanford University Press, 2009.

Courtemanche, Eleanor. *The "Invisible Hand" and British Fiction, 1818–1860: Adam Smith, Political Economy, and the Genre of Realism.* Houndmills, Basingstoke: Palgrave Macmillan, 2011.

Craciun, Adriana. "Writing the Disaster: Franklin and *Frankenstein.*" *Nineteenth-Century Literature* 65, no. 4 (March 2011): 433–80.

Craig, Cairns. *Associationism and the Literary Imagination: From the Phantasmal Chaos.* Edinburgh: Edinburgh University Press, 2007.

Crawford, Robert. "Walter Scott and European Union." *Studies in Romanticism* 40, no. 1 (Spring 2001): 137–52.

Croker, John Wilson. "Mrs. Barbauld's *Eighteen Hundred and Eleven.*" *Quarterly Review* 7, no. 14 (June 1812): 309–13. Reprinted as "A Review of *Eighteen Hundred and Eleven*" in *The Longman Anthology of British Literature.* 3rd edition, Volume 2A, edited by Susan Wolfson and Peter Manning. New York: Pearson Education, 2006.

Cronin, Richard. *Paper Pellets: British Literary Culture after Waterloo.* Oxford: Oxford University Press, 2010.

Darwin, John. *The Empire Project: The Rise and Fall of the British World-System, 1830–1970.* Cambridge: Cambridge University Press, 2009.

Debray, Régis. *Transmitting Culture*, translated by Eric Rauth. New York: Columbia University Press, 2000.

Dekker, George. *The Fictions of Romantic Tourism: Radcliffe, Scott, and Mary Shelley.* Stanford, CA: Stanford University Press, 2005.

Deleuze, Gilles, and Félix Guattari. *A Thousand Plateaus: Capitalism and Schizophrenia Volume II*, translated by Brian Massumi. Minneapolis: University of Minnesota Press, 1987.

Deligiorgi, Katerina. *Kant and the Culture of Enlightenment*. Albany, NY: State University of New York Press, 2005.
DeLucia, JoEllen. "From the Female Gothic to a Feminist Theory of History: Ann Radcliffe and the Scottish Enlightenment." *The Eighteenth Century: Theory and Interpretation* 50, no. 1 (2010): 101–15.
Dentith, Simon. *Epic and Empire in Nineteenth-Century Britain*. Cambridge: Cambridge University Press, 2006.
Derrida, Jacques. "Autoimmunity: Real and Symbolic Suicides." In *Philosophy in a Time of Terror: Dialogues with Jürgen Habermas and Jacques Derrida*, edited by Giovanni Borradori. Chicago: University of Chicago Press, 2003.
———. *Dissemination*, translated by Barbara Johnson. Chicago: University of Chicago Press, 1981.
———. *The Gift of Death*, translated by David Wills. Chicago: University of Chicago Press, 1995.
———. "Globalization, Peace, and Cosmopolitanism." In *Negotiations: Interventions and Interviews, 1971–2001*, edited and translated by Elizabeth Rottenberg. Stanford, CA: Stanford University Press, 2002.
———. *Of Hospitality*, translated by Rachel Bowlby. Stanford, CA: Stanford University Press, 2000.
———. *Specters of Marx: The State of the Debt, the Work of Mourning, and the New International*, translated by Peggy Kamuf. New York: Routledge, 1994.
Dick, Alexander J. *Romanticism and the Gold Standard: Money, Literature, and the Economic Debate in Britain, 1790–1830*. Houndmills, Basingstoke: Palgrave Macmillan, 2013.
Doyle, Laura. *Freedom's Empire: Race and the Rise of the Novel in Atlantic Modernity, 1640–1940*. Durham, NC: Duke University Press, 2008.
Duffy, Michael. "Contested Empires, 1756–1815." In *The Eighteenth Century, 1688–1815*, edited by Paul Langford. Oxford: Oxford University Press, 2002.
Duncan, Ian. *Modern Romance and Transformations of the Novel: The Gothic, Scott, Dickens*. Cambridge: Cambridge University Press, 1992.
———. "Primitive Inventions: *Rob Roy*, Nation, and World System." *Eighteenth-Century Fiction* 15, no. 1 (2002): 81–102.
———. "Scott's Romance of Empire: The *Tales of the Crusaders*." In *Scott in Carnival: Selected Papers from the Fourth International Scott Conference*, edited by J. H. Alexander and David Hewitt. Aberdeen: Association for Scottish Literary Studies, 1993.
———. *Scott's Shadow: The Novel in Romantic Edinburgh*. Princeton, NJ: Princeton University Press, 2007.
Eagleton, Terry. *The English Novel: An Introduction*. Oxford: Blackwell, 2004.
Edwards, Simon. "Home and Away with Walter Scott." In Gottlieb and Duncan, eds., *Approaches to Teaching Scott's Waverley Novels*.
Elden, Stuart. *Terror and Territory: The Spatial Extent of Sovereignty*. Minneapolis: University of Minnesota Press, 2009.
Elfenbein, Andrew. "Byron: Gender and Sexuality." In *The Cambridge Companion to Byron*, edited by Drummond Bone. Cambridge: Cambridge University Press, 2005.
Ellis, Elisabeth. *Kant's Politics: Provisional Theory for an Uncertain World*. New Haven, CT: Yale University Press, 2005.
Ellis, Markman. "Enlightenment or Illumination: The Spectre of Conspiracy in Gothic Fictions of the 1790s." In *Recognizing the Romantic Novel: New Histories of British Fiction, 1780–1830*, edited by Jillian Heydt-Stevenson and Charlotte Sussman. Liverpool: Liverpool University Press, 2008.

Esdaile, Charles J. *Fighting Napoleon: Guerillas, Bandits, and Adventurers in Spain, 1808–1814*. New Haven, CT: Yale University Press, 2004.
Fabricant, Carole. "The Literature of Domestic Tourism and the Public Consumption of Private Property." In *The New Eighteenth Century: Theory, Politics, English Literature*, edited by Felicity Nussbaum and Laura Brown. New York: Methuen, 1987.
Favret, Mary. "Everyday War." *ELH* 72, no. 3 (2005): 605–33.
———. *War at a Distance: Romanticism and the Making of Modern Wartime*. Princeton, NJ: Princeton University Press, 2010.
Feldman, Paula R. Introduction to Felicia Hemans, *Records of Women with Other Poems*, edited by Feldman. Lexington: University Press of Kentucky, 1999.
Fenves, Peter. *Late Kant: Towards Another Law of the Earth*. London: Routledge, 2003.
Ferguson, Adam. *An Essay on the History of Civil Society*. New Brunswick, NJ: Transaction, 1980.
Ferris, Ina. *The Achievement of Literary Authority: Gender, History, and the Waverley Novels*. Ithaca, NY: Cornell University Press, 1991.
Fielding, Penny. *Scotland and the Fictions of Geography: North Britain, 1760–1830*. Cambridge: Cambridge University Press, 2008.
Fletcher, Richard. *The Cross and the Crescent: The Dramatic Story of the Earliest Encounters Between Christians and Muslims*. New York: Penguin, 2003.
Forbes, Duncan. "The Rationalism of Sir Walter Scott." *The Cambridge Journal* 7 (1953): 20–35.
Foucault, Michel. *Discipline and Punish: The Birth of the Prison*, translated by Alan Sheridan. New York: Vintage, 1979.
———. *The Order of Things: An Archaeology of the Human Sciences*. New York: Vintage, 1970.
———. *Security, Territory, Population: Lectures at the Collège de France, 1977–78*, edited by Michel Senellart, translated by Graham Burchell. New York: Picador, 2009.
François, Anne-Lise. *Open Secrets: The Literature of Uncounted Experience*. Stanford, CA: Stanford University Press, 2008.
Franklin, Caroline. *Byron's Heroines*. Oxford: Clarendon Press, 1992.
———. "The Influence of Madame de Staël's Account of *Goethe's Die Braut von Korinth* in *De l'Allemagne* on the Heroine of Byron's *Siege of Corinth*." *Notes and Queries* 35, no. 3 (Sept. 1988): 307–10.
Frey, Anne. *British State Romanticism: Authorship, Agency, and Bureaucratic Nationalism*. Stanford, CA: Stanford University Press, 2010.
Fukuyama, Francis. *The End of History and the Last Man*. New York: Free Press, 1992.
Fulford, Timothy. *Romantic Indians: Native Americans, British Literature, and Transatlantic Culture, 1756–1830*. Cambridge: Cambridge University Press, 2006.
Fulford, Timothy, Debbie Lee, and Peter J. Kitson. *Literature, Science and Exploration in the Romantic Era: Bodies of Knowledge*. Cambridge: Cambridge University Press, 2004.
Gallagher, John, and Ronald Robinson. "The Imperialism of Free Trade." *Economic History Review* 6, no. 1 (1953): 1–15.
Galli, Carlo. *Political Spaces and Global War*, edited by Adam Sitze, translated by Elisabeth Fay. Minneapolis: University of Minnesota Press, 2010.
Garofalo, Daniela. "Political Seductions: The Show of War in Byron's *Sardanapalus*," *Criticism* 44, no. 1 (Winter 2002): 43–63.
Garside, Peter. "Scott and the 'Philosophical Historians.'" *Journal for the History of Ideas* 36 (1975): 497–512.
Geertz, Clifford. "A Strange Romance: Anthropology and Literature." *Profession* (2003): 28–36.

Gellner, Ernest. *Nations and Nationalism*. 2nd edition. Ithaca, NY: Cornell University Press, 2006.
Gephardt, Katarina. "Hybrid Gardens: Travel and the Nationalization of Taste in Ann Radcliffe's Continental Landscapes." *European Romantic Review* 21, no. 1 (February 2010): 3–28.
Giddings, Robert. "Scott and Opera." In *Sir Walter Scott: The Long-Forgotten Melody*, edited by Alan Bold. London: Barnes and Noble, 1983.
Gikandi, Simon. *Slavery and the Culture of Taste*. Princeton, NJ: Princeton University Press, 2011.
Gilmartin, Kevin. *Writing against Revolution: Literary Conservatism in Britain, 1790–1830*. Cambridge: Cambridge University Press, 2007.
Gleckner, Robert. *Byron and the Ruins of Paradise*. Baltimore: The Johns Hopkins University Press, 1967.
Golinski, Jan. *British Weather and the Climate of Enlightenment*. Chicago: University of Chicago Press, 2007.
Goodman, Kevis. *Georgic Modernity and British Romanticism: Poetry and the Mediation of History*. Cambridge: Cambridge University Press, 2004.
Gottlieb, Evan. *Feeling British: Sympathy and National Identity in Scottish and English Writing, 1707–1832*. Lewisburg, PA: Bucknell University Press, 2007.
——. "No Place Like Home: From Local to Global (and back Again) in the Gothic Novel." In Gottlieb and Shields, eds., *Representing Place in British Literature and Culture*.
——. *Walter Scott and Contemporary Theory*. London: Bloomsbury Academic, 2013.
Gottlieb, Evan, and Ian Duncan, eds. *Approaches to Teaching Scott's Waverley Novels*. New York: MLA, 2009.
Gottlieb, Evan, and Juliet Shields, eds. *Representing Place in British Literature and Culture, 1660–1830: From Local to Global*. Aldershot, UK: Ashgate, 2013.
Grant, Anne. *Eighteen Hundred and Thirteen*. Edinburgh: James Ballantyne and Co., 1814.
Greenfeld, Liah. *Nationalism: Five Roads to Modernity*. Cambridge, MA: Harvard University Press, 1993.
Grenby, M. O. *The Anti-Jacobin Novel: British Conservatism and the French Revolution*. Cambridge: Cambridge University Press, 2005.
Gunn, Giles, ed. "Globalizing Literary Studies." Special issue of *PMLA* 116, no. 1 (January 2001): 16–188.
Gupta, Suman. *Globalization and Literature*. Malden, MA: Polity, 2009.
Haakonssen, Knud. *Natural Law and Moral Philosophy: From Grotius to the Scottish Enlightenment*. Cambridge: Cambridge University Press, 1996.
Habermas, Jürgen. *The Philosophical Discourse of Modernity: Twelve Lectures*, translated by Frederick Lawrence. Cambridge, MA: The MIT Press, 1987.
——. *The Postnational Constellation: Political Essays*, edited and translated by Max Pensky. Cambridge, MA: The MIT Press, 2001.
——. *The Structural Transformation of the Public Sphere: An Inquiry into a Category of Bourgeois Society*, translated by Thomas Burger with Frederick Lawrence. Cambridge, MA: The MIT Press, 1989.
Han, Suh-Reen. "When Theory Meets the World: Kant's Post-Revolutionary Renegotiation of the Cosmopolitan Ideal," *European Romantic Review* 21, no. 6 (December 2010): 673–92.
Hardin, Russell. *David Hume: Moral and Political Theorist*. New York: Oxford University Press, 2007.
Hardt, Michael, and Antonio Negri. *Commonwealth*. Cambridge, MA: Belknap Press, 2009.

———. *Empire*. Cambridge, MA: Harvard University Press, 2000.
Harkin, Maureen. "Adam Smith's Missing History: Primitives, Progress, and the Problems of Genre." *ELH* 72, no. 2 (Summer 2005): 429–51.
Harris, Jocelyn. "'Domestic Virtues and National Importance': Lord Nelson, Captain Wentworth, and the English Napoleonic War Hero." *Eighteenth-Century Fiction* 19, nos. 1–2 (Fall/Winter 2006–07): 181–205.
Harvey, David. *Justice, Nature and the Geography of Difference*. Malden, MA: Blackwell, 1996.
Haywood, Ian. *Bloody Romanticism: Spectacular Violence and the Politics of Representation, 1776–1832*. Houndmills, Basingstoke: Palgrave Macmillan, 2006.
Heinowitz, Rebecca Cole. *Spanish America and British Romanticism, 1777–1826: Rewriting Conquest*. Edinburgh: Edinburgh University Press, 2010.
Heller-Roazen, Daniel. *The Enemy of All: Piracy and the Law of Nations*. New York: Zone Books, 2009.
Hemans, Felicia (Dorothea Browne). *England and Spain: Or, Valour and Patriotism*. London: Cadell, 1808.
Hill, Richard J. *Picturing Scotland through the Waverley Novels: Walter Scott and the Origins of the Victorian Illustrated Novel*. Aldershot, UK: Ashgate, 2010.
Hinton, Laura. *The Perverse Gaze of Sympathy: Sadomasochistic Sentiments from* Clarissa *to* Rescue 911. Albany, NY: State University of New York Press, 1999.
Holton, Robert J. *Cosmopolitanisms: New Thinking and New Directions*. Houndmills, Basingstoke: Palgrave Macmillan, 2009.
Horkheimer, Max, and Theodor Adorno. *Dialectic of Enlightenment*, edited by Gunzelin Schmid Noerr, translated by Edmund Jephcott. Stanford, CA: Stanford University Press, 2002.
Horrocks, Ingrid. "'Her ideas arranged themselves': Re-membering Poetry in Radcliffe." *Studies in Romanticism* 47, no. 4 (Winter 2008): 507–27.
———. "More Than a Gravestone: *Caleb Williams, Udolpho*, and the Politics of the Gothic." *Studies in the Novel* 39, no. 1 (Spring 2007): 31–47.
Hume, David. *Essays: Moral, Political, and Literary*, edited by Eugene F. Miller. Indianapolis: Liberty Fund, 1985.
———. *The Letters of David Hume*, edited by J. Y. T. Grieg. Oxford: Oxford University Press, 1932.
———. *A Treatise of Human Nature*. 2nd edition, edited by L. A. Selby-Bigge and P. H. Nidditch. Oxford: Oxford University Press, 1978.
Hunt, Lynn. *Inventing Human Rights: A History*. New York: Norton, 2007.
Huntington, Samuel. "The Clash of Civilizations?" *Foreign Affairs* 72, no. 3 (Summer 1993): 22–49.
———. *The Clash of Civilizations and the Remaking of World Order*. New York: Simon & Schuster, 1996.
Ingham, Geoffrey. *Capitalism*. Malden, MA: Polity, 2008.
Israel, Jonathan. *Enlightenment Contested: Philosophy, Modernity, and the Emancipation of Man, 1670–1752*. Oxford: Oxford University Press, 2006.
Jackson, Emily A. Bernhard. "*Manfred*'s Mental Theater and the Construction of Knowledge." *SEL* 47, no. 4 (Autumn 2007): 799–824.
Jameson, Fredric. "Cognitive Mapping." In *Marxism and the Interpretation of Culture*, edited by Cary Nelson and Lawrence Grossberg. Urbana, IL: University of Illinois Press, 1988.
———. "Notes on Globalization as a Philosophical Issue." In *The Cultures of Globalization*, edited by Fredric Jameson and Masao Miyoshi. Durham, NC: Duke University Press, 1998.

———. *The Political Unconscious: Narrative as a Socially Symbolic Act*. Ithaca, NY: Cornell University Press, 1982.

———. "The Realist Floor-Plan." In *On Signs*, edited by Marshall Blonsky. Baltimore: The Johns Hopkins University Press, 1985.

Jay, Paul. *Global Matters: The Transnational Turn in Literary Studies*. Ithaca, NY: Cornell University Press, 2010.

Jenkins, Eugenia Zuroski. *A Taste for China: English Subjectivity and the Prehistory of Orientalism*. Oxford: Oxford University Press, 2013.

Johnson, Claudia. *Jane Austen: Women, Politics, and the Novel*. Chicago: University of Chicago Press, 1988.

Jones, Vivien. "Reading for England: Austen, Taste, and Female Patriotism." *European Romantic Review* 16, no. 2 (April 2005): 221–30.

Judson, Barbara. "Tragicomedy, Bisexuality, and Byronism; or, Jokes and Their Relation to Sardanapalus." *Texas Studies in Language and Literature* 45, no. 3 (Fall 2003): 245–63.

Kames, Lord, Henry Home. *Sketches of the History of Man*, 3 vols., edited by James A. Harris. Indianapolis: Liberty Fund, 2007.

Kant, Immanuel. *Practical Philosophy*, edited and translated by Mary J. Gregor. Cambridge: Cambridge University Press, 1996.

Kaul, Suvir. *Poems of Nation, Anthems of Empire: English Verse in the Long Eighteenth Century*. Charlottesville: University of Virginia Press, 2000.

Keach, William. "A Regency Prophecy and the End of Anna Barbauld's Career." *Studies in Romanticism* 33, no. 4 (Winter 1994): 569–77.

Keane, John. *Global Civil Society?* Cambridge: Cambridge University Press, 2003.

Kenyon, John. *The History Men*. London: Weidenfeld and Nicolson, 1983.

Kittler, Friedrich. *Discourse Networks 1800/1900*, translated by Michael Metteer with Chris Cullens. Stanford, CA: Stanford University Press, 1990.

Kleingeld, Pauline. "Kant's Theory of Peace." In *The Cambridge Companion to Kant and Modern Philosophy*, edited by Paul Guyer. Cambridge: Cambridge University Press, 2006.

Knox-Shaw, Peter. *Jane Austen and the Enlightenment*. Cambridge: Cambridge University Press, 2004.

Koselleck, Reinhart. *The Practice of Conceptual History: Timing History, Spacing Concepts*, translated by Todd Samuel Presner and others. Stanford, CA: Stanford University Press, 2004.

Lackey, Lionel. "Plausibility and the Romantic Plot Construction of *Quentin Durward*." *Studies in Philology* 90, no. 1 (1993): 101–14.

Lamb, Jonathan. *Preserving the Self in the South Seas, 1680–1840*. Chicago: University of Chicago Press, 2001.

Langan, Celeste. "Understanding Media in 1805: Audiovisual Hallucination in *The Lay of the Last Minstrel*." *Studies in Romanticism* 40, no. 1 (Spring 2001): 49–70.

Latour, Bruno. *Irreductions*. In *The Pasteurization of France*, translated by Alan Sheridan and John Law. Cambridge, MA: Harvard University Press, 1988.

———. *On the Modern Cult of the Factish Gods*, translated by Catherine Porter and Heather Maclean. Durham, NC: Duke University Press, 2010.

Leask, Nigel. *British Romantic Writers and the East: Anxieties of Empire*. Cambridge: Cambridge University Press, 1993.

———. *Curiosity and the Aesthetics of Travel Writing, 1770–1840: 'From an Antique Land.'* Cambridge: Cambridge University Press, 2002.

Le Carré, John. *The Constant Gardener: A Novel*. New York: Scribner, 2001.

Levecq, Christine. *Slavery and Sentiment: The Politics of Feeling in Black Atlantic Antislavery Writing, 1770–1860*. Durham, NH: University of New Hampshire Press, 2008.

Lewis, Matthew. *The Monk*, edited by Howard Anderson, introduction by Emma McEvoy. New York: Oxford University Press, 1995.

Lincoln, Andrew. *Walter Scott and Modernity*. Edinburgh: Edinburgh University Press, 2007.

Löwy, Michael, and Robert Sayre. *Romanticism against the Tide of Modernity*, translated by Catherine Porter. Durham, NC: Duke University Press, 2001.

Lumsden, Alison, and Ainsley McIntosh. "The Narrative Poems." In *The Edinburgh Companion to Walter Scott*, edited by Fiona Robertson. Edinburgh: Edinburgh University Press, 2012.

Lynch, Deidre. *The Economy of Character: Novels, Market Culture, and the Business of Inner Meaning*. Chicago: University of Chicago Press, 1998.

———. "Gothic Fiction." In *The Cambridge Companion to Fiction in the Romantic Era*, edited by Richard Maxwell and Katie Trumpener. Cambridge: Cambridge University Press, 2008.

———. "Gothic Libraries and National Subjects." *Studies in Romanticism* 40, no. 1 (Spring 2001): 29–48.

Mack, Douglas, and Suzanne Gilbert. "Scottish History in the Waverley Novels." In Gottlieb and Duncan, eds., *Approaches to Teaching Scott's Waverley Novels*.

Makdisi, Saree. "Romantic Cultural Imperialism." In *The Cambridge History of English Romantic Literature*, edited by James Chandler. Cambridge: Cambridge University Press, 2009.

———. *Romantic Imperialism: Universal Empire and the Culture of Modernity*. Cambridge: Cambridge University Press, 1998.

———. *William Blake and the Impossible History of the 1790s*. Chicago: University of Chicago Press, 2003.

———. "Worldly Romanticism." Special issue of *Nineteenth-Century Literature* 65, no. 4 (March 2011): 429–32.

Malherbe, Michael. "The Impact on Europe." In *The Cambridge Companion to the Scottish Enlightenment*, edited by Alexander Broadie. Cambridge: Cambridge University Press, 2003.

Manning, Peter J. *Byron and His Fictions*. Detroit: Wayne State University Press, 1978.

———, ed. "Nostalgia, Melancholy, Anxiety: Discursive Mobility and the Circulation of Bodies." Special issue of *Studies in Romanticism* 49, no. 2 (Summer 2010): 195–336.

Marx Karl, and Frederick Engels. *The German Ideology*. In *The Marx-Engels Reader*. 2nd edition, edited by Robert C. Tucker. New York: W. W. Norton, 1978.

Maxwell, Richard. *The Historical Novel in Europe, 1650–1950*. Cambridge: Cambridge University Press, 2009.

McCracken-Flesher, Caroline. *Possible Scotlands: Walter Scott and the Story of Tomorrow*. Oxford: Oxford University Press, 2005.

McDayter, Ghislaine. *Byromania and the Birth of Celebrity Culture*. Albany, NY: State University of New York Press, 2009.

McGann, Jerome J. "Hero With a Thousand Faces: The Rhetoric of Byronism." *Studies in Romanticism* 31, no. 3 (Fall 1992): 295–313.

McLane, Maureen N. *Balladeering, Minstrelsy, and the Making of British Romantic Poetry*. Cambridge: Cambridge University Press, 2008.

McMaster, Graham. *Scott and Society*. Cambridge: Cambridge University Press, 1981.

McNeil, Kenneth. *Scotland, Britain, Empire: Writing the Highlands, 1760–1860*. Columbus: The Ohio State University Press, 2007.
Meek, Ronald. *Social Science and the Ignoble Savage*. Cambridge: Cambridge University Press, 1976.
Mehta, Uday Singh. *Liberalism and Empire: A Study in Nineteenth-Century British Liberal Thought*. Chicago: University of Chicago Press, 1999.
Meillassoux, Quentin. *After Finitude: An Essay on the Necessity of Contingency*, translated by Ray Brassier. London: Continuum, 2008.
Mellor, Anne K. *Mothers of the Nation: Women's Political Writing in England, 1780–1830*. Bloomington: Indiana University Press, 2000.
Melnick, Arthur. "Kant's Proofs of Substance and Causation." In *The Cambridge Companion to Kant and Modern Philosophy*, edited by Paul Guyer. Cambridge: Cambridge University Press, 2006.
Mergenthal, Sylvia. "'An Imaginary Line Drawn Through Waste and Wilderness': Scott's *The Talisman*." In *Romantic Localities: Europe Writes Place*, edited by Christoph Bode and Jacqueline Labbe. London: Pickering and Chatto, 2010.
Miles, Robert. *Ann Radcliffe: The Great Enchantress*. Manchester: Manchester University Press, 1995.
Millar, John. *An Historical View of the English Government*, edited by Mark Salber Phillips and Dale R. Smith. Indianapolis, IN: Liberty Fund, 2006.
———. *The Origin of the Distinction of Ranks*, edited by Aaron Garrett. Indianapolis, IN: Liberty Fund, 2006.
Mitchell, Robert. "Global Flows: Romantic-era Terraforming." Unpublished manuscript.
———. *Sympathy and the State in the Romantic Era: Systems, State Finance, and the Shadows of Futurity*. New York: Routledge, 2007.
Moers, Ellen. *Literary Women*. Garden City, NY: Doubleday, 1976.
Mole, Tom. *Byron's Romantic Celebrity: Industrial Culture and the Hermeneutic of Intimacy*. Houndmills, Basingstoke: Palgrave Macmillan, 2007.
Moretti, Franco. *Graphs, Maps, Trees*. London: Verso, 2005.
Mortensen, Peter. "The Englishness of the English Gothic Novel: Romance Writing in an Age of Europhobia." In *"Better in France?": The Circulation of Ideas across the Channel in the Eighteenth Century*, edited by Frédéric Ogée. Lewisburg, PA: Bucknell University Press, 2005.
Morton, Graeme. *Unionist-Nationalism: Governing Urban Scotland, 1830–1860*. Edinburgh: Tuckwell Press, 1999.
Mulholland, James. *Sounding Imperial: Poetic Voice and the Politics of Empire*. Baltimore: The Johns Hopkins University Press, 2013.
Muthu, Sankar. *Enlightenment against Empire*. Princeton, NJ: Princeton University Press, 2003.
Nancy, Jean-Luc. *The Creation of the World or Globalization*, translated by François Raffoul and David Pettigrew. Albany, NY: State University of New York Press, 2007.
Nord, Deborah Epstein. *Gypsies and the British Imagination, 1807–1930*. New York: Columbia University Press, 2006.
Norton, Richter. *Mistress of Udolpho: The Life of Ann Radcliffe*. Liverpool: Liverpool University Press, 1999.
Nussbaum, Felicity, ed. *The Global Eighteenth Century*. Baltimore: The Johns Hopkins University Press, 2003.
Nussbaum, Martha. *Not for Profit: Why Democracy Needs the Humanities*. Princeton, NJ: Princeton University Press, 2010.

O'Brien, Karen. "Poetry, Knowledge, and Imperial Globalization." In *The Postcolonial Enlightenment: Eighteenth-Century Colonialism and Postcolonial Theory*, edited by Daniel Carey and Lynn Festa. Cambridge: Cambridge University Press, 2009.
Oliver, Susan. *Scott, Byron, and the Poetics of Cultural Encounter*. Houndmills, Basingstoke: Palgrave Macmillan, 2005.
Omori, Ikuo. "The 'Scottish Triangle' in the Shaping of Political Economy: David Hume, Sir James Steuart, and Adam Smith." In *The Rise of Political Economy in the Scottish Enlightenment*, edited by Tatsuya Sakamoto and Hideo Tanaka. London: Routledge, 2003.
Osterhammel, Jürgen, and Niels P. Petersson. *Globalization: A Short History*, translated by Dona Geyer. Princeton, NJ: Princeton University Press, 2005.
Oz-Salzburger, Fania. *Translating the Enlightenment: Scottish Civic Discourse in Eighteenth-Century Germany*. Oxford: Oxford University Press, 1995.
Paulson, Ronald. "Gothic Fiction and the French Revolution." *ELH* 48, no. 3 (Fall 1981): 532–54.
Peck, Jamie, Nik Theodore, and Neil Brenner. "Neoliberalism Resurgent? Market Rule after the Great Recession." *South Atlantic Quarterly* 111.2 (Spring 2012): 265–88.
Perkins, Pam. "John Moore, Ann Radcliffe and the Gothic Vision of Italy." *Gothic Studies* 8, no. 1 (May 2006): 35–51.
Phillips, Mark Salber. *Society and Sentiment: Genres of Historical Writing in Britain, 1740–1820*. Princeton, NJ: Princeton University Press, 2000.
Piper, Andrew. *Dreaming in Books: The Making of the Bibliographic Imagination in the Romantic Age*. Chicago: University of Chicago Press, 2009.
Pittock, Murrary G. H. "Historiography." In *The Cambridge Companion to the Scottish Enlightenment*, edited by Alexander Broadie. Cambridge: Cambridge University Press, 2003.
―――, ed. *The Reception of Sir Walter Scott in Europe*. London: Continuum, 2006.
Poovey, Mary. *Genres of the Credit Economy: Mediating Value in Eighteenth- and Nineteenth-Century Britain*. Chicago: University of Chicago Press, 2008.
―――. *A History of the Modern Fact: Problems of Knowledge in the Sciences of Wealth and Society*. Chicago: University of Chicago Press, 1998.
―――. "Ideology in *The Mysteries of Udolpho*." *Criticism* 21 (1979): 307–30.
Pope, Alexander. *Selected Poetry and Prose*, edited by William K. Wimsat. New York: Holt, Rinehart and Winston, n.d.
Porter, Bernard. *The Absent-Minded Imperialists: Empire, Society, and Culture in Britain*. Oxford: Oxford University Press, 2005.
Price, Richard. "One Big Thing: Britain, Its Empire, and Their Imperial Culture." *Journal of British Studies* 45, no. 3 (July 2006): 602–27.
Radcliffe, Ann. *The Italian, or The Confessional of the Black Penitents*, edited by Frederick Garber, introduction and notes by E. J. Clery. Oxford: Oxford University Press, 1998.
―――. *A Journey made in the Summer of 1794, through Holland and the Western Frontier of Germany, with a Return down the Rhine: to which are added, Observations during a tour to the Lakes of Lancashire, Westmoreland, and Cumberland*. London: G. G. and J. Robinson, 1795.
―――. *The Mysteries of Udolpho*, edited by Bonamy Dobrée, introduction and notes by Terry Castle. Oxford: Oxford University Press, 1998.
―――. *The Romance of the Forest*, edited by Chloe Chard. Oxford: Oxford University Press, 1986.

Raj, Kapil. *Relocating Modern Science: Circulation and the Construction of Knowledge in South Asia and Europe, 1650–1900*. Houndmills, Basingstoke: Palgrave Macmillan, 2007.
Rancière, Jacques. *The Politics of Aesthetics*, translated by Gabriel Rockhill. London: Continuum, 2004.
Reston, James Jr. *Warriors of God: Richard the Lionheart and Saladin in the Third Crusade*. New York: Doubleday, 2001.
Robertson, Fiona. *Legitimate Histories: Scott, Gothic, and the Authorities of Fiction*. Oxford: Clarendon Press, 1994.
Robertson, John. *The Case for the Enlightenment: Scotland and Naples, 1680–1760*. Cambridge: Cambridge University Press, 2005.
Robertson, Roland. *Globalization*. New York: Sage, 1992.
Rogers, Deborah, ed. *The Critical Response to Ann Radcliffe*. Westport, CT: Greenwood Press, 1994.
Rohrbach, Emily. "Anna Barbauld's History of the Future: A Deviant Way to Poetic Agency." *European Romantic Review* 17, no. 2 (2006): 179–87.
Ross, Marlon B. "Configurations of Feminine Reform: The Woman Writer and the Tradition of Dissent." In *Re-Visioning Romanticism: British Women Writers, 1776–1837*, edited by Carol Shiner Wilson and Joel Haefner. Philadelphia: University of Pennsylvania Press, 1994.
———. *The Contours of Masculine Desire: Romanticism and the Rise of Women's Poetry*. Oxford: Oxford University Press, 1989.
———. Foreword to *Felicia Hemans: Reimagining Poetry in the Nineteenth Century*, edited by Nanora Sweet and Julie Melnyk. Houndmills, Basingstoke: Palgrave Macmillan, 2001.
Rothschild, Emma. *Economic Sentiments: Adam Smith, Condorcet, and the Enlightenment*. Cambridge, MA: Harvard University Press, 2001.
———. *The Inner Life of Empires: An Eighteenth-Century History*. Princeton, NJ: Princeton University Press, 2011.
Ruppert, Timothy. "Waterloo, Napoleon, and the Vision of Peace in Louisa Stuart Costello's *The Maid of the Cyprus Isle*." *Studies in Romanticism* 51, no. 4 (Winter 2012): 555–78.
Russett, Margaret. "Narrative as Enchantment in *The Mysteries of Udolpho*." *ELH* 65, no. 1 (1998): 159–86.
Rutherford, Andrew, ed. *Byron: The Critical Heritage*. New York: Barnes & Noble, 1970.
Ryan, Dermot. *Technologies of Empire: Writing, Imagination, and the Making of Imperial Networks, 1750–1820*. Newark, NJ: University of Delaware Press, 2013.
Saglia, Diego. "'A deeper and richer music': The Poetics of Sound and Voice in Felicia Hemans's 1820s Poetry." *ELH* 74, no. 2 (Summer 2007): 351–70.
———. "Looking at the Other: Cultural Difference and the Traveler's Gaze in *The Italian*." *Studies in the Novel* 28, no. 1 (Spring 1996): 12–38.
———. *Poetic Castles in Spain: British Romanticism and Figurations of Iberia*. Amsterdam: Rodopi, 2000.
———. "War Romances, Historical Analogies and Coleridge's *Letters on the Spaniards*." In *Romantic Wars: Studies in Culture and Conflict, 1789–1822*, edited by Philip Shaw. Aldershot, UK: Ashgate, 2000.
Said, Edward. "The Clash of Ignorance." *The Nation*, October 4, 2001. Accessed 14 July 2008. www.thenation.com/doc/20011022/said.
———. *Culture and Imperialism*. New York: Vintage, 1993.
———. *Orientalism*. New York: Vintage, 1978.
Sassen, Saskia. *A Sociology of Globalization*. New York: W. W. Norton, 2007.

———. "Spatialities and Temporalities of the Global: Elements for a Theorization." *Public Culture* 12, no. 1 (2000): 215–32.
———. *Territory, Authority, Rights: From Medieval to Global Assemblages*. Princeton, NJ: Princeton University Press, 2006.
Schmidt, Claudia. *David Hume: Reason in History*. University Park, PA: Penn State University Press, 2003.
Schmitt, Cannon. *Alien Nation: Nineteenth-Century Gothic Fictions and English Nationality*. Philadelphia: University of Pennsylvania Press, 1997.
———. "Techniques of Terror, Technologies of Nationality: Ann Radcliffe's *The Italian*." *ELH* 61, no. 4 (Winter 1994): 853–77.
Scott, Walter. *Anne of Geierstein*, edited by J. H. Alexander. Edinburgh: Edinburgh University Press, 2000.
———. *The Journal of Sir Walter Scott*, edited by W. E. K. Anderson. Edinburgh: Canongate, 1998.
———. *Letters of Sir Walter Scott*, edited by H. J. C. Grierson. London: Constable, 1933.
———. *The Poetical Works of Sir Walter Scott*, edited by J. Robertson. London: Oxford University Press, 1940.
———. *Quentin Durward*, edited by J. H. Alexander and G. A. M. Wood. Edinburgh: Edinburgh University Press, 2001.
———. *Quentin Durward*, edited by Susan Manning. Oxford: Oxford University Press, 1992.
———. *The Talisman*, edited by J. B. Ellis with J. H. Alexander, P. D. Garside and David Hewitt. Edinburgh: Edinburgh University Press, 2009.
———. *The Talisman*. London: J. M. Dent & Sons, 1977.
———. *Waverley, or 'Tis Sixty Years Since*, edited by Claire Lamont. Oxford: Oxford University Press, 1986.
———. *The Works of Sir Walter Scott*. Ware, Hertfordshire: Wordsworth Editions, 1995.
Semmel, Bernard. *The Rise of Free-Trade Imperialism: Classical Political Economy, the Empire of Free Trade and Imperialism, 1750–1850*. Cambridge: Cambridge University Press, 1970.
Sen, Amartya. "Civilizational Imprisonments." *The New Republic* 226, no. 22 (June 10, 2002): 28–33.
Shapira, Yael. "Where the Bodies Are Hidden: Ann Radcliffe's 'Delicate' Gothic." *Eighteenth-Century Fiction* 18, no. 4 (Summer 2006): 1–24.
Shaw, Philip. *Waterloo and the Romantic Imagination*. Houndmills, Basingstoke: Palgrave Macmillan, 2002.
Shelley, Percy. *A Defence of Poetry*, edited by Mary Shelley. New York: Bobbs-Merrill, 1904.
Sher, Richard B. *The Enlightenment and the Book: Scottish Authors and their Publishers in Eighteenth-Century Britain, Ireland, and America*. Chicago: University of Chicago Press, 2006.
Shields, Juliet. *Sentimental Literature and Anglo-Scottish Identity, 1745–1820*. Cambridge: Cambridge University Press, 2010.
Simpson, David. *Romanticism, Nationalism, and the Revolt against Theory*. Chicago: University of Chicago Press, 1993.
———. "'Which is the merchant here? and which the Jew?': Friends and Enemies in Walter Scott's Crusader Novels." *Studies in Romanticism* 47, no. 4 (Winter 2008): 437–53.
Simpson, Erik. "'A Good One Though Rather for the Foreign Market': Mercenary Writing and Scott's *Quentin Durward*." *Studies in Romanticism* 48, no. 4 (Winter 2009): 667–85.
Simpson, Michael. "Wavering on Europe: Walter Scott and the Equilibrium of Empires." *Romanticism* 11, no. 2 (2005): 127–42.

Singh, Jyotsna G., ed. *A Companion to the Global Renaissance*. Malden, MA: Wiley-Blackwell, 2009.
Siskin, Clifford. "Mediated Enlightenment: The System of the World." In *This Is Enlightenment*, edited by Siskin and William Warner. Chicago: University of Chicago Press, 2010.
———. "Novels and Systems." *Novel: A Forum on Fiction* 34, no. 2 (Spring 2001): 202–15.
———. *The Work of Writing: Literature and Social Change in Britain, 1700–1830*. Baltimore: Johns Hopkins University Press, 1998.
Siskin, Clifford, and William Warner. "This Is Enlightenment: An Invitation in the Form of an Argument." In *This is Enlightenment*, edited by Siskin and Warner. Chicago: University of Chicago Press, 2010.
Skinner, Andrew S. "Economic Theory." In *The Cambridge Companion to the Scottish Enlightenment*, edited by Alexander Broadie. Cambridge: Cambridge University Press, 2003.
———. *A System of Social Science: Papers Relating to Adam Smith*. 2nd edition. Oxford: Oxford University Press, 1996.
Sloterdijk, Peter. "The Space of Global Capitalism and Its Imaginary Imperialism: An Interview with Peter Sloteridjk." In *Peter Sloterdijk's Spherological Poetics of Being*, edited by Willem Schinkel and Liesbeth Noordegraaf-Eelens. Amsterdam: University of Amsterdam Press, 2011.
Smith, Adam. *The Correspondence of Adam Smith*, edited by Ernest Campbell Mossner and Ian Simpson Ross. Oxford: Clarendon, 1977.
———. *An Inquiry into the Nature and Causes of the Wealth of Nations*, 2 volumes, edited by R. H. Campbell and A. S. Skinner. Indianapolis, IN: Liberty Fund, 1981.
———. *Lectures on Jurisprudence*, edited by R. L. Meek, D. D. Raphael, and P. G. Stein. Indianapolis, IN: Liberty Fund, 1982.
Smith, Neil. *Uneven Development: Nature, Capital, and the Production of Space*. New York: Blackwell, 1984.
Soule, George. "*The Prelude* and the French Revolution." *Charles Lamb Bulletin* 129 (2005): 9–19.
Spivak, Gayatri Chakravorty. *An Aesthetic Education in the Era of Globalization*. Cambridge, MA: Harvard University Press, 2012.
St. Clair, William. *The Reading Nation in the Romantic Period*. Cambridge: Cambridge University Press, 2004.
Steger, Manfred. *Globalization: A Very Short Introduction*. New York: Oxford University Press, 2003.
———. *Globalization: A Very Short Introduction*. 2nd edition. New York: Oxford University Press, 2009.
———. *The Rise of the Global Imaginary: Political Ideologies from the French Revolution to the Global War on Terror*. Oxford: Oxford University Press, 2008.
Sudan, Rajani. *Fair Exotics: Xenophobic Subjects in English Literature, 1720–1850*. Philadelphia: University of Pennsylvania Press, 2002.
Sulkes, Stanley. "The Code of Hospitality in the Waverley Novels: A Study of Sir Walter Scott's Fiction." PhD dissertation, 1976.
Sutherland, John. *The Life of Walter Scott*. Oxford: Blackwell, 1995.
Sweet, Nanora. "Felicia Hemans' 'A Tale of the Secret Tribunal': Gothic Empire in the Age of Jeremy Bentham and Walter Scott." *European Journal of English Studies* 6, no. 2 (2002): 159–71.
———. "History, Imperialism, and the Aesthetics of the Beautiful: Hemans and the Post-Napoleonic Moment." In *At the Limits of Romanticism: Essays in Cultural, Feminist,*

and Materialist Criticism, edited by Mary A. Favret and Nicola Watson. Bloomington: Indiana University Press, 1994.

Teichgraeber, Richard F. III. *"Free Trade" and Moral Philosophy: Rethinking the Sources of Adam Smith's* Wealth of Nations. Durham, NC: Duke University Press, 1986.

Trivedi, Harish. "From Bollywood to Hollywood: The Globalization of Hindi Cinema." In *The Postcolonial and the Global,* edited by Revathi Krishnaswamy and John C. Hawley. Minneapolis: University of Minnesota Press, 2008.

Trumpener, Katie. *Bardic Nationalism: The Romantic Novel and the British Empire.* Princeton, NJ: Princeton University Press, 1997.

Vermeule, Blakey. *Why Do We Care About Literary Characters?* Baltimore: The Johns Hopkins University Press, 2010.

Virilio, Paul. *The Great Accelerator,* translated by Julie Rose. Malden, MA: Polity, 2012.

———. *Speed and Politics,* translated by Mark Polizzoti. Los Angeles: Semiotext(e), 1986.

Wagner, Peter. *Modernity: Understanding the Present.* Malden, MA: Polity, 2012.

Wallace, Miriam L., ed. *Enlightening Romanticism, Romancing the Enlightenment: British Novels from 1750 to 1832.* Aldershot, UK: Ashgate, 2009.

Wallace, Tara Ghoshal. *Imperial Characters: Home and Periphery in Eighteenth-Century Literature.* Lewisburg, PA: Bucknell University Press, 2010.

———. "Thinking Globally: *The Talisman* and *The Surgeon's Daughter."* In Gottlieb and Duncan, eds., *Approaches to Teaching Scott's Waverley Novels.*

Wallerstein, Immanuel. *The Capitalist World-Economy.* Cambridge: Cambridge University Press, 1979.

———. *The Modern World System I: Capitalist Agriculture and the Origins of the European World-Economy in the Sixteenth Century.* New York: Academic Press, 1974.

———. *Utopistics, or, Historical Choices of the Twenty-First Century.* New York: New Press, 1998.

———. *World-Systems Analysis: An Introduction.* Durham, NC: Duke University Press, 2004.

Walmsley, Peter. "The Melancholy Briton: Enlightenment Sources of the Gothic." In *Enlightening Romanticism, Romancing the Enlightenment,* edited by Miriam L. Wallace. Aldershot, UK: Ashgate, 2009.

Walpole, Horace. *The Castle of Otranto,* edited by W. S. Lewis, introduction and notes by E. J. Clery. Oxford: Oxford University Press, 1996.

Watson, David. Preface to *The Worlding Project: Doing Cultural Studies in the Era of Globalization,* edited by Rob Wilson and Christopher Leigh Connery. Santa Cruz, CA: New Pacific Press and North Atlantic Books, 2007.

Watt, James. *Contesting the Gothic: Fiction, Genre, and Cultural Conflict, 1764–1832.* Cambridge: Cambridge University Press, 1999.

———. "Scott, the Scottish Enlightenment, and Romantic Orientalism." In *Scotland and the Borders of Romanticism,* edited by Leith Davis, Ian Duncan, and Janet Sorensen. Cambridge: Cambridge University Press, 2004.

Wein, Toni. *British Identities, Heroic Nationalisms, and the Gothic Novel, 1764–1824.* Houndmills, Basingstoke: Palgrave Macmillan, 2002.

Weinbrot, Howard. *Britannia's Issue: The Rise of British Literature from Dryden to Ossian.* Cambridge: Cambridge University Press, 1993.

Welsh, Alexander. *The Hero of the Waverley Novels: With New Essays on Scott.* Princeton, NJ: Princeton University Press, 1992.

Wheeler, Roxann. *The Complexion of Race: Categories of Difference in Eighteenth-Century British Culture.* Philadelphia: University of Pennsylvania Press, 2000.

White, Daniel E. *Early Romanticism and Religious Dissent.* Cambridge: Cambridge University Press, 2006.
Wickman, Matthew. "Alba Newton and Alasdair Gray." In *Scotland as Science Fiction*, edited by Caroline McCracken-Flesher. Lewisburg, PA: Bucknell University Press, 2012.
Wiley, Michael. *Romantic Migrations: Local, National, and Transnational Dispositions.* Houndmills, Basingstoke: Palgrave Macmillan, 2008.
Wilt, Judith. "Transmutations: From Alchemy to History in *Quentin Durward* and *Anne of Geierstein.*" *European Romantic Review* 13, no. 3 (2002): 249–60.
Winch, Donald. *Riches and Poverty: An Intellectual History of Political Economy in Britain, 1750–1834.* Cambridge: Cambridge University Press, 1996.
Withers, Charles W. J. "Geography, Natural History and the Eighteenth-Century Enlightenment: Putting the World in Place." *History Workshop Journal* 39 (1995): 137–63.
Wohlgemut, Esther. *Romantic Cosmopolitanism.* Houndmills, Basingstoke: Palgrave Macmillan, 2009.
Womack, Peter. *Improvement and Romance: Constructing the Myth of the Highlands.* London: Macmillan, 1989.
Woodring, Carl. "Three Poets of Waterloo." *The Wordsworth Circle* 18, no. 2 (1987): 54–57.
Wordsworth, William. *The Prelude, or Growth of a Poet's Mind*, edited by Ernest de Selincourt. Oxford: Oxford University Press, 1960.
Wordsworth, William, and Samuel Taylor Coleridge. *Lyrical Ballads: 1798 and 1800*, edited by Michael Gamer and Dahlia Porter. Peterborough, Ontario: Broadview Press, 2008.
———. *Lyrical Ballads and Related Writings*, edited by William Richey and Daniel Robinson. Boston: Houghton Mifflin, 2002.
Wright, Angela. *Britain, France, and the Gothic: The Import of Terror, 1764–1820.* Cambridge: Cambridge University Press, 2013.
———. *Gothic Fiction: A Reader's Guide to Essential Criticism.* Houndmills, Basingstoke: Palgrave Macmillan, 2007.
———. "Inspiration, Toleration and Relocation in Ann Radcliffe's *A Journey Made in the Summer of 1794, through Holland and the Western Frontier of Germany* (1795)." In *Romantic Localities: Europe Writes Place*, edited by Christoph Bode and Jacqueline Labbe. London: Pickering and Chatto, 2010.
Yadav, Alok. *Before the Empire of English: Literature, Provinciality, and Nationalism in Eighteenth-Century Britain.* Houndmills, Basingstoke: Palgrave Macmillan, 2004.
Young, Robert J. C. *Colonial Desire: Hybridity in Theory, Culture and Race.* London: Routledge, 1995.
Žižek, Slavoj. "Against Human Rights," *New Left Review* 34 (July-August 2005): 115–31.
———. *First as Tragedy, Then as Farce.* London: Verso, 2009.
———. *For They Know Not What They Do: Enjoyment as a Political Factor.* 2nd edition. London: Verso, 2002.
———. "Multiculturalism, the Reality of an Illusion." Accessed 24 February 2010. http://www.lacan.com/essays/?page_id=454.
———. *Tarrying with the Negative: Kant, Hegel, and the Critique of Ideology.* Durham, NC: Duke University Press, 1993.
———. "Tolerance as an Ideological Category." *Critical Inquiry* 34, no. 4 (Summer 2008): 660–82.
———. *Violence: Six Sideways Reflections.* New York: Picador, 2008.
———. *Welcome to the Desert of the Real!: Five Essays on September 11 and Related Dates.* New York: Verso, 2002.

INDEX

Addison, Joseph, 20–21
Adorno, Theodor, 44
Agamben, Giorgio, 66, 132–36, 143
Ahern, Stephen, 168n13
Al-Andalus, 75–76, 77
"Albion," 174n19
Alexander, J. H., 185n67
Alliston, April, 58
alter-globalist movements, 152, 187n17
"The Ancient Mariner, A Poet's Reverie" (Coleridge), 149
Anderson, Benedict, 81
Anne of Geierstein (Scott), 119, 136–45, 184n52
Appadurai, Arjun, 3
Appiah, Kwame Anthony, 55
Aravamudan, Srinivas, 97
Arendt, Hannah, 185n60
Armstrong, Nancy, 149–50
Arrighi, Giovanni, 163n50
Ashcroft, Bill, 3
Austen, Jane: *Northanger Abbey*, 65, 167n5; *Persuasion*, 68, 149; Said on *Mansfield Park*, 7, 157n28
autoimmunity, 82

Badiou, Alain, 106, 166n84
Bainbridge, Simon, 92–93, 175n39
Baker, Samuel, 8, 57, 164n53, 175n28
Balibar, Étienne, 145

ban, Agamben's logic of the, 132–33
Barbauld, Anna Laetitia: *Eighteen-Hundred and Eleven*, 76, 78–83; Grant compared to, 83–89; on Radcliffe, 64–65
Barber, Benjamin, 119
bare lives, 66, 136, 141
Barrell, John, 77, 157n32
Baucom, Ian, 8, 153, 158n33
Bauman, Zygmunt, 3
Bayly, C. A., 5
Behrendt, Stephen, 69, 71
Belich, James, 5–6
Bell, David A., 91, 176n60
Benhabib, Seyla, 41, 42, 142, 185n60
Berdell, John, 162n27
Bewell, Alan, 8, 113
Birns, Nicholas, 79
Blake, William, 133, 157n31, 170n44
Bohls, Elizabeth, 158n43
Brennan, Timothy, 65
The Bride of Abydos (Byron), 95, 100
The Bride of Lammermoor (Scott), 125, 179n66
British Empire, imperialism, and colonialism: globalization, relation with, 6; poets' predictions on, 81–83, 85–86, 94; Romantic globalism and, 148; Smith on, 26–27
Broadie, Alexander, 30, 160n4
Brown, Tony, 165n64

Brown, Wendy, 65
Bruzelius, Margaret, 118
Buck-Morss, Susan, 54–55, 99
Buffon, Georges-Louis, Comte, 33, 35
Burke, Edmund, 15, 46, 66
Butler, Judith, 101, 179n40
Butler, Marilyn, 96
Byron, George Gordon, Lord: *The Bride of Abydos*, 95, 100; *Childe Harold's Pilgrimage*, 69, 89, 97, 178n21; *The Corsair*, 95, 99–100, 104; death of, 113; *Don Juan*, 109; *The Giaour*, 95, 100, 104; *The Island*, 109; *Lara*, 97, 99–104; *Manfred*, 102, 179n40; popularity of, 96–97; *Sardanapalus*, 109–13, 114; *The Siege of Corinth*, 97, 100, 102, 104–9, 112–13; "turning Turk" or "going native" trope and, 97

Cadell, Robert, 137
Calhoun, Craig, 141, 183n30
Canuel, Mark, 63
capitalism: destabilizing, inequitable tendencies of, 28–29; print capitalism, 81; Wallerstein on, 24, 151; Watson on, 152; Žižek on, 181n75. *See also* Smith, Adam
"Casabianca" (Hemans), 174n22
Casanova, Pascale, 181n3, 186n72
Castells, Manuel, 15
Chakrabarty, Dipesh, 161n15
Chandler, James, 29–30, 32, 36, 78–79, 165n65
Chang, Elizabeth, 8
Cheah, Pheng, 152–53
Chibber, Vivek, 7, 157n29
Childe Harold's Pilgrimage (Byron), 69, 89, 97, 178n21
chilvaric romance idiom, 72–73
choice, freedom of, 135
Chow, Rey, 37
Christensen, Jerome, 100, 111, 179n49, 181n76, 183n31, 185n69
Christianity and Islam in Byron's *The Siege of Corinth*, 106–8
civilizational clashes. *See* clash of civilizations mentality

clash of civilizations mentality: Byron's *Lara* and, 99–104; Byron's *Sardanapalus* and, 109–13; Byron's *The Island* and, 109; Byron's *The Siege of Corinth* and, 104–9; critiques of, 98–99, 119, 179n57, 181n75; Huntington's concept, 98–99; levantinization and, 97, 100–105, 111–12; Scott's *The Talisman* and, 113–19
Clery, E. J., 46
Cochran, Peter, 179n40
cognitive mapping, 160n12
Cohen, Margaret, 122
Coleridge, Samuel Taylor, 1–2, 149
Colley, Linda, 169n24
colonialism. *See* British Empire, imperialism, and colonialism
commerce and trade, foreign: free trade, 22–23, 25–26, 162n28; Hume on, 20, 21; Smith on, 25
conjectural history. *See* stadial theory and conjectural history
The Constant Gardener (Le Carré), 147–48
Cooper, James Fennimore, 121
The Corsair (Byron), 95, 99–100, 104
cosmopolitanism: Appiah on strands of, 55; limits of, 65–66; sympathetic, 54, 55–58, 60–67, 142–43
"cosmopolitan right" (Kant), 42, 142
Count Robert of Paris (Scott), 179n59
Cowper, William, 9
Crawford, Robert, 14
Croker, John Wilson, 78, 80, 83
Crusades, in Scott's *The Talisman*, 114–19
cryptoliberalism, policy of, 181n76
Culture and Imperialism (Said), 7, 157n28
Curran, Stuart, 70

Darwin, John, 6, 156n23
Defauconpret, A. J. B., 181n3
Defence of Poetry (Shelley), 149
Dekker, George, 51
Deleuze, Gilles, 132
Deligiorgi, Katerina, 167n96
DeLucia, JoEllen, 168n13
Derrida, Jacques, 10–11, 29, 82, 115, 142–43, 159n44

The Deserted Village (Goldsmith), 176n42
Dever, Carolyn, 122
Distinction of Ranks (Millar), 32, 35–39
Don Juan (Byron), 109
Doyle, Laura, 8
Duncan, Ian, 123, 184n54, 185n69

East India Company, 27
Eighteen-Hundred and Eleven (Barbauld), 76, 78–89
Eighteen-Hundred and Thirteen (Grant), 83–89
Elfenbein, Andrew, 110
Ellis, Markman, 168n12
England and Spain (Hemans), 70–78
Enlightenment: Gothic genre and, 44–46, 168n13; historicity, shift in, 38; mediation and, 150. *See also* Scottish Enlightenment
Enquiry Concerning the Principles of Morals (Hume), 161n19
Essay on Man (Pope), 85
Essay on the Military Policy and Institutions of the British Empire (Pasley), 148
Essays on the Superstitions of the Highlands of Scotland (Grant), 83
European Union, 163n43

Fanon, Franz, 7
Favret, Mary, 8–9, 69, 77, 80, 85
"Fears in Solitude" (Coleridge), 1–2
Fenves, Peter, 42
Ferguson, Adam, 82, 164n60
Fielding, Penny, 88, 123
The Field of Waterloo (Scott), 89–90, 92–94
Fletcher, Richard, 174n24
foreign trade. *See* commerce and trade, foreign
Foucault, Michel, 6, 20, 130
France, war with. *See* Napoleonic Wars in British poetry
Franklin, Caroline, 107, 178n32, 179n38
freedom: in Barbauld's *Eighteen Hundred Eleven*, 79–80; of choice, 135; Hemans on, 77
free trade, 22–23, 25–26, 162n28

French Revolution, 49–50
Frey, Anne, 130–31
Fukuyama, Francis, 177n7

Galli, Carlo, 21
Garofalo, Daniela, 111
Geertz, Clifford, 114
geographies. *See* landscapes and geographies
George IV, 121, 145
Gephardt, Katarina, 62, 172n71
The Giaour, 95, 100, 104
"global integration," 141
globalism, Romantic, 3–4, 10–12, 14–15, 45, 148–53. *See also specific authors and works*
globalization: Cheah on, 152–53; definitions of, 3–4; humanistic learning and, 153; imperialism, conflation with, 5–6, 7, 23; internationalization vs., 28; long-durational view of, 3–9; mediation, in Romantic era vs. today, 15; *mondialisation* vs., 10–11; postcolonialism and, 7–8, 9
globalization studies, 5
"going native" trope, 97
Goldsmith, Oliver, 176n42
Goodman, Kevis, 9, 175n39
Gothic genre: Enlightenment rationalism and, 44–45; Lewis' *The Monk*, 59–60, 63–64; loyalist Gothic subgenre, 59. *See also* Radcliffe, Ann
governmentality, 20, 21, 130, 136. *See also* nation-states
Graham, James, Earl of Montrose, 88
Graham, Thomas, 88
Grant, Anne ("Mrs. Grant of Laggan"): *Eighteen-Hundred and Thirteen*, 83–88; *Essays on the Superstitions of the Highlands of Scotland*, 83; Hemans and Barbauld compared to, 88–89
Guattari, Félix, 132
Guest, Harriet, 77
Guy Mannering (Scott), 131
gypsies (Roma), 131–35, 183n39

Haakonssen, Knud, 165n75

Habermas, Jürgen, 18, 103, 140, 178n25
Han, Suh-Renn, 185n64
Hardin, Russell, 161n19
Hardt, Michael, 4, 141
Hartley, L. P., 32, 165n65
Harvey, David, 29
Heinowitz, Rebecca Cole, 75
Heller-Roazen, Daniel, 167n96
Hemans, Felicia: Bainbridge on, 175n39; Barbauld and Grant compared to, 78–83, 88–89; "Casabianca," 174n22; *England and Spain*, 70–78; *Records of Women*, 89
An Historical Survey of the Foreign Affairs of Great Britain (Leckie), 148
Historical View of the English Government (Millar), 37, 166n81
historiography, Scottish Enlightenment and, 29–30, 31–32. *See also* stadial theory and conjectural history
Holton, Robert, 43
Homer, 71
homo sacer (*homines sacri*), 133, 134, 135–36, 143
Horkheimer, Max, 44
Horrocks, Ingrid, 57
hospitality: Derrida on, 142–43; global, 137, 142–44, 149; Kant on, 42
humanistic study, 153, 187n24
humanity and sympathy in Racliffe's *Romance of the Forest*, 53–54
Hume, David: *Enquiry Concerning the Principles of Morals*, 161n19; Gothic novels and, 45–46; Kant and, 40; limits of, 28–29; "Of the Origin of Government," 161n19; "Of the Study of History," 30; *Political Discourses*, 21–23; *Principles of Political Economy and Taxation*, 28; Scottish Enlightenment and, 17–18; on slave trade, 166n85; *Treatise on Human Nature*, 19–21
Huntington, Samuel P., 98–99, 177n7. *See also* clash of civilizations mentality
hybridity: in Byron's *Laura*, 100, 104; in Byron's *Sardanapalus*, 112, 113; in Byron's *The Siege of Corinth*, 105; in Hemans' *England or Spain*, 76; postcolonial theory and, 7; in Radcliffe's *The*

Mysteries of Udolpho, 58–59; in Scott's *Quentin Durward*, 132; in Scott's *The Talisman*, 117–18

Iliad (Homer), 71
imperialism: conflation of globalization with, 5–6, 7, 23; Hume's disarticulation of globalization and, 23. *See also* British Empire, imperialism, and colonialism
indifference, universalizing, 106
Ingham, Geoffrey, 28
Inquisition, 63
internationalization vs. globalization, 28
Islam and Christianity in Byron's *The Siege of Corinth*, 106–8
Islamic stereotypes, 114
The Island (Byron), 109
Israel, Jonathan, 18, 162n30, 163n46
The Italian (Radcliffe), 47–48, 54, 60–64
Ivanhoe (Rossini opera), 121–22
Ivanhoe (Scott), 115, 123, 179n55

Jackson, Emily A. Bernhard, 102
Jameson, Fredric, 18, 59, 150–51, 160n12
Jay, Paul, 9
Jeffrey, Francis, 95–96
Jenkins, Eugenia Zuroski, 157n32
Jerusalem Delivered (Tasso), 76
A Journey Made in the Summer of 1794 (Radcliffe), 61–62
Judson, Barbara, 109
justice systems, in Scott's *Quentin Durward*, 138–41

Kames, Henry Home, Lord, 32–35
Kant, Immanuel, 40–42, 142, 185n64
Keach, William, 78, 79
Keane, John, 152, 187n17
Kleingeld, Pauline, 41
Kosseleck, Reinhart, 38

Lacan, Jacques, 127
Lackey, Lionel, 184n44
The Lady of the Lake (Scott), 89

landscapes and geographies: Radcliffe and, 50–51, 62; Scott and, 184n52
Lara (Byron), 97, 99–104
Latour, Bruno, 15–16, 160n56
The Lay of the Last Minstrel (Scott), 72, 89
"league of nations" (Kant), 40–41
Leask, Nigel, 8, 101, 178n16
Le Carré, John, 147–48
Leckie, Gould Francis, 148
levantinization, 97, 100–105, 111–12. *See also* clash of civilizations mentality
Lewis, Matthew, 59–60, 63–64, 171n59
Lincoln, Andrew, 132, 179n58
Lowth, Robert, 61
Löwy, Michael, 153
Lynch, Deidre, 44–45, 171n54

Maclaurin, Colin, 18
Makdisi, Saree, 7, 103, 148, 157n31
Mandeville, Bernard, 21
Manfred (Byron), 102, 179n40
Manning, Peter J., 101
Manning, Susan, 124
Marmion (Scott), 72, 89
Marx, Karl, 31, 124, 182n11
Maxwell, Richard, 106
McNeil, Kenneth, 123
mediation: Armstrong on, 149–50; Enlightenment and, 150; Favret on, 69; globalization and, 15; Scott and, 150; vanishing mediators, 130, 131
Mehta, Uday Singh, 19, 23
Mellor, Ann, 68
mercantilism, 22, 24–25
The Metaphysics of Morals (Kant), 40–42
Miles, Robert, 48
Mill, James, 164n53
Millar, John, 32, 35–40, 165nn75–76, 166n81
Miller, Eugene F., 21–22
Milton, John, 84
Mistress of Udolpho (Norton), 48–49
Mitchell, Robert, 11
Moers, Ellen, 47
mondialisation, 10–11, 29, 36, 159n44
The Monk (Lewis), 59–60, 63–64, 171n59
Montesquieu, Baron de, 31, 33

More, Hannah, 59–60, 68
Moretti, Franco, 13
Mortensen, Peter, 60
Mulholland, James, 157n32
multiculturalism: in Byron's *The Island*, 109; in Byron's *The Siege of Corinth*, 104–9; Žižek on, 65
The Mysteries of Udolpho (Radcliffe), 56–59, 65

Nancy, Jean-Luc, 10–11, 36, 151–52
Napoleonic Wars in British poetry: Barbauld's *Eighteen-Hundred and Eleven*, 76, 78–88; emphasis on changing global position in Hemans, Barbauld, and Grant, 88–89; Grant's *Eighteen-Hundred and Thirteen*, 83–88; Hemans' *England and Spain*, 70–78, 79–80; levantinization and, 97; Scott's *The Field of Waterloo*, 89–90, 92–94; Scott's *Vision of Don Roderick*, 89–92; "total war" phenomenon and, 69–70, 91, 176n60; war events and Britain's situation, 72, 78, 79, 84, 182n6; women in the discursive public sphere and, 68–69
nationalism: Calhoun on, 183n30; in Grant's *Eighteen Hundred Thirteen*, 87; Radcliffe and, 54, 58, 62; Scott's *Waverley* and, 122. *See also* Napoleonic Wars in British poetry; patriotism
nation-states: decline of, 4–5; freedom of choice and, 135; Hume on commerce and development of, 21; sovereignty and, 4–5, 128–36, 140–42
Native Americans, 34–35
Negri, Antonio, 4, 141
neoclassicism, Hemans and, 71, 76, 77
neoliberalism: clash of civilizations and, 98; hegemony of, 66, 151–52; Hume and, 23; Le Carré's *The Constant Gardener* and, 147–48; Smith and, 25; Žižek on cosmopolitanism and, 65
North American Colonies, 26–27
Northanger Abbey (Austen), 65, 167n5
Norton, Rictor, 48–49
Not for Profit (Nussbaum), 153

Nussbaum, Martha, 153, 187n24

O'Brien, Karen, 23
"Of the Origin of Government" (Hume), 161n19
"Of the Study of History" (Hume), 30
Oliver, Susan, 107, 109, 113
Orientalism (Said), 6–7
Osterhammel, Jürgen, 9
Oz-Salzburger, Fania, 40
"Ozymandias" (Shelley), 82

Palgrave, Francis, 140
Pasley, Charles, 148
pastoral governmentality, 130
patriotism: in Coleridge's "Fears in Solitude," 1, 78; in Hemans' *England and Spain*, 74–76, 76–77; Radcliffe and, 59–60; Scott and, 89. *See also* Napoleonic Wars in British poetry; nationalism
Paulson, Ronald, 172n74
Peninsular War. *See* Napoleonic Wars in British poetry
Persuasion (Austen), 68, 149
Petersson, Niels P., 9
Phillips, Mark Salber, 33
Pittock, Murray, 146
poetry, wartime. *See* Napoleonic Wars in British poetry
Political Discourses (Hume), 21–23
political economy: destabilizing, inequitable tendencies of capitalism, 28–29; Hume's *Treatise on Human Nature* and *Political Discourses*, 19–23; Smith's *Wealth of Nations*, 23–27. *See also* nation-states
Poovey, Mary, 158n33
Pope, Alexander, 71, 77, 85
Porter, Bernard, 6
postcolonial theory, 7–8, 9, 158n43
The Prelude (Wordsworth), 49–50
price-specie-flow mechanism, 22, 162n27
Principles of Political Economy and Taxation (Hume), 28
progress: Barbauld and, 82; Hume on, 21–22; stadial theory and, 32; Worthington on, 164n63
Prussia, 72

Quentin Durward (Scott), 123–26, 128–37, 140, 145, 146

race, Kames on, 34–35. *See also* stadial theory and conjectural history
Radcliffe, Ann: *The Castles of Athlin and Dunbayne*, 50; context and personal life of, 48–50, 66; critical dismissal of, 47–48; Enlightened themes and, 46, 168n13; *The Italian*, 47–48, 54, 60–64; *A Journey Made in the Summer of 1794*, 61–62; Lewis' *The Monk* and, 59–60, 63–64; *The Mysteries of Udolpho*, 56–59, 65; national mood and waning popularity of, 66–67; *The Romance of the Forest*, 51–56; *A Sicilian Romance*, 50–51; sympathetic cosmopolitanism and, 55–58, 60–64, 65–66, 142–43; tolerance theme and, 61–63, 64–65
Raj, Kapil, 9
Rancière, Jacques, 182n9
"The Realist Floor-Plan" (Jameson), 18, 150–51
Records of Women (Hemans), 89
Reeve, Clara, 45, 58
religious conversion in Byron's *The Siege of Corinth*, 106–8
republicanism of Kant, 41–43
Ricardo, David, 28
Richardson, Samuel, 52
Robertson, John, 23
Robertson, Roland, 4, 156n12
Robertson, William, 164n60
Rob Roy (Scott), 123
Rohrbach, Emily, 82
The Romance of the Forest (Radcliffe), 51–56
Romantic globalism, 3–4, 10–12, 14–15, 45, 148–53. *See also specific authors and works*
Romantic Imperialism (Makdisi), 7

Romanticism, 7–8, 153. *See also specific authors and works*
Rome, Hemans' comparison of Britain to, 73
Ross, Marlon B., 70, 80, 175n32
Rossetti, Christina, 48
Rousseau, Jean-Jacques, 41
Ryan, Dermot, 157n31, 163n46

sacrifice, 135–36
Saglia, Diego, 72, 172n65, 174n18
Said, Edward: on clash of civilizations thesis, 98–99, 179n57; *Culture and Imperialism*, 7, 157n28; Jenkins on, 158n32; *Orientalism*, 6–7
Saint Pierre, Abbé de, 41
salvific global force, Grant on Britain as, 85–86
Samson Agonistes (Milton), 84
Sardanapalus (Byron), 109–13, 114
Sassen, Saskia, 5, 21, 183n22
"savages," Millar on, 37–38
Sayre, Robert, 153
Schmitt, Cannon, 47, 54, 61, 62, 169n24
Scott, Walter: *Anne of Geierstein*, 119, 136–45, 184n52; authorial identity and, 124–26; Barbauld and, 83; *The Bride of Lammermoor*, 125, 179n66; *Count Robert of Paris*, 179n59; *The Field of Waterloo*, 89–90, 92–94; *Guy Mannering*, 131; *Ivanhoe*, 115, 123, 179n55; *The Lady of the Lake*, 89; *The Lay of the Last Minstrel*, 72, 89; *Life of Napoleon*, 121; *Marmion*, 72, 89; mediation and, 150; popularity and influence of, 89, 122, 146; *Quentin Durward*, 123–26, 128–37, 140, 145, 146; on Radcliffe, 46; *Rob Roy*, 123; systems and, 151; *Tales of the Crusaders*, 114; *The Talisman*, 113–19, 133; travel to London and Paris (1826), 121–22; *The Vision of Don Roderick*, 89–92, 174n17; *Waverley*, 122–23
Scottish Enlightenment: about, 17–19; Gothic novels and, 45–46; Hume on conjectural history, 30; Hume's economics, 19–23; Kames' stadial theory, 32–35; Kant's globalism, 40–43; limits to Hume's and Smith's visions, 28–29; Millar's stadial theory, 35–40; Smith's stadial theory, 29–32; Smith's *Wealth of Nations*, 23–27; systems and, 150–51. *See also* Enlightenment
Sen, Amartya, 99
Seven Years' War, 176n60
Shapira, Yael, 60
Shaw, Philip, 90
Shelley, Percy, 82, 149
A Sicilian Romance (Radcliffe), 50–51
The Siege of Corinth (Byron), 97, 100, 102, 104–9, 112–13
Simpson, David, 115, 159n52
Simpson, Erik, 183n42, 184n46
Simpson, Michael, 123
Siskin, Clifford, 139, 150–51, 162n34
Sketches of the History of Man (Kames), 32–35
slavery, 39–40, 166n85
Sloterdijk, Peter, 159n55
Smith, Adam: on British "nation of shopkeepers," 27, 130; Gothic novels and, 45–46; "invisible hand," 32, 45, 150; limits of, 28–29; on slave trade, 166n85; on stadial theory, 30–32; *Theory of Moral Sentiments*, 169n15; *Wealth of Nations*, 23–27, 165n67, 169n15
social contract theory, Hume on, 19–20
"The Solitary Reaper" (Wordsworth), 102
Southey, Robert, 96
sovereignty: Hume on commerce and development of, 21; limited, advantages of, 140–42; in Scott's *Anne of Geierstein*, 137, 140; Scott's new world order and, 145–46; in Scott's *Quentin Durward*, 128–36
Spadafora, David, 164n63
Specters of the Atlantic (Baucom), 8, 158n33
Spivak, Gayatri Chakravorty, 7, 157n29, 187n24
stadial theory and conjectural history: difference between, 164n56; Ferguson on, 164n60; Hume on, 30; Jeffrey on Byron's Eastern Tales and, 95–96; Kames on, 32–35; Mill and, 164n53; Millar on, 35–40; Smith on, 29–32; Whig progress narrative and, 82

State Romanticism, 130–31
St. Clair, William, 122
Steger, Manfred, 3
Sterne, Laurence, 52
Steuart, James, 24
Stewart, Dugald, 25, 30
subjectivity, modern: Armstrong on mediation and, 149–50; bare lives and, 136; global hospitality and, 143; in Scott's *Quentin Durward*, 123–28, 135–36; Žižek on, 126–28, 135, 138, 143, 182n21
Sudan, Rajani, 8
Sutherland, John, 91
Sweet, Nanora, 71
sympathetic cosmopolitanism, 54, 55–58, 60–67, 142–43
sympathy: Nussbaum on, 187n24; Radcliffe and, 51–58, 60–66; Scottish Enlightenment and, 46; Shelley on, 149; utopian sympathetic communities, 58
system, concept of, 4, 139, 150–51

Tales of the Crusaders (Scott), 114
The Talisman (Scott), 113–19, 133
The Task (Cowper), 9
Tasso, Torquato, 76
Teichgraeber, Richard F., 26
Thakeray, William, 47
Theory of Moral Sentiments (Smith), 169n15
This Is Enlightenment (Siskin and Warner), 150
"Tintern Abbey" (Wordsworth), 54
tolerance, 61–66. See also sympathy
"total war" phenomenon, 69–70, 91, 176n60
"Toward Perpetual Peace" (Kant), 40, 42
trade. See commerce and trade, foreign
Treatise on Human Nature (Hume), 19–21
Trivedi, Harish, 151
Trumpener, Katie, 7–8, 185n71
"turning Turk" trope, 97

unequal distribution of wealth, 39
unequal exchange, 28–29
utopian sympathetic communities, 58

utopistics, 16

vanishing mediators, 130, 131
Vehme Gericht, 138–41
Vico, Giambattista, 31
Virilio, Paul, 15
The Vision of Don Roderick (Scott), 89–92, 174n17
Volney, Comte de, 175n39

Wallace, Tara Ghoshal, 8
Wallerstein, Immanuel: on capitalism, 24; on free trade, 162n28; on protectionism, 151; on unequal exchange, 28; "utopistics," 16; world-systems analysis, 4, 156n14
Walpole, Horace, 44, 45
war: Favret's "everyday war," 80; Hume on governmentality and, 20; Kant on, 40–41, 166n90; "total war" phenomenon and, 69–70, 91, 176n60. See also Napoleonic Wars in British poetry
War at a Distance (Favret), 8–9
Warburton, William, 61
Warner, William, 150
War of 1812, 84. See also Napoleonic Wars in British poetry
Watson, David, 152
Watt, Ian, 47
Watt, James, 59, 181n74
Waverley Novels (Scott): *Anne of Geierstein*, 119, 136–45, 184n52; Barbauld's influence on, 83; *The Bride of Lammermoor*, 125; Defauconpret's French translations of, 181n3; *Guy Mannering*, 131; *Ivanhoe*, 115, 121–22, 123, 179n55; new world order and, 145–46; *Quentin Durward*, 123–26, 128–37, 140, 145, 146; *Rob Roy*, 123; Scottish Enlightenment and, 45; *The Talisman*, 113–19, 133; *The Vision of Don Roderick* compared to, 91; *Waverley*, 122–23
Wealth of Nations (Smith), 23–27, 165n67, 169n15
Wein, Tony, 48
Welsh, Alexander, 138

Wheeler, Roxann, 32
Wickman, Matthew, 18
Williams, Helen Maria, 68
Wilt, Judith, 129
Winch, Donald, 24
"Windsor Forest" (Pope), 71, 77
women: female-centered view of war in Barbauld's *Eighteen Hundred Eleven*, 79–81; Millar on evolution of social positions of, 37
Woodring, Carl, 177n62
Wordsworth, William, 7, 49–50, 54, 102
The Worlding Project (Watson), 152
world-systems analysis, 4

Worthington, William, 164n63
Written on the Water (Baker), 8, 175n28

Young, Robert J. C., 174n19

Žižek, Slavoj: on capitalism, 28; on clash of civilizations, 119, 181n75; on "forced choice," 135, 142; on modern subjectivity, 126–28, 135, 138, 143, 182n21; "obscene underside," 59, 171n58; on tolerance, 65; on vanishing mediators, 130

www.ingramcontent.com/pod-product-compliance
Lightning Source LLC
Chambersburg PA
CBHW030137240426
43672CB00005B/162